The New Texas Challenge

The New Texas Challenge: Population Change and the Future of Texas

Steve H. Murdock
Steve White
Md. Nazrul Hoque
Beverly Pecotte
Xuihong You
Jennifer Balkan

Texas A&M University Press
College Station

Library of Congress Cataloging-in-Publication Data

The new Texas challenge : population change and the future of Texas /
Steve H. Murdock ... [et al.].-- 1st ed.
      p. cm.
Includes bibliographical references and index.
  ISBN 1-58544-305-0 (pbk. : alk. paper)
  1. Population forecasting--Texas. 2. Texas--Population. I. Murdock,
Steven H.
  HB3525.T4 N48 2003
  304.6'09764--dc21
                                    2003006495

To our colleagues who have worked
diligently to make Texas better:

Dr. James H. Copp
Dr. William P. Kuvlesky
Dr. Bardin H. Nelson
Dr. Albert Schaffer
Dr. Ruth C. Schaffer
Dr. Robert L. Skrabanek

This book has been prepared with the general assistance of
the following people, to whom appreciation is expressed:

Patricia Bramwell
Andrea Chrietzberg
Sheila Dos Santos–Dierking
Hongmei Wang
Jeffrey Jordan
Darrell Fannin
Teresa Ray
Xiaodong Wang

Contents

List of Tables

List of Figures

Foreword by State Senator
Teel Bivins

To be a true Texan is to be a romantic. I believe all Texans possess a certain degree of romanticism about our great state. It is instilled in us from birth as our imaginations are nurtured by the riches of our heroic history, our robust and diverse culture, and our seemingly endless display of natural beauty. We Texans are a proud people who rightfully believe our state is unique and unrivaled among all the states in the country, and for that matter, all the places in the world.

It is wonderful to ruminate and rhapsodize about the greatness of Texas. However, there is a danger inherent in romance if we carry it too far and get mired in identifying with our glorious past. We cannot consider our state's legacy to be a guarantee of eternal self-perpetuating greatness, for Texas has been jolted by enormous change.

Our sense of identity was seeded by the exploits of daring cattle-drive leaders and gutsy oil wildcatters. Yet, hopefully, we have all come to realize by now that our days as an oil and cattle state are over. We still have a lot of pump-jacks and steers scattered across the landscape, but we are no longer the Texas where people could prosper with little more than a willingness to work hard and some "cowboy" know-how.

Quicker than we could add the words *gigabyte* and *modem* to our vocabularies, Texas and the rest of the world have been absorbed into the high-tech Information Age. With our global economy no longer dominated by manufacturing, the field of play has been recast. Assuring Texas' ability to compete depends on how we confront the demands placed upon us by the new economy.

One thing Texans have always liked to brag about is our state's size. In the changing Texas, we are getting even bigger, at least in population. We added approximately 4 million people to our population during the decade of the nineties. Texas is awash in a wave of young people and how we respond to their arrival will determine whether they become a longtime asset or a longtime liability.

How do we meet the needs of this new economy? What is the best resource for insuring prosperity for our expanding population? I believe I have a one-word answer: Education.

Those who know me will not be surprised that I tout education as the mechanism for enabling Texas to flourish. Since first being elected to the Texas Senate in 1989, I have had a part, for good or bad, in tackling the very wide array of issues that state government encounters. However, if I have found my focus in any one area, it has been education. I have chaired the Senate Education Committee since 1997 and I am very passionate about the subject. I stand in solidarity with the wise person who described education as "the ticket out of poverty." I see education as the answer to just about any problem you can name. My argument receives a strong boost in the findings included in *The New Texas Challenge: Population Change and the Future of Texas* .

I know of no work that offers a clearer vision of what is at stake for our state than the book you currently hold in your hands. *The New Texas Challenge* has had a greater impact on me as a legislator than any other scholarly work I have received. In a resounding fashion, it underscores the need for our state to continue building on the progress we have made toward increasing the quality and accessibility of our educational system from prekindergarten through all levels of higher education.

There is much within this book to demonstrate why our state must remain committed to education. Herewith, I cite a major example. For many who are about to read *The New Texas Challenge: Population Change and the Future of Texas* , perhaps the most jarring revelation will be found in the data pertaining to our state's racial and ethnic mix. In the year 2000, slightly more than half the Texas population was Anglo. By the year 2040, the demographic projections indicate the Anglo portion of the population will constitute as little as one-fourth to one-third of the total population. Obviously, one treads on highly sensitive, politically charged ground when interpreting what such a demographic recomposition communicates about Texas' future.

As an education advocate, I am very pleased that the data and analysis within *The New Texas Challenge: Population Change and the Future of Texas* make a strong case for the incomparable value of education. In addressing the ramifications of the changes in our racial/ethnic mix, this book does not serve up an impression filtered through the prism of political correctness. Instead, it points out with sober realism what I hope no one would attempt to dispute: There is a profound gap in the levels of educational attainment reached by Anglos and the levels of educational attainment reached by Hispanics and African Americans. The data in this book illustrate a direct correlation between levels of education and levels of income. Thus, the researchers posit, and I concur, how Texas fares in the years to come relies heavily on how much we eliminate those gaps in educational attainment. This work asserts that completely closing the gaps could deliver an annual income windfall of $300 billion for our state's economy by the year 2040.

Fortunately, we in Texas state government have long been aware of the need to eliminate the disparities in levels of educational attainment. The state has developed programs and policies aimed at closing the disturbing chasms. In my opinion, the single greatest tool the state has implemented for improving education is the accountability system we use to evaluate how well public schools are preparing students to meet the demands

of postsecondary education and the workplace. Under the
Texas accountability system, each school district is held
accountable for the test scores of all student groups, including
each minority group and economically disadvantaged students.

We have a long way to go to achieve all of our goals, but
we are making tremendous progress as evidenced by the
performance of our students on the accountability test known
as the Texas Assessment of Academic Skills (TAAS). Between
1994 and 2001, the percentage of African-American students
passing the TAAS math test rose from 38 percent to 82 percent.
At the same time, Hispanic students passing the TAAS math
test climbed from 47 percent to 87 percent and economically
disadvantaged student scores in math have risen from 45
percent passing to 85 percent. The improvement in student
performance can be directly linked to the creation of statewide
curriculum standards on which both the TAAS test and the
state's textbooks are based. I have made the linking of
standards, curriculum, and testing the cornerstone of my efforts
in educational policy and I am pleased to see the gains made by
the various demographic groups *The New Texas Challenge:
Population Change and the Future of Texas* identifies as being
most critical to our state's future success.

While the TAAS scores show advancement in preparing
public school students for higher education, more must be done
to provide those students access to colleges and universities.
Texas is working to address that concern. A new state law
gives students who graduate in the top 10 percent of their high
school class automatic admission to any Texas state university.
The state has also established the Texas Grant Program, which
provides scholarships to Texas students in need.

Although I am happy with the inroads Texas is making, I
believe we need to continue the mission of enhancing what our
state's educational system offers. The findings in *The New
Texas Challenge: Population Change and the Future of Texas*
will help me make my case.

The research and analysis conducted by Dr. Steve Murdock and his colleagues present two realistic but distinct visions of Texas' future. In one scenario, our state aggressively grasps the awesome task at hand, labors to subdue it, and comes out victorious with the reward of a vastly improved quality of life for our citizens. In the less cheery alternative scenario, our state responds meekly to the daunting undertaking and Texas plunges into a condition of increased privation and diminished independence.

Certainly, no proud Texan would ever want to see our state left behind in the dust as our competitors gallop away from us. Yet, I believe that will be our fate unless we turn our reconstituted economy and demographics into forces that empower rather than ensnare us.

Over the years I have developed a great respect for Dr. Murdock and his work. This book is just the latest of many endeavors in which he has proven the importance of demography to public policy. *The New Texas Challenge: Population Change and the Future of Texas* might not be the kind of leisurely read we get from a John Grisham or Sue Grafton novel, but it will provide compelling reading for anyone who truly cares to be involved in shaping our state's future.

As for the story of Texas, it is still being written. It is up to our state leaders, and all Texas citizens, to develop a plot line that delivers a happy ending.

Foreword by Former Lt. Governor William P. Hobby, Jr.

We have been given a wakeup call here: Texas needs more students and doctors and fewer prisoners.

This book is about the implications for Texas (and the nation) of population growth between 2000 and 2040. Texas is now a microcosm of the nation.

Texas' growth is staggering, and so are the implications of its growth.

We have heard many times that Texas is becoming more diverse. Soon (2005) Texas will have another huge new minority population: Anglos. Then, by 2040, Texas will again have a majority population group: Hispanics (see page 27)

As shown in Table 2.1, Texas population has grown faster than that of the nation ever since it became a state. In the 1990s the state's population grew to 20,851,820 or by 22.8 percent. This increase of 3,865,310 was the largest of any decade in Texas history and moved Texas past New York to become the nation's second largest state (Table 2.2).

But we have not seen anything yet! By 2040, population could increase by as much as 29.7 million and 142.6 percent.

What follows are the implications for the state.

EDUCATION

Under the most likely projection, there will be nearly 3.8 million *more* students in our public elementary and secondary schools, colleges, and universities in 2040 than there were in 2000 (see page 152).

The educational disparity among Anglos and Hispanics and African Americans is historic and will not be corrected in our lifetimes. We can seek to reduce that disparity and continue to prosper, or we can let that disparity widen and watch the rest of the United States leave us in self-inflicted poverty.

HEALTH AND HUMAN SERVICES

Texans are getting older, and therefore sicker.

In 2000, there were 3.3 million Texans getting health and human services. By 2040 there will be 9.6 million. The cost will go up by more than 8 billion constant (2000) dollars.

CORRECTIONS

The most striking findings affect our prison system. Texas locks up a higher percentage of its population than any other state in the nation. Between 1979 and 1999, the population in juvenile correctional facilities in Texas increased by 155.1 percent compared to 51.5 percent for the nation. The prison population in Texas increased by 414.2 percent from 1980 to 2000, compared to a 310.6 percent increase in the nation (see Table 9.1).

If current incarceration rates continue, Texas will have 17,118 youth in TYC facilities and more than 340,000 prison inmates in 2040. That would mean nearly $510 million for TYC and $5.1 billion for adult prison facilities in 2040.

Nationwide there are more than 2 million inmates currently in state and federal prisons and local jails. However, unlike Texas, Iowa has laid off prison guards, Ohio and Illinois are closing prisons; and Montana, Arkansas, and Kentucky are releasing convicted felons early, getting around no-parole policies passed in the 1990s, according to the *New York Times* ("Inmates Go Free to Reduce Deficits," *New York Times,* December 19, 2002). The bottom line is that getting tough on crime is going to be tough on taxpayers.

The New Texas Challenge: Population Change and the Future of Texas is important reading for any policy maker and any other resident of Texas. The policy implications of the numbers are clear. Do we face up to them, or do we once again lapse into the economic and educational mediocrity that characterized Texas fifty years ago. The information in this book projects the future of Texas—unless we wise up.

Texas was a part of the Mexican state of Coahuila y Tejas. Texas revolted from Mexico in part because Mexico did not provide adequate public education for Texans. If Texas does not provide adequate education for its citizens, should we secede and rejoin Coahuila?

Preface

In the latter part of the twentieth century, many policy makers, analysts, and academics began to recognize that Texas' population was changing rapidly with dramatic implications for the state. By 1950, Texas was no longer a state that was primarily rural. By the end of the century, Texas had become the second largest state in the United States with a population of nearly 21 million persons and three of the ten largest cities in the nation.

Its demographic characteristics reflected those of the nation in some regards but differed in others. As with other states, Texas' median age was increasing as the baby-boom generation (those persons born from 1946–64) aged. By 2000, the median age of Texas' population was 32.3 years compared to 18.7 in 1900 and 26.4 years in 1970. Households in Texas were also changing rapidly, such that households involving married couples with children were only 27.1 percent of all households by 2000.

Particularly notable, however, was the change in the racial/ethnic composition of the state's population. Although its Hispanic heritage is older than Texas' existence either as a nation or as a state, self-enumeration of Hispanics as a group did not begin until 1980, providing the first opportunity to accurately record the growth of this population group. Moreover, data on the population by race/ethnicity have shown dramatic differences in rates of population growth among racial/ethnic groups. During the 1980s, the Anglo population increased by 10.1 percent and in the 1990s by about 7.6

percent, whereas the Black population increased by 16.8 percent in the 1980s and 22.5 percent in the 1990s, the Hispanic population by 45.4 percent in the 1980s and 53.7 percent in the 1990s, and the population of persons from the Other racial/ethnic group by 88.8 percent in the 1980s and 81.2 percent in the 1990s. The result was that, by 2000, Texas was 53.1 percent Anglo, 11.6 percent Black, 32.0 percent Hispanic, and 3.3 percent members of the Other racial/ethnic group. Between 2005 and 2006, Texas' population is projected to be less than one-half Anglo.

Against the background of such change, the Texas Legislative Council (TLC) commissioned the Center for Demographic and Socioeconomic Research and Education (CDSRE) in the mid-1990s to examine the implications of current and future patterns of population change for state services. With sponsorship from the TLC under the leadership of House Speaker Pete Laney and Lt. Gov. Bob Bullock, the CDSRE contracted to examine the implications of demographic change on the demand for, and delivery and financing of, state services. The CDSRE's efforts resulted in a report that became the book entitled *The Texas Challenge: Population Change and the Future of Texas.* The study examined the implications of recent and future population change on the demand for housing, education, welfare, and employment services, as well as for income and wealth and for state costs and revenues. The findings portrayed a sober future for the state if the population changed as projected and the socioeconomic differences among population groups remained stagnant. The conclusions suggested that the challenge for Texas was to ensure that all Texans have the skills and other resources necessary to compete in the global economy so that the resources necessary to drive private-sector growth and fund public services would be available.

This volume addresses several basic questions that logically follow from the work presented in the original *Texas Challenge* volume: Has the dramatic demographic and economic expansion of the 1990s changed the outlook for Texas' future in the twenty-first century? In what ways have the demographic and economic changes affected the need for state services? When, where, and how have changes occurred that may alter the future of different population groups in Texas? The purpose of this volume is thus threefold: (1) to update its readers on the progress that Texas has made in meeting the challenges suggested by the original (Murdock et al., 1995, 1996, 1997) volumes; (2) to use current data and recent trends to provide updated projections of the implications of population change for socioeconomic resources and services, including previously unexamined services, in Texas; and (3) to provide an expanded discussion of the policy implications of the state's future demographic trends. This volume thus provides both a report card of sorts and a prognosis for the future, assuming recent and projected trends prevail.

This publication begins with overviews of recent and projected population and housing change, which provide the underlying basis for socioeconomic change and change in demand for public- and private-sector services in Texas. It then presents a series of chapters that examine the implications of population change on specific socioeconomic characteristics of the population or for key public, or selected privately provided, services. Each of these topical chapters examines recent and historical changes in the subjects under consideration, including change in service demand and provision during the 1990s; provides an overview of the projected changes in the service area; and examines the implications of the projected changes. The work concludes with a chapter that assesses the overall implications of the past and projected changes for Texas' future.

The data used in this volume are based on values that are either directly or indirectly derived from historical population and socioeconomic statistics, population projections, and projections of population-based factors impacting the topics under examination. In so doing, we do not intend to suggest that demography is destiny. Economic, policy, societal, and other factors may also result in equally large or larger levels of change and related challenges. We believe, however, that demographics will play a sufficiently large role to merit close examination. We also clearly acknowledge that demographic projections, like all forms of projections, are subject to substantial errors. This is especially true for projections made for extended periods of time into the future. Projections are generally more accurate for periods closer to their base date and become increasingly inaccurate the farther they are extended into the future. Anyone using the work reported in this volume should use the results with full recognition of the limitations of projections.

We also assume that current relationships between demographic and socioeconomic and service factors will continue across time. We do not, in fact, expect this to be the case. Nevertheless, such assumptions are made for two reasons. First, there often is little data available to allow us to extend trends other than those prevailing during the current period or those resulting from relatively short historical periods. Second, by examining the implications of current trends projected into the future, we provide information on what is likely to occur in the state if no new actions are taken to change these trends. It thus provides a base against which to measure the implications of alternative policy and other options.

In examining the implications of population change for selected topics, we make no claim to inclusiveness. That is, we have clearly chosen to examine only some of the areas of importance to the state. Many other equally important dimensions could have been examined had time, data availability, and space allowed.

We also wish to acknowledge that our discussion of differences impacting services and conditions often focus on racial/ethnic differences as potential drivers of change. Our intention is not to suggest that race or ethnicity, as social and/or cultural or other phenomena, are determinants of service or socioeconomic factors in and of themselves. Rather, we argue that due to a variety of historical, discriminatory, and other factors, many socioeconomic conditions and differences that are major drivers of service usage have become associated with race/ethnicity. Clearly, many of the racial/ethnic differences are largely social class differences for which race/ethnicity are but indicators. At the same time, we do not wish to suggest that race/ethnicity-related forms of discrimination do not continue to play a role in society. We attempt to recognize the reality of race/ethnicity and to use it to explicate the potential future of Texas through such groups for which data are often available when socioeconomic or social class data are not available.

Similarly, we recognize that our selection of the racial/ethnic categories used in this volume is somewhat arbitrary. We examine patterns for non-Hispanic Whites or Anglos, non-Hispanic Blacks, Hispanics from all races, and for persons in a category that includes persons from all Other racial/ethnic groups (who are not Hispanic and not members of the other groups noted above). The definition of such groups became increasingly difficult with the multiple-race identification allowed in the 2000 Census. We thus were forced to make certain assumptions to provide comparability between 2000 data and that for earlier periods (see the description of our procedures in the section on comparing 2000 to earlier racial/ethnic categories on our Web site: txsdc.tamu.edu). Our reason for including these groups was largely dictated by the size of the groups in all parts of the state. Analysis for specific subgroups included in our Other category such as Asians, Native Americans, Multi-race, and other persons would have been useful if group size, time, and resources had been sufficient. We trust that members of those groups not specifically noted will understand that our failure to include them was not intended to suggest that they are of diminished importance for Texas, but rather was a result of data availability, size, and resource considerations.

Finally, we trust that the names we use to refer to groups will not offend our readers. That is, we use Anglos to refer to non-Hispanic Whites, Blacks rather than African Americans, Hispanics rather than Latinos, and Other (without differentiating between different subgroups within). We use Anglo because of its widespread use in the Southwest, Black because Blacks of non-African origin are included in this category, Hispanic because this category is not limited to Hispanics of a given set of origins, and Other simply because there are too many specific subgroups to list all of them. We have found no uniform acceptance of any terms and hope that those used here are generally acceptable.

We received assistance from numerous organizations and agencies in completing the work reported in this volume. We wish to thank especially the Texas Legislative Council and its Executive Director, Steve Collins, and its Director of Research, Debbie Irvine, for supporting the work from which this volume is derived. We also wish to thank the Texas Agricultural Experiment Station and the Vice Chancellor for Agriculture and Director of the Texas Agricultural Experiment Station, Dr. Edward A. Hiler, who has provided ongoing support for this activity in the Department of Rural Sociology.

We are also grateful to the Texas state agencies that have so generously provided data for use in this study. Among these are the Texas Youth Commission, Texas Department of Criminal Justice, Criminal Justice Policy Council, Texas Education Agency, Texas Higher Education Coordinating Board, Office of the Texas Comptroller of Public Accounts, Texas Legislative Budget Board, Texas Workforce Commission, Texas Department of Human Services, and Texas Department of Health. It should be noted, however, that the views expressed here are those of the authors and do not necessarily reflect those of any of the agencies listed above. Similarly, any errors in the use of data from those agencies should be attributed to the authors. Finally, it is essential to note that the projections presented here for specific state services are long-term projections and are not intended to supplant or substitute for those made by the agencies that clearly use more detailed procedures for short-term projections of service needs, usage, and costs.

We extend our appreciation to numerous persons who participated in this work. We acknowledge the careful and extensive computer analysis of Darrell Fannin, Jeffrey Jordan, and Hongmei Wang. Xiaodong Wang provided extensive graduate assistance. We especially appreciate the tireless efforts in typing and retyping drafts provided by Andrea Chrietzberg and Teresa Ray. We owe very special appreciation to Patricia Bramwell and Sheila Dos Santos-Dierking, who ensured that all parts of the production of this work were carefully coordinated and completed. They are our friends as well as our colleagues.

We also wish to thank former Lieutenant Governor William P. Hobby, Jr.; Dr. Don Warren of the Texas Legislative Council; Al Mirabal, Director of the Dallas regional office of the U.S. Bureau of the Census; and Dr. David Gardner of the Texas Higher Education Coordinating Board, who carefully read the draft of this work and provided constructive comments. We wish to especially thank Karen White, who edited the entire volume and prevented the authors from making numerous egregious errors. We sincerely appreciate her efforts and friendship.

We thank our families and friends for bearing with us as we neglected them to finish this work. Finally, we wish to thank the many Texans who have provided many of the insights suggested here in numerous conversations and forms of correspondence over the years and who must ultimately ensure that the *Texas Challenge* is successfully addressed.

The New Texas Challenge

CHAPTER 1

Introduction

Texans have generally maintained an optimistic view of the future of their state. This optimism has been supported by extensive economic and population growth that has made Texas a land of opportunity for many natives and new residents alike. However, parts of Texas and some Texas residents have failed to share in that growth, such that the state had sixty-eight counties in which population declined from 1990 to 2000 and some of the highest county-level poverty rates in the nation.

What will Texas' future be like? Will its population continue to increase? If so, how rapidly and where will this growth be most extensive? Will its wealth increase with its population or will per capita levels of income and wealth decrease? What are the opportunities and challenges likely to impact governments in Texas in the first decades of the twenty-first century?

We first attempted to address such questions in the mid-1990s with the publication of a report and related book entitled *The Texas Challenge: Population Change and the Future of Texas* (Murdock et al. 1996, 1997). In that work, we generally projected a sober future for Texas if the socioeconomic characteristics (differences in income, education, and program participation) of the fastest growing segments of Texas' population did not change and the state showed the rapid, diverse, and relatively pervasive growth projected to occur. The work suggested that the challenge for the state was to ensure that all Texans have the skills and education necessary to compete in the increasingly international economy impacting Texas and the rest of the nation and world, and that failing to meet this challenge could result in a Texas that is poorer and less competitive.

The 2000 Census revealed a Texas population that had increased even more rapidly in size and diversity than anticipated and a state that showed rapid levels of economic expansion in many areas. At the same time, many public programs changed substantially. For example, welfare programs have been dramatically altered by the Personal Responsibility and Work Opportunity Reconciliation Act (PRWORA) of 1996 and higher education access programs by the *Hopwood v State of Texas* decision of 1994. Educational programs such as the Texas Higher Education Coordinating Board's "Closing the Gaps" program and financial aid programs such as the "TEXAS Grant" program have been instituted. In light of such changes, have the realities underlying the original projections contained in *The Texas Challenge* been altered?

This volume attempts to address both the original questions raised by *The Texas Challenge* in light of new 2000 and post-2000 data and to address the question of how—and in what ways—recent trends, patterns, and policies may have changed its conclusions. In so doing, the intent is both to provide an overview of how far Texas has come and to suggest where it may be going under conditions prevailing in the first years of this century.

To accomplish these goals, we again examine the effects of four major demographic trends that continue to markedly impact Texas and other parts of the nation. Those trends are:

1. changes in the rates and sources of population growth;
2. the aging and age structure of the population;
3. growth in the non-Anglo population; and
4. the changing composition of Texas households.

These four factors not only continue to impact numerous aspects of Texas and United States society and public programs (see Murdock 1995; Murdock et al. 1996), but also continue to show trends that are critical for understanding the future.

Texas' population increased by nearly 4 million persons in the 1990s to about 21 million, representing a growth rate of 22.8 percent. That growth was due nearly equally to the two determinant processes of population change: natural increase (the difference between births and deaths) and net migration (including both inmigration from other states and immigration from other nations). The fact that so much of this growth was due to net migration reflected the state's economic expansion and helped to propel that expansion because new growth through migration results in new households with needs for housing and other services. Overall, Texas' population was the second fastest growing in the nation in numerical terms and the eighth fastest growing state in percentage terms and its growth exceeded projected growth for the decade by at least four hundred thousand persons.

The population also diversified more rapidly than expected with the Anglo (non-Hispanic White) population increasing by only 7.6 percent, compared to 22.5 percent for the Black (non-Hispanic Black) population, 53.7 percent for the Hispanic population, and 81.2 percent for the Other (non-Hispanic persons of all Other races) population. Of the total net increase in Texas' population in the 1990s, almost 80 percent was due to non-Anglo populations compared to roughly 66 percent in the 1980s. As a result, Texas' population was only 53 percent Anglo in 2000 (compared to nearly 66 percent in 1980 and nearly 61 percent in 1990), and projections (Texas Population Estimates and Projections Program 2001) suggest that its population will be less than one-half Anglo by 2005 or 2006 and will become a majority Hispanic between 2026 and 2035. In addition, by 2000 Hispanics had come to form the single largest racial/ethnic group in the cities of Houston, Dallas, San Antonio, and El Paso. Thus, in four of the five largest cities in Texas (the exception being Austin), Hispanics are now the largest single racial/ethnic group.

Two basic characteristics continued to describe the age structure of Texas' population and the changes taking place

within it. The population continued to age overall, with the
state's median age increasing from 30.8 years in 1990 to 32.3
years in 2000. This trend is a result of the aging of the baby-
boom generation (those born from 1946 through 1964) that is
expected to move the overall population in Texas and the
nation as a whole toward increasing proportions of elderly
whose numbers will challenge health care, retirement, and
other systems. The second important characteristic of the age
structure is the clear relationship between non-Anglo status and
youth status. Whereas 53 percent of the total population was
Anglo and 32 percent Hispanic, 73 percent of the population
sixty-five years of age or older was Anglo and 17 percent
Hispanic; for the population less than five years of age, 40
percent was Anglo and 44 percent Hispanic. In total, 57 percent
of the population less than eighteen years of age in 2000 was
non-Anglo.

Household composition has continued to change as well.
Although some demographers anticipated a marked reversal of
the trend toward greater diversity in households in the 1990s,
this reversal did not occur. Despite the extensive growth in
Hispanic and Other non-Anglo population groups that are more
likely to be in married-couple households, the percentage of
Texas households involving married couples increased by only
16.1 percent, while the total number of Texas households
increased by 21.8 percent. Married-couple households
decreased as a share of all households from 56.6 in 1990 to
54.0 percent in 2000.

When combined with the fact that differences in age,
race/ethnicity, and household composition tend to be associated
with differences in income, poverty, and other socioeconomic
factors that affect private-sector markets and public service
usage, such demographic trends provide the impetus for
substantial change in Texas. For example, Table 1.1 shows that
income tends to peak at middle age, Hispanic and Black
incomes are less than two-thirds of the income for Anglos, and
married-couple families tend to have incomes substantially

Table 1.1

Median Household Income
in Texas by Age of Householder, Race/Ethnicity
of Householder, and Household Type, 1999

Characteristics of Householder	Median Income
Age of Householder	
Total	$ 39,927
<25	21,570
25-34	37,732
35-44	47,418
45-54	52,926
55-64	44,905
65-74	30,296
75+	21,734
Race/Ethnicity of Householder	
Total	$ 39,927
Anglo	47,162
Black	29,305
Hispanic	29,873
Other	44,834
Household Type	
All households	$ 39,927
Family households	45,861
Married couple	53,338
Female householder	23,583
Male householder	31,739
Nonfamily households	25,623

Source: U.S. Census Bureau, Census 2000 Summary File 3, [machin-readable data files], 2002a.

higher than those for single-parent (male- and female-householder) families. It is the patterns of population change, along with these socioeconomic differences and differences related to policy changes, that are addressed in this volume. Specifically, we examine these demographic changes, their socioeconomic implications, and their implications for state and selected private-sector services for the period from 2000 to 2040.

ORGANIZATION

This volume is organized with two general chapters that describe recent and projected future trends in Texas' population (Chapter 2) and Texas households (Chapter 3). These chapters provide the demographic base for the socioeconomic and service impacts that are delineated in subsequent chapters. In these two chapters, the patterns of the past are examined and alternative projections of the population and of households are described.

The remainder of the volume consists of chapters examining the impact of population and household change on selected characteristics and services. Chapter 4 examines the impact of changes in population and households on socioeconomic factors—including income, poverty, and tax revenues. Chapter 5 examines the effects of these changes on the private sector. It includes analyses of consumer expenditures, net worth, and assets, and provides more detailed analysis of two selected industries—housing and health care—as examples of private-sector impacts. Chapter 6 provides an overview of effects on the labor force and labor force programs. Chapter 7 examines impacts on primary and secondary and higher education. Chapter 8 presents information on human services and related programs, and Chapter 9 describes effects likely to occur in the area of youth and adult corrections.

Each of these latter chapters (4–9) presents data on recent historical changes and a discussion of the factors affecting such changes, projections of the underlying factors driving change in the area under examination, an examination of the implications of the historical patterns and projected changes, and an examination of alternative simulations when appropriate. In sum, each chapter attempts to describe for each topic where it has been, where it is going, and what the changes described mean for those requiring—and those providing—such services and for the state as a whole.

The final chapter, Chapter 10, provides a broad overview of the implications of the patterns described in the preceding nine chapters. It presents not only a summary but also an examination of several alternative futures potentially impacted by changes that were not apparent when the previous volume was written. It attempts to summarize what is likely to occur if current conditions continue and what might occur under different patterns of change.

LIMITATIONS

This work is obviously limited in several regards. First, we examine the implications of only population change for a limited number of services and conditions. Numerous other social, economic, and policy factors also affect socioeconomic and service conditions. We maintain that demography plays an important role in determining characteristics of the future, but any analysis stressing only one dimension, be it demographic or any other single dimension, is admittedly incomplete. Similarly, we assume that socioeconomic conditions are associated with demographic characteristics. In particular, we assume that differences in age, household composition, and race/ethnicity tend to differentiate the levels of socioeconomic resources available to persons and households. This assumption is not intended to suggest that such relationships are immutable, but rather that they have tended to prevail across time and thus can be used in the absence of more direct indicators to assess likely socioeconomic change. This is not an indictment of persons with certain characteristics for the socioeconomic conditions they are experiencing or for the effects these conditions may have on overall population patterns. This work simply recognizes that, because of a variety of historical, discriminatory, and other factors, certain demographic characteristics (such as very young or old age or non-Anglo status) tend to be associated with reduced levels of socioeconomic resources.

Since the volume examines only some services and conditions, it does not address all of the important dimensions or issues likely to affect Texas in the coming years. Because this volume is derived from a larger study that examines patterns for substate areas, only services and conditions for which consistent county-level data could be obtained were included. Important areas such as transportation, environmental factors such as water supply and quality and air quality, and numerous other quality of life dimensions could not be examined. No claim is made that this analysis is inclusive or exhaustive.

The work is also limited by the fact that many of its conclusions are based on population projections that make certain assumptions about the future of the demographic processes of fertility, mortality, and migration (see Texas Population Estimates and Projections Program 2001 for a description of these assumptions) and—when applied to socioeconomic and service projections—about the future age-, sex-, and race/ethnicity-specific rates of acquisition of resources or use of different types of services. Uncertainty and inaccuracy are evident in all projections, especially those made for relatively small areas, specific forms of participation, and for long periods of time into the future (Ascher 1978; Brody 1993; Murdock et al. 1991; Murdock and Ellis 1991; Siegel 2002; Smith et al. 2001). Uncertainty is compounded when there is a need to create comparability between population subgroups (such as racial/ethnic groups) used as major components in the projections. Thus, the procedures used to create similar racial/ethnic groups for 2000 and 1990 described on our Web site (txsdc.tamu.edu) may have affected the accuracy of projections in ways that cannot be determined with absolute certainty. It must also be recognized that projections are less accurate for extended periods in the future such that projections for the near term, (for example, 5–10 years) tend to be more accurate than those for the long term (for example, 30–40 years). In sum, population projections, like projections of any phenomena, must be used with full recognition of their limitations.

The work is also affected by data limitations. Although numerous data sources were used and every attempt was made to use the best data available in each topical area, there were numerous instances in which data were insufficient in several regards. These limitations are noted in the substantive chapters.

The work is further limited by the fact that we emphasize only the demographically determined demand for services and do so in many cases assuming that either 2000 conditions prevail throughout the projection period from 2000 to 2040 or that 1990 to 2000 trends continue in the future. Supply issues that reflect funding, policy, and other factors simply are not examined. It is obvious that in most situations current (2000) conditions will not continue unchanged through a forty-year projection period; nor will the trends of the 1990s. However, in the absence of adequate historical data for modeling change, there are few alternatives to assuming historical continuity. The use of assumptions of constant rates or trended rates thus may be useful in identifying the conditions that are likely to prevail in the absence of change. Additionally, because of differences in reporting periods and procedures used for reporting the number of people using specific services among agencies, the numbers of persons noted in the descriptive data at the beginning of each chapter may differ from that used in the projections sections of these chapters.

The work thus has numerous limitations. Despite these limitations, we hope that readers will find this publication useful in describing the conditions that have prevailed in the past and those that may characterize Texas' future.

CHAPTER 2

Current and Future State of the Texas Population

Texas' population has shown dramatic change since the state was formed, and projections of its future suggest that equally substantial changes may be expected in the coming decades. In this chapter we give an overview of recent and projected change in the population of Texas, with an emphasis placed on three of the four major demographic trends that are the focus of this volume. Specifically we examine total population change, change in the racial/ethnic composition of the population, and change in the age structure of the population. Household change and projections are examined in Chapter 3. The purpose of this chapter is to describe the basic demographic trends underlying the socioeconomic and service changes described in the remainder of the volume.

HISTORICAL AND CURRENT PATTERNS OF POPULATION CHANGE

Patterns of Population Change

The demographic history of Texas has been one of growth. As shown in Table 2.1, Texas' population has increased more rapidly (in percentage terms) than that of the nation in every decade since it became a state. The decade of the 1990s was notable in several regards, however, with the state's population growing to 20,851,820 by 2000, an increase of 22.8 percent since 1990. This increase of 3,865,310 persons was the largest of any decade in Texas' history and moved Texas past New York to become the nation's second largest state. It was an

Table 2.1

Total Population and Percent Population Change
in Texas and the United States, 1850–2000

Year	Total Population		Percent Change from Previous Time Period	
	Texas	U.S.	Texas	U.S.
1850	212,592	23,191,876	—	—
1860	604,215	31,443,321	184.2	35.6
1870	818,579	39,818,449	35.5	26.6
1880	1,591,749	50,155,783	94.5	26.0
1890	2,235,527	62,947,714	40.4	25.5
1900	3,048,710	75,994,575	36.4	20.7
1910	3,896,542	91,972,266	27.8	21.0
1920	4,663,228	105,710,620	19.7	14.9
1930	5,824,715	122,775,046	24.9	16.1
1940	6,414,824	131,669,275	10.1	7.2
1950	7,711,194	150,697,361	20.2	14.5
1960	9,579,677	179,323,175	24.2	19.0
1970	11,196,730	203,302,031	16.9	13.4
1980	14,229,191	226,545,805	27.1	11.4
1990	16,986,510	248,709,873	19.4	9.8
2000	20,851,820	281,421,906	22.8	13.2

Source: U.S. Census Bureau, "Census of Population and Housing," April 1 population counts for each year indicated.

increase roughly equivalent to adding to Texas' population, in a single decade, the sum of the 1990 populations of the cities of Houston, Dallas, San Antonio, and Corpus Christi. It was an increase larger than the total populations of twenty-four of the fifty states and meant that more than one of every nine persons added to the population of the United States in the 1990s was added in Texas. Texas' population increase was second only to California in numerical size (California increased by 4.1 million persons in the 1990s) and the eighth largest in percentage terms among all states (see Table 2.2).

Growth in the 1990s came nearly equally from the two components of population growth, with 49.7 percent due to natural increase (the difference between the number of births

Table 2.2

Population and Population Change by State for the United States, 1990–2000

State	1990 Census	2000 Census	Population Change Number	Population Change Percent
United States	248,709,873	281,421,906	32,712,033	13.2
Alabama	4,040,587	4,447,100	406,513	10.1
Alaska	550,043	626,932	76,889	14.0
Arizona	3,665,228	5,130,632	1,465,404	40.0
Arkansas	2,350,725	2,673,400	322,675	13.7
California	29,760,021	33,871,648	4,111,627	13.8
Colorado	3,294,394	4,301,261	1,006,867	30.6
Connecticut	3,287,116	3,405,565	118,449	3.6
Delaware	666,168	783,600	117,432	17.6
Florida	12,937,926	15,982,378	3,044,452	23.5
Georgia	6,478,216	8,186,453	1,708,237	26.4
Hawaii	1,108,229	1,211,537	103,308	9.3
Idaho	1,006,749	1,293,953	287,204	28.5
Illinois	11,430,602	12,419,293	988,691	8.6
Indiana	5,544,159	6,080,485	536,326	9.7
Iowa	2,776,755	2,926,324	149,569	5.4
Kansas	2,477,574	2,688,418	210,844	8.5
Kentucky	3,685,296	4,041,769	356,473	9.7
Louisiana	4,219,973	4,468,976	249,003	5.9
Maine	1,227,928	1,274,923	46,995	3.8
Maryland	4,781,468	5,296,486	515,018	10.8
Massachusetts	6,016,425	6,349,097	332,672	5.5
Michigan	9,295,297	9,938,444	643,147	6.9
Minnesota	4,375,099	4,919,479	544,380	12.4
Mississippi	2,573,216	2,844,658	271,442	10.5
Missouri	5,117,073	5,595,211	478,138	9.3
Montana	799,065	902,195	103,130	12.9
Nebraska	1,578,385	1,711,263	132,878	8.4
Nevada	1,201,833	1,998,257	796,424	66.3
New Hampshire	1,109,252	1,235,786	126,534	11.4
New Jersey	7,730,188	8,414,350	684,162	8.9
New Mexico	1,515,069	1,819,046	303,977	20.1
New York	17,990,455	18,976,457	986,002	5.5
North Carolina	6,628,637	8,049,313	1,420,676	21.4
North Dakota	638,800	642,200	3,400	0.5
Ohio	10,847,115	11,353,140	506,025	4.7
Oklahoma	3,145,585	3,450,654	305,069	9.7
Oregon	2,842,321	3,421,399	579,078	20.4
Pennsylvania	11,881,643	12,281,054	399,411	3.4
Rhode Island	1,003,464	1,048,319	44,855	4.5
South Carolina	3,486,703	4,012,012	525,309	15.1
South Dakota	696,004	754,844	58,840	8.5
Tennessee	4,877,185	5,689,283	812,098	16.7
Texas	16,986,510	20,851,820	3,865,310	22.8
Utah	1,722,850	2,233,169	510,319	29.6
Vermont	562,758	608,827	46,069	8.2
Virginia	6,187,358	7,078,515	891,157	14.4
Washington	4,866,692	5,894,121	1,027,429	21.1
West Virginia	1,793,477	1,808,344	14,867	0.8
Wisconsin	4,891,769	5,363,675	471,906	9.6
Wyoming	453,588	493,782	40,194	8.9

Sources: U.S. Census Bureau 2001a and 1991a.

and deaths) and 50.3 percent due to net migration (which can be immigration from nations outside the United States or inmigration from other states). The relatively large proportion attributable to net migration is reflective of the dramatic economic expansion of the decade, which brought substantial numbers of new households and the economic impact of moving these new households into the state. The number attributable to natural increase is notable as well because this 1.9 million increase in the 1990s was greater than the total population increase in all other states except California and Florida. Because natural increase rates change relatively slowly, and their response to economic change is less immediate than that for migration, Texas has a natural impetus to growth that is likely to lead to substantial future population growth in the state under a variety of economic conditions.

The growth in Texas' population was also relatively pervasive. All twenty-four of Texas council of governments (COG) regions experienced population growth, as did all twenty-seven of its metropolitan statistical areas (MSAs), 186 (73.2 percent) of its counties, and 945 (74 percent) of its places (that is, towns and cities). However, growth was not the same everywhere and it tended to be larger in the state's large urban centers and in three major regions of the state. The three parts of Texas that showed the highest levels of population growth in either numerical or percentage terms were areas along the Texas-Mexico border, areas in the central corridor of Texas (along Interstate 35) from Dallas–Fort Worth through San Antonio, and the Houston-Galveston area.

The slowest rates of growth were in the Panhandle, West Texas, and Beaumont–Port Arthur areas. Rural areas continued to show reduced levels of growth. By 2000, nonmetropolitan counties accounted for only 15.2 percent of the state's total population (and only 8.8 percent of the state's population increase in the 1990s), whereas metropolitan counties accounted for 84.8 percent of the population (and 91.2 percent of the population increase). Central city counties accounted for

67.1 percent of the total population (and 61.5 percent of the population growth from 1990 to 2000), whereas suburban counties accounted for 17.7 percent of the population (and 29.7 percent of the 1990 to 2000 population increase).

Overall, Texas has shown rapid population growth resulting from both natural increase and net migration, and its high level of natural increase suggests future growth. Its growth was relatively pervasive but was highest in the Texas-Mexico border area, the Central Texas corridor, and the Houston-Galveston area and lowest in the Panhandle, South Plains, West Texas, and Beaumont–Port Arthur regions. Population growth was generally less in rural areas, extensive in central cities, and fastest in suburban areas in the state.

Changes in Racial/Ethnic Composition

An extensive diversification of the racial/ethnic composition of Texas' population has occurred in recent decades. Table 2.3 shows recent patterns of population change by race/ethnicity. In both the 1980s and 1990s, non-Anglo population groups showed substantially larger percentage increases than the Anglo population, with the Anglo population increasing by only 10.1 percent in the 1980s and 7.6 percent in the 1990s compared to 16.8 and 22.5 percent increases in the Black population, 45.4 and 53.7 percent increases in the Hispanic population, and 88.8 and 81.2 percent increases in the population of persons from the Other racial/ethnic group. As a result of these trends, Texas' population was 53.1 percent Anglo by 2000 (down from 65.7 percent in 1980 and 60.6 percent in 1990), 11.6 percent Black (compared to 11.9 in 1980 and 11.6 percent in 1990), and 32 percent Hispanic (compared to 21 percent in 1980 and 25.6 percent in 1990), and 3.3 percent (compared to 1.4 percent in 1980 and 2.2 percent in 1990) were members of the Other racial/ethnic group.

By 2000, Texas had the second largest total population among all the states in the United States and also had the third largest Anglo population (11,074,716), second largest Black

Table 2.3

Population, Population Change, Percent Population Change,
Proportion of Population, and Proportion of Net Change in Texas
by Race/Ethnicity, 1980–2000

Race/ Ethnicity	Population			Numerical Change		Percent Change	
	1980	1990	2000	1980– 90	1990– 2000	1980– 90	1990– 2000
Anglo	9,350,297	10,291,680	11,074,716	941,383	783,036	10.1	7.6
Black	1,692,542	1,976,360	2,421,653	283,818	445,293	16.8	22.5
Hispanic	2,985,824	4,339,905	6,669,666	1,354,081	2,329,761	45.4	53.7
Other	200,528	378,565	685,785	178,037	307,220	88.8	81.2
Total	14,229,191	16,986,510	20,851,820	2,757,319	3,865,310	19.4	22.8

Race/ Ethnicity	Proportion of Population			Proportion of Net Change	
	1980	1990	2000	1980– 90	1990– 2000
Anglo	65.7	60.6	53.1	34.1	20.3
Black	11.9	11.6	11.6	10.3	11.5
Hispanic	21.0	25.6	32.0	49.1	60.3
Other	1.4	2.2	3.3	6.5	7.9
Total	100.0	100.0	100.0	100.0	100.0

Sources: U.S. Census Bureau 2001a, 1991b, and 1982.

(2,421,653), second largest Hispanic (6,669,666), and fourth
largest population of persons from the Other racial/ethnic group
(685,785) of any state in the nation. Equally important, its
growth across these groups was such that it had the second
largest numerical increase in the Anglo population in the 1990s
(an increase of 783,036), the third largest increase in the Black
population (445,293), the second largest increase in the
Hispanic population (2,329,761), and the third largest increase
(307,220) in the Other population.

Particularly notable is the increase in the Hispanic
population. Not only does Texas have the second largest
Hispanic population in the nation (behind California, which
had 11 million in 2000), but Hispanic population growth has
also been the single largest determinant of population growth in
the state for each of the last two decades. In the 1980s, 49.1
percent of the state's net population growth and 60.3 percent of
its net increase in the 1990s were due to the Hispanic

population, and this growth was pervasive across the state. For example, Hispanic population increases occurred in all twenty-four COGs, all twenty-seven MSAs, 89.4 percent of the counties, and 88 percent of the places in Texas. By comparison, fifteen of the COGs, twenty-three of the MSAs, 56.3 percent of counties, and 56 percent of places showed increases in their Anglo populations. Similarly, if one examines the relative contributions of Hispanic population growth to total net population growth in different types of counties (metropolitan central city, metropolitan suburban, nonmetropolitan adjacent counties [nonmetropolitan counties that share a common boundary with a metropolitan central city or suburban county], and nonmetropolitan nonadjacent counties), one finds that Hispanics accounted for 78.1 percent of the net increase in the population in central city counties, 23.3 percent of the net growth in suburban counties, 54.7 percent in nonmetropolitan adjacent counties, and 82.2 percent of the net change in the population of nonmetropolitan nonadjacent counties. For the State of Texas as a whole and pervasively across the state, population change has come to be increasingly determined by change in non-Anglo populations.

Age Structure of the Population

Two aspects of the Texas population's age structure are critical to understanding the impact of population change. First, as with the rest of the United States, Texas' population is aging as a result of increased longevity and the aging of the baby-boom generation (those persons born between 1946 and 1964). As shown in Table 2.4, Texas' median age (the age at which half the people are younger and half are older) was 18.7 years in 1900 but was 28 in 1980, 30.8 in 1990, and 32.3 in 2000. Although still younger than the nation as a whole (which had a median age of 35.3 years in 2000), Texas' population is likely to continue to age in a manner similar to that of the nation as a whole and to have nearly one in five persons who are 65 years of age or older by 2040 compared to fewer than one in ten in

Table 2.4

Median Age in the United States and Texas, 1900–2000

Year	United States	Texas
1900	22.9	18.7
1910	24.1	20.2
1920	25.3	22.0
1930	26.5	23.7
1940	29.0	26.8
1950	30.1	27.9
1960	29.5	27.0
1970	28.1	26.4
1980	30.0	28.0
1990	32.9	30.8
2000	35.3	32.3

Source: U.S. Census Bureau, "Census of Population and Housing," for each year indicated.

2000. Services and conditions affecting older persons will become of increasing relevance to Texas and the nation as a whole in the coming decades.

The second characteristic of the age structure in Texas and in the United States is the clear relationship between youth status and non-Anglo status. For example, the median age for Anglos in 2000 was 38 years but for Blacks it was 29.6 years, for Hispanics 25.5, and for the Other population 31.1 years. The differences in age structure are especially obvious when data for specific age groups are examined. Figure 2.1 shows the percentages of the population in each of several age groups that are Anglo and Hispanic (data for the Black and Other population groups are not shown in this figure). For the population 65 years of age or older, 73 percent is Anglo and 17 percent is Hispanic, while for the group that is less than 5 years of age, 40 percent is Anglo and 44 percent is Hispanic. When Other non-Anglo population groups are included, 60 percent of the Texas population less than 5 years of age and 57 percent of the total population less than 18 years of age are non-Anglo. Clearly, issues related to older persons are more likely to affect Anglo populations and those related to children to affect

Figure 2.1

Percent of Texas Population by Age Group
and Race/Ethnicity, 2000

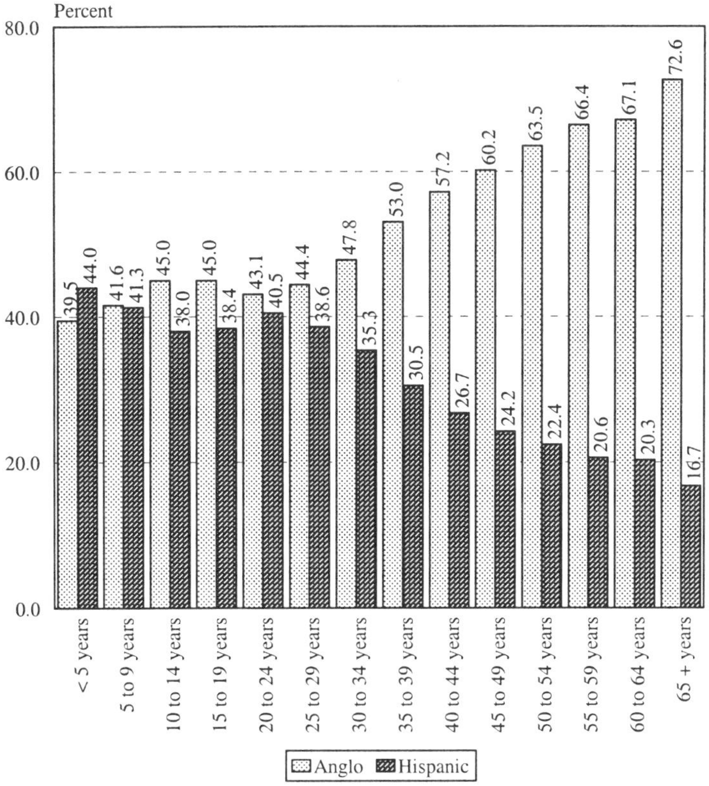

non-Anglo populations. Issues related to race/ethnicity and age may become increasingly interrelated.

FUTURE PATTERNS OF POPULATION CHANGE

In this section, we examine alternative projections of Texas' population. These projections were produced by the Texas State Population Projections Program in the Texas State Data Center in the Office of the State Demographer in the Department of Rural Sociology in the Texas A&M University System (Texas Population Estimates and Projections Program 2001).

The projections were made using the cohort-component projection method, which is a widely accepted method for projecting populations (see Murdock and Ellis 1991; Smith et al. 2001). It consists of the development of assumptions for projecting the three major demographic processes of fertility, mortality, and migration for different population cohorts (a cohort being a population subgroup that shares one or more common characteristics). The Texas State Data Center provides projections for both sexes for Anglos, Blacks, Hispanics, and persons from the Other racial/ethnic group for age groups from less than one through eighty-five years of age or older for each year from 2001 to 2040 using 2000 Census data as a base and alternative assumptions about age-, sex-, and race/ethnicity-specific net migration that result in alternative population projection scenarios. Projections are completed for each of Texas' 254 counties and the state as a whole, and the sum of the county values is controlled to the state total for each age, sex, and race/ethnicity cohort for each year for each scenario. The methodology for these projections is described in detail on the Texas State Data Center's Web site (txsdc.tamu.edu). As noted above, these and any other projections should be used with the full realization of their limitations.

The projection scenarios share common assumptions about birth and death rates but they employ three different assumptions about age-, sex-, and race/ethnicity-specific net migration that differentiate the three projection scenarios; these are the zero (0.0) scenario, the one-half of 1990 to 2000 age-, sex-, and race/ethnicity-specific net migration rates (0.5) scenario, and the scenario that assumes a continuation of age-, sex-, and race/ethnicity-specific rates of net migration at the 1990 to 2000 level (1.0 scenario). The zero migration scenario is provided for comparison only. It indicates what the population would be if the population increased only as a result of natural increase with net migration being zero, either because no one moved into or out of the state or the amounts of in- and outmigration were equal. This scenario is unlikely to characterize future population growth, but its inclusion allows one to compare the relative importance of both natural increase and net migration for future population growth. Because it is unlikely to characterize the future, it is examined only in this chapter. The 1.0 scenario assumes that the rates of the 1990s will continue throughout the projection period, whereas the 0.5 scenario assumes migration levels equal to half those in the 1990 to 2000 decade.

Values based on both the 0.5 and 1.0 scenarios are discussed in several parts of this analysis because of the uncertainty inherent in population projections (see Murdock and Ellis 1991). This uncertainty is increased because of characteristics of the 2000 Census that may affect the net migration rates upon which the projection scenarios are based. The 2000 Census revealed substantially more persons than anticipated by the U.S. Bureau of the Census for the nation and nearly all states, including Texas. This finding suggests that one or more of the following factors may have occurred: (1) the 2000 Census provided a more complete count of the existing population than other recent censuses (that is, the rate of undercount was less), (2) the number of undocumented persons counted in this census was substantially higher than in earlier censuses, or (3) the U.S. Census Bureau's 1990 to 2000 estimates were less accurate than at earlier periods. The difficulty presented by either a reduced undercount or a better count of undocumented persons is that it is impossible to determine what proportion of those in the 2000 count lived in the nation in 1990. Since the migration rates used to project population are residual net migration rates, meaning that they are computed as the difference between the 1990 and 2000 population counts after the effects of births and deaths have been removed, any undercount or other differences become part of the residual and affect the migration rates. Therefore, somewhat greater uncertainty may exist in the migration rates computed from 1990 to 2000 than those from earlier censuses, and the factors leading to such uncertainty tend to be ones that would increase migration rates. As a result, the 1.0 scenario's projections may, in most cases, be seen as a high-growth projection and the 0.5 scenario's as a moderate-growth projection scenario.

Population Growth Projected to Continue

The data in Tables 2.5 and 2.6 suggest there would be substantial population increases under all of the scenarios. Texas' population would be 24.2 million by 2010 under the 0.5 scenario and 25.9 million under the 1.0 scenario. Under the 0.5 scenario the state would have a population of more than 35 million by 2040, including 11.4 million Anglos, 3.3 million Blacks, 18.4 million Hispanics, and nearly 2 million persons in the Other racial/ethnic group. The state's population under the 1.0 scenario would be nearly 50.6 million by 2040, with 12.2

Table 2.5

Population in Texas by Race/Ethnicity in 2000 and Projections
to 2040 Assuming Alternative Projection Scenarios

Year	Anglo	Black	Hispanic	Other	Total
2000	11,074,716	2,421,653	6,669,666	685,785	20,851,820
Assuming Rates of Zero Net Migration (0.0 Scenario)					
2010	11,292,858	2,604,162	7,986,640	776,088	22,659,748
2020	11,320,857	2,727,365	9,220,971	828,786	24,097,979
2030	11,086,475	2,756,470	10,406,060	856,437	25,105,442
2040	10,599,190	2,697,888	11,408,456	856,047	25,561,581
Assuming Rates of Net Migration Equal to One-Half of 1990–2000 (0.5 Scenario)					
2010	11,494,673	2,730,659	8,999,827	953,348	24,178,507
2020	11,735,043	3,004,173	11,742,820	1,256,342	27,738,378
2030	11,701,065	3,191,230	14,900,692	1,596,578	31,389,565
2040	11,382,992	3,283,413	18,391,333	1,954,592	35,012,330
Assuming Rates of Net Migration Equal to 1990–2000 (1.0 Scenario)					
2010	11,700,471	2,863,397	10,164,378	1,168,772	25,897,018
2020	12,165,004	3,309,068	15,056,028	1,897,182	32,427,282
2030	12,350,427	3,694,283	21,533,219	2,960,361	40,538,290
2040	12,225,486	3,995,349	29,926,210	4,435,916	50,582,961

Source: Texas Population Estimates and Projections Program 2001.

Table 2.6

Percent Change in Projected Population in Texas by Race/Ethnicity
Assuming Alternative Projection Scenarios, 2000–40

Time Period	Anglo	Black	Hispanic	Other	Total
Assuming Rates of Zero Net Migration (0.0 Scenario)					
2000–10	2.0	7.5	19.7	13.2	8.7
2010–20	0.2	4.7	15.5	6.8	6.3
2020–30	-2.1	1.1	12.9	3.3	4.2
2030–40	-4.4	-2.1	9.6	0.0	1.8
2000–40	-4.3	11.4	71.0	24.8	22.6
Assuming Rates of Net Migration Equal to One-Half of 1990–2000 (0.5 Scenario)					
2000–10	3.8	12.8	34.9	39.0	16.0
2010–20	2.1	10.0	30.5	31.8	14.7
2020–30	-0.3	6.2	26.9	27.1	13.2
2030–40	-2.7	2.9	23.4	22.4	11.5
2000–40	2.8	35.6	175.7	185.0	67.9
Assuming Rates of Net Migration Equal to 1990–2000 (1.0 Scenario)					
2000–10	5.7	18.2	52.4	70.4	24.2
2010–20	4.0	15.6	48.1	62.3	25.2
2020–30	1.5	11.6	43.0	56.0	25.0
2030–40	-1.0	8.1	39.0	49.8	24.8
2000–40	10.4	65.0	348.7	546.8	142.6

Source: Texas Population Estimates and Projections Program 2001.

million Anglos, 4 million Blacks, 29.9 million Hispanics, and 4.4 million persons in the Other racial/ethnic group. Even the 0.0 scenario would result in the state's population increasing by more than 4.7 million persons during the period 2000 to 2040. Increases under the 0.5 scenario would add nearly 14.2 million, and under the high-growth (1.0) scenario, the increase would be more than 29.7 million. The rates of growth for the total projection period from 2000 to 2040 would be 67.9 percent under the 0.5 scenario and 142.6 percent under the 1.0 scenario. The projected population would increase by decennial rates that are between 70 and 50 percent of the 1990s' growth rate under the middle scenario and, as might be expected, decennial growth rates are about 100 percent of the rates of growth for the 1990s under the 1.0 scenario.

The alternative projections also show how large a role migrants and their descendants will play in the state's future growth and how the role of migration varies by racial/ethnic group. If one compares the growth of the total population under the 0.0 scenario (which shows growth resulting only from natural increase) to that for the other scenarios (which include growth from both natural increase and net migration), one finds that 66.7 percent of the net growth in the state from 2000 to 2040 under the 0.5 scenario and 84.2 percent under the 1.0 scenario would be due to net migration (that is to migrants and their descendants). Because its birth rate is below the replacement level, the Anglo population would actually decline by 2040 under the 0.0 migration scenario, so all of the growth in the Anglo population under both the 0.5 and 1.0 scenarios is due to net migration. Under the 0.5 scenario, 68 percent of the net growth in the Black population, 59.6 percent of the growth in the Hispanic, and 86.6 percent of the growth in the Other population would be due to migrants and their descendants, while under the 1.0 scenario 82.4 percent of the Black, 79.6 percent of the Hispanic, and 95.5 percent of the growth in the Other population would be due to migrants and their descendants. Although some may see a lack of migration as benefiting the state because it reduces the number of persons for whom the state must provide services, others view the lack of migration as inhibiting business expansion (the average decennial growth rates under the 0.0 scenario would be lower than at any period in the state's history except that which occurred during the decade of the 1930s, which reflected the effects of the Great Depression). Similarly, the 0.0 scenario results in the oldest age structure of any of the scenarios and in lower levels of employment and a proportionate increase in services for the elderly compared to the other scenarios. In general, then, net migration at some level seems likely to be desired by most persons from the public and private sectors in Texas.

An Increasingly Diverse Population

When differences in rates of population growth among racial/ethnic groups (see Tables 2.5 and 2.6) are examined in conjunction with data in Tables 2.7 and 2.8, the extensive growth of non-Anglo populations is evident. Although all racial/ethnic groups show population increases under the 0.5 and 1.0 scenarios, the Anglo population increases by only 2.8 percent from 2000 to 2040 under the 0.5 scenario and by 10.4 percent under the 1.0 scenario, while the Black population increases by 35.6 percent and 65 percent, the Hispanic population by 175.7 percent and 348.7 percent, and the Other population by 185 percent and 546.8 percent. As a result, the Anglo population decreases as a proportion of the total population, from 53.1 percent in 2000 to 32.5 percent in 2040

Table 2.7

Percent of Population in Texas by Race/Ethnicity in 2000 and Projections to 2040 Assuming Alternative Projection Scenarios

Year	Anglo	Black	Hispanic	Other
2000	53.1	11.6	32.0	3.3
Assuming Rates of Zero Net Migration (0.0 Scenario)				
2010	49.9	11.5	35.2	3.4
2020	47.0	11.3	38.3	3.4
2030	44.2	11.0	41.4	3.4
2040	41.5	10.6	44.6	3.3
Assuming Rates of Net Migration Equal to One-Half of 1990–2000 (0.5 Scenario)				
2010	47.6	11.3	37.2	3.9
2020	42.4	10.8	42.3	4.5
2030	37.2	10.2	47.5	5.1
2040	32.5	9.4	52.5	5.6
Assuming Rates of Net Migration Equal to 1990–2000 (1.0 Scenario)				
2010	45.2	11.1	39.2	4.5
2020	37.5	10.2	46.4	5.9
2030	30.5	9.1	53.1	7.3
2040	24.2	7.9	59.1	8.8

Source: Texas Population Estimates and Projections Program 2001.

Table 2.8

Number and Percent of Net Change in the Texas
Population Due To Each Race/Ethnicity Group,
Assuming Alternative Projection Scenarios, 2000–40

Race/ Ethnicity	Number	Percent
Assuming Rates of Zero Net Migration (0.0 Scenario)		
Anglo	-475,526	-10.1
Black	276,235	5.9
Hispanic	4,738,790	100.6
Other	170,262	3.6
Total	4,709,761	100.0
Assuming Rates of Net Migration Equal to One-Half of 1990–2000 (0.5 Scenario)		
Anglo	308,276	2.2
Black	861,760	6.1
Hispanic	11,721,667	82.8
Other	1,268,807	8.9
Total	14,160,510	100.0
Assuming Rates of Net Migration Equal to 1990–2000 (1.0 Scenario)		
Anglo	1,150,770	3.9
Black	1,573,696	5.3
Hispanic	23,256,544	78.2
Other	3,750,131	12.6
Total	29,731,141	100.0

Source: Texas Population Estimates and Projections Program
2001.

under the 0.5 scenario and to 24.2 percent by 2040 under the
1.0 scenario, and the Black population decreases from 11.6
percent of the population in 2000 to 9.4 percent by 2040 under
the 0.5 scenario and to 7.9 percent by 2040 under the 1.0
scenario. On the other hand, the Hispanic population increases
from 32 percent in 2000 to 52.5 percent by 2040 under the 0.5
scenario and to 59.1 percent under the 1.0 scenario and the
Other population increases from 3.3 percent in 2000 to 5.6
percent in 2040 under the 0.5 scenario and to 8.8 percent under
the 1.0 scenario. Texas' population would be less than one-half
Anglo by 2005 under the 1.0 scenario and by 2006 under the
0.5 scenario. The Hispanic population is projected to become a

majority of the state's population by 2026 under the 1.0 scenario and by 2035 under the 0.5 scenario. Under either the 0.5 or 1.0 scenarios, the Anglo population would account for no more than one-third of the total population by 2040, and even under the highest growth scenario (the 1.0 scenario), the Anglo population would account for only 3.9 percent of net population growth from 2000 to 2040 (see Table 2.8 and Figure 2.2), meaning that more than 96 percent of the total net increase in Texas' population from 2000 to 2040 would be due to the growth of the non-Anglo population.

The extent to which slow Anglo population growth and rapid growth for Hispanics will become pervasive patterns is evident in the fact that under even the high-growth scenario (1.0), which shows the maximum increase in Anglo populations, the Anglo population would show an absolute

Figure 2.2

Projected Percent of Net Change Due To Each
Race/Ethnicity Group in Texas for 2000 to 2040*

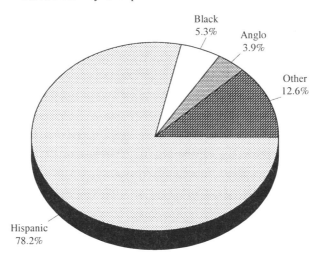

* Using U.S. Census count for 2000 and Texas Population
  Estimates and Projections Program 1.0 population projection
  scenario for 2040.

numerical decline between 2000 and 2040 in 19 of 24 COG
regions, with declines of at least 25 percent occurring in 13
regions. On the other hand, the Hispanic population increases
in all 24 regions, with increases exceeding 100 percent in 21 of
24 regions.

Texas' projected population will clearly become more
diverse over the next few decades. By about 2005 no single
racial/ethnic group will account for a majority of the population
and the majority of Texas' population will be Hispanic before
the end of the projection period. The diverse, multiracial
population that many (Skrabanek et al. 1985; Bouvier and
Poston 1993; Murdock et al. 1997) have foreseen as
characterizing the future of Texas is projected to become a
reality during the first decades of this century.

An Aging and Age-Stratified Population

As noted above, Texas' population, although aging in a manner
similar to other parts of the nation, is nevertheless somewhat
younger than the populations of most other states. In fact,
Texas was the second youngest state in the nation in 2000, with
only Utah (which has a median age of 27.1 years) having a
lower median age. The aging of the population and the pattern
showing that non-Anglo populations tend to be younger and
Anglo populations to be older are evident throughout the
alternative projections for Texas (see Table 2.9).

The trend toward a generally older population is evident
under all projection scenarios. The median age increases from
32.3 years in 2000 to 39.7 years by 2040 under the 0.0 scenario,
to 38.8 years by 2040 under the 0.5 scenario, and to 38.3 years
by 2040 under the 1.0 scenario. The patterns are not uniform
across time or age groups, however. For example, the
percentage of the population that is 65 years of age or older,
which is 9.9 percent in 2000 but 16 to 20 percent by 2040,
changes by less than 1 percent from 2000 to 2010 (depending
on the scenario) but by 1 to 4 percent for each decade
thereafter. The proportion of the population that is between 45

Table 2.9

Percent of Population in Texas by Age and Race/Ethnicity of the
Population and Median Age by Race/Ethnicity in 2000 and
Projections to 2040 Assuming Alternative Projection Scenarios

Age Group	Anglo	Black	Hispanic	Other	Total Percent
2000					
<18	23.0	31.7	35.8	26.1	28.2
18–24	8.8	11.2	13.2	11.2	10.6
25–44	30.1	32.1	31.8	37.7	31.1
45–64	24.4	17.7	14.0	20.1	20.2
65+	13.7	7.3	5.2	4.9	9.9
Median Age	38.0	29.6	25.5	31.1	32.3
Assuming Rates of Zero Net Migration (0.0 Scenario)					
2010					
<18	21.1	27.3	34.0	24.6	26.5
18–24	9.1	11.8	11.1	8.7	10.1
25–44	25.4	29.1	30.0	31.3	27.6
45–64	29.5	24.2	18.8	26.8	25.1
65+	14.9	7.6	6.1	8.6	10.7
Median Age	40.7	32.0	28.2	36.8	34.6
2040					
<18	17.4	19.8	27.4	17.0	22.1
18–24	7.7	8.9	10.1	6.7	8.8
25–44	24.0	27.3	26.7	23.8	25.6
45–64	25.2	27.0	20.8	22.9	23.3
65+	25.7	17.0	15.0	29.6	20.2
Median Age	45.8	40.8	34.1	47.2	39.7
Assuming Rates of Net Migration Equal to One-Half of 1990–2000 (0.5 Scenario)					
2010					
<18	21.0	27.3	32.9	23.3	26.2
18–24	9.1	12.0	11.7	9.0	10.4
25–44	25.5	29.2	31.9	32.7	28.6
45–64	29.4	24.0	17.9	26.7	24.4
65+	15.0	7.5	5.6	8.3	10.4
Median Age	40.7	31.8	28.2	36.8	34.1
2040					
<18	17.2	19.8	26.0	15.5	22.0
18–24	7.6	9.2	10.1	6.5	9.0
25–44	23.9	27.6	29.4	24.2	27.1
45–64	25.4	26.8	22.3	25.5	23.9
65+	25.9	16.6	12.2	28.3	18.0
Median Age	46.0	40.4	34.2	47.9	38.8

Table 2.9, continued

Age Group	Anglo	Black	Hispanic	Other	Total Percent
Assuming Rates of Net Migration Equal to 1990–2000 (1.0 Scenario)					
2010					
<18	20.8	27.3	31.8	22.1	25.9
18–24	9.2	12.3	12.3	9.4	10.8
25–44	25.7	29.2	33.8	34.0	29.6
45–64	29.3	23.7	16.9	26.4	23.7
65+	15.0	7.5	5.2	8.1	10.0
Median Age	40.7	31.7	28.2	36.9	33.6
2040					
<18	17.0	19.9	24.4	14.1	21.4
18–24	7.5	9.4	10.2	6.4	9.1
25–44	23.9	27.9	31.9	24.5	29.0
45–64	25.6	26.6	23.6	28.0	24.7
65+	26.0	16.2	9.9	27.0	15.8
Median Age	46.3	40.1	34.4	48.4	38.3

Source: Texas Population Estimates and Projections Program 2001.

and 64 years of age increases by about 3 to 5 percent over the projection period, and the percentage of the population that is under 18 years of age declines by about 5 to 7 percent from 2000 to 2040. The slower aging under the higher-growth scenarios reflects the fact that such scenarios project more growth from non-Anglo populations that have higher birth rates and younger populations. Under all scenarios, however, the population will age substantially.

The differentials by race/ethnicity are marked as well, and although non-Anglo and Anglo populations show aging population structures, racial/ethnic differences in age remain important. For example, in 2000, 13.7 percent of the Anglo population was 65 years of age or older and the median age of Anglos was 38 years. By comparison, only 5.2 percent of the Hispanic population was 65 years of age or older in 2000 and the median age of Hispanics was 25.5 years. Under the 0.5 scenario in 2040, the percentage of persons 65 years of age or older would be 25.9 percent for Anglos and 12.2 percent for Hispanics and median ages would be 46 for Anglos and 34.2

for Hispanics. Under the 1.0 scenario, the percentage of persons 65 years of age or older increases to 26 percent for Anglos but is only 9.9 percent for Hispanics and median ages are 46.3 and 34.4 years, respectively. The aging of populations occurs across race/ethnicity groups, but younger populations remain more characteristic of non-Anglo than Anglo populations and older populations of Anglo than non-Anglo populations.

Overall, the data on aging suggest that Texas' population will become older, that the aging will become more obvious after 2010 when the baby boomers begin to reach 65 years of age, and that marked differences in the age structures of Anglos and non-Anglos will continue across the projection period. These patterns suggest that issues related to aging and issues related to younger non-Anglo populations and older Anglo populations are likely to be important in the coming decades.

SUMMARY

In this chapter we have described recent and projected changes in the size, race/ethnicity, and age composition of Texas' population. The results suggest several important conclusions:

1. Texas' population is likely to increase substantially under the alternative scenarios of future growth. For the total projection period from 2000 to 2040, the population increase would be at least 4.7 million persons and could be as high as 29.7 million under the high-growth (1.0) scenario, with percentage increases of between 67.9 and 142.6 percent under the 0.5 and 1.0 scenarios, respectively. Under the two most likely scenarios (the 0.5 and 1.0 scenarios), between 66.7 and 84.2 percent of the population increase will result from migrants and their descendants.

2. The state's racial/ethnic diversity will also increase substantially. Under all scenarios, the Texas population becomes more diverse over the next few decades. Texas' population will be less than one-half Anglo by 2005 under the

high-growth (1.0) scenario and by 2006 under the moderate rate of growth (0.5) scenario. Under either scenario, the Texas population is projected to be more than one-half Hispanic before the end of the projection period. Moreover, by the end of the projection period (depending on whether one employs the 1.0 or 0.5 scenario), Texas' population will be between 24.2 and 32.5 percent Anglo, 7.9 and 9.4 percent Black, 59.1 and 52.5 percent Hispanic, and 8.8 and 5.6 percent Other.

3. Both the aging of Texas' population and the racial/ethnic diversification in the age structure are projected to continue. By 2040, the median age in Texas will be at least 38.3 years, compared to 32.3 in 2000. Anglo populations will continue to be older, with the median age of Anglos increasing to about 46 years (from 38 in 2000) under all scenarios, while that of Hispanics increases to at most 34.4 years by 2040 (compared to 25.5 in 2000).

Overall, the projections of the Texas population examined in this chapter suggest that a population that is larger, older, and increasingly diverse will impact socioeconomic and service structures. It is a population that seems likely to increasingly challenge the state's resources in the coming decades.

CHAPTER 3

Current and Future Trends in Texas Households

Together with population growth, change in racial/ethnic diversity, and the aging of the population, a fourth major demographic factor is shaping Texas' future; change in the number and composition of Texas households. The forms of households—that is, how Texans are grouped together to live—impact numerous aspects of the state's public and private sectors. For example, the number of persons in a household affects the level of demand for different types of housing, households with single parents tend to have higher levels of need for public assistance, and married-couple households tend to have higher incomes. Services such as long-term care are often impacted by the family's characteristics (for example, the number of caregivers), and even the level of public versus private care that is required may be affected by household characteristics. Understanding how households in Texas have changed and are projected to change in the future is thus instrumental to understanding the state's future. In this chapter we examine both the past and future of Texas households and families.

HISTORICAL TRENDS

For a number of decades, household growth in Texas has mirrored the extensive growth of the population. In fact, because of the population's rapid growth in those ages associated with initial stages of household formation, the decennial percentage increases in households have tended to exceed those in the population. For example, population growth in the 1960s, 1970s, and 1980s of 16.9 percent, 27.1 percent, and 19.4 percent (see Table 2.1) was surpassed by increases in the number of households of 23.6, 43.7, and 23 percent during the same decades (see Table 3.1). The movement of baby boomers into household formation ages resulted in substantial growth in the number of households.

In the 1990s, the percentage increase in the number of Texas households was less than the percentage increase in the population (21.8 percent for households and 22.8 percent for the population). This change can be attributed to two factors: (1) large parts of the population were aging out of the ages in which initial household formation occurs, so that fewer households were being formed, and (2) non-Anglo populations, which accounted for roughly 80 percent of the net population growth in the 1990s, have larger average household sizes, resulting in larger population increases per housing unit. Overall, however, these data suggest that, although the pace of growth has varied by decade, the number of Texas households has increased rapidly in all recent decades.

Table 3.1

Number and Percent Change in Households in the
United States and Texas, 1960–2000

	1960	1970	1980	1990	2000
	Number of Households				
U.S.	53,021,343	63,616,135	80,467,427	91,947,410	105,480,101
Texas	2,777,982	3,433,996	4,934,936	6,070,937	7,393,354

	Percent Change in Households			
	1960–70	1970–80	1980–90	1990–2000
U.S.	20.0	26.5	14.3	14.7
Texas	23.6	43.7	23.0	21.8

Source: U.S. Census Bureau, "Census of Population and Housing," for each year indicated.

Texas and U.S. households have also shown substantial changes in size (see Figure 3.1) and composition (Table 3.2). Since 1940, the size of the average Texas household has decreased by one person, representing a 36.5 percent decrease. Similar declines occurred in both Texas and the nation during more recent periods (see Figure 3.1). This decline is important because having fewer persons per household results in a larger number of households. This means that changes in household size affect changes in the number of households—that is, growth in the number of both consumer units and taxing units.

Like growth in the number of households, change in the average size of Texas households was impacted by the characteristics of the population changes of the 1990s. The 1990s witnessed relatively little change in average household size in Texas, while the average size of households continued

Figure 3.1

Average Persons Per Household in the United States and Texas, 1950–2000

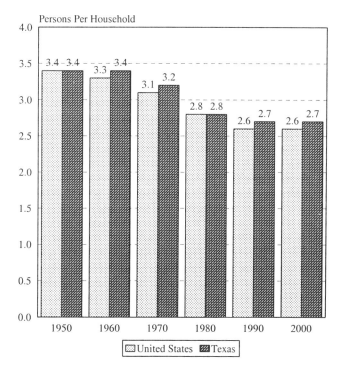

Table 3.2

Percent of and Percent Change in Texas Households
by Size and Type, 1970–2000

Size/Type of Household	Year				Percent Change in Number of Households		
	1970	1980	1990	2000	1970–80	1980–90	1990–2000
Total Households							
(in thousands)	3,434	4,929	6,071	7,393	43.5	23.2	21.8
Households by Size							
One-person	16.2	21.6	23.9	23.7	90.5	36.4	20.6
Two-person	30.0	30.8	30.1	30.5	47.5	20.4	23.6
Three-person	17.4	17.5	17.3	17.1	44.6	21.6	20.1
Four-person	15.6	15.6	15.7	15.3	43.8	23.2	18.6
Five-person	9.8	8.0	7.5	7.8	17.6	15.7	26.5
Six or more	11.0	6.5	5.5	5.6	-14.9	2.4	25.2
Households by Type							
Family	81.8	74.6	71.6	71.0	30.9	18.1	20.8
Married couple	71.5	62.6	56.6	54.0	25.7	11.2	16.1
Male householder	2.0	2.5	3.4	4.3	75.9	69.3	55.2
Female householder	8.3	9.5	11.6	12.7	64.4	50.2	33.6
Nonfamily	18.2	24.4	28.4	29.0	100.5	38.0	24.2

Source: U.S. Census Bureau, "Census of Population and Housing," for each year indicated.

to decline from 2.63 in 1990 to 2.59 in 2000 in the nation as a whole. The difference between the Texas and national patterns reflects differences in the composition of population growth. In Texas, average household size decreased for nearly all racial/ethnic groups during the 1990s, but the larger household size of Hispanic and Other non-Anglo populations (for example, the average household size in 2000 for Hispanics was 3.6 and that for non-Hispanics was 2.5) and the large proportion of the population increase that is due to non-Anglo populations resulted in the addition of a larger proportion of larger households. As a result, the overall average size of households in the total state population did not decline in the 1990s as it had in earlier decades. The substantial difference in the size of households being added to Texas' population in the 1990s compared to earlier decades is very evident in the data in the top panel of Table 3.2. These data show that although households with five or more persons showed the smallest percentage increases in both the 1970s and 1980s, the number of households with five or six persons showed the largest percentage increases in the 1990s. The rapid growth of populations with larger households played a significant role in household change in Texas in the 1990s. Despite such changes, the data on households continue to show that a majority of all households are one- and two-person households, with 23.7 percent of all households in 2000 involving only one individual and 30.5 having only two persons.

The diversification of household forms was evident in both Texas and the United States as a whole. Texas households, like those in the nation as a whole, have become increasingly characterized by nonfamily, single-parent, and unmarried-partner households (see Table 3.2). The percentage increase in nonfamily households (that is, households consisting of a single person or two or more unrelated persons living in the same housing unit) has exceeded that for family households (households with two or more persons who are related by kinship, marriage, or adoption and living in the same housing unit) in each of the last three decades (see the bottom panel of Table 3.2). Married-couple (including both those with and those without children) households have shown smaller percentage increases than male- or female-family householder (that is, single-parent) households, and the percentage of married-couple households declined and showed smaller rates of growth than unmarried-partner households. For example, the number of family households in Texas increased by 30.9, 18.1, and 20.8 percent in the 1970s, 1980s, and 1990s, respectively, while the number of nonfamily households increased by 100.5, 38.0, and 24.2 percent during the same decades; the number of married-couple families increased by 16.1 percent in the 1990s but the number of male-householder families increased by 55.2 percent and the number of female-householder families by 33.6 percent, and the percentage of all households in Texas that were married-couple households declined from 71.5 percent of all households in 1970 to 54 percent in 2000; and while the number of married-couple households increased by 16.1 percent from 1990 to 2000, the number of unmarried-partner households increased by 87.7 percent. Although a majority of Texas and U.S. households (54 percent in Texas and 51.7 percent in the United States) remained married-couple households in 2000, the forms and types of households are clearly diversifying.

Overall, recent patterns of household change suggest that the number of Texas households has increased substantially and that households have become smaller in size and more diverse in form than in the past. The larger non-Anglo population in Texas has resulted in slower rates of change toward nonfamily, single-parent, and unmarried-partner households than in the United States as a whole, but it is evident that Texas households are changing. This growth in the number and diversity of household forms affects the magnitude of services needed in the state, the types of services, and how those services can be delivered most effectively.

FUTURE PATTERNS OF HOUSEHOLD CHANGE

The number of Texas households is likely to continue to grow extensively in the coming years and the characteristics of such households to reflect the diversity and age structure of the population. Household projections based on the population projection scenarios discussed in the preceding chapter are shown in Tables 3.3–3.8.

The data in these tables point to substantial change in the number of Texas households. From 2000 to 2040 the number of Texas households is projected to increase by more than 6.2 million from 7.4 million households in 2000 to 13.6 million households in 2040 under the 0.5 scenario and by nearly 12 million to 19.4 million households in 2040 under the 1.0 scenario (Table 3.3). These numbers represent increases of 84.2 percent and 162.1 percent, respectively (Table 3.4). The rate of

Table 3.3

Number of Households in Texas by Race/Ethnicity in 2000 and
Projections to 2040 Assuming Alternative Projection Scenarios

Year	Anglo	Black	Hispanic	Other	Total
2000	4,540,078	843,712	1,789,623	219,941	7,393,354
Assuming Rates of Net Migration Equal to One-Half of 1990–2000 (0.5 Scenario)					
2010	4,855,688	1,022,198	2,607,216	333,617	8,818,719
2020	5,126,311	1,207,150	3,614,696	467,026	10,415,183
2030	5,262,528	1,351,408	4,821,738	617,857	12,053,531
2040	5,203,862	1,441,747	6,200,085	770,565	13,616,259
Assuming Rates of Net Migration Equal to 1990–2000 (1.0 Scenario)					
2010	4,950,419	1,068,979	2,956,070	414,118	9,389,586
2020	5,327,431	1,324,961	4,676,499	717,860	12,046,751
2030	5,571,513	1,557,897	7,051,958	1,166,697	15,348,065
2040	5,610,322	1,746,730	10,231,880	1,787,865	19,376,797

Sources: Derived by the authors from Texas Population Estimates and Projections
Program 2001; U.S. Census Bureau 2001b.

Table 3.4

Percent Change in the Projected Number of Households in Texas
by Race/Ethnicity Assuming Alternative Projection Scenarios, 2000–40

Time Period	Anglo	Black	Hispanic	Other	Total
Assuming Rates of Net Migration Equal to One-Half of 1990–2000 (0.5 Scenario)					
2000–10	7.0	21.2	45.7	51.7	19.3
2010–20	5.6	18.1	38.6	40.0	18.1
2020–30	2.7	12.0	33.4	32.3	15.7
2030–40	-1.1	6.7	28.6	24.7	13.0
2000–40	14.6	70.9	246.4	250.4	84.2
Assuming Rates of Net Migration Equal to 1990–2000 (1.0 Scenario)					
2000–10	9.0	26.7	65.2	88.3	27.0
2010–20	7.6	23.9	58.2	73.3	28.3
2020–30	4.6	17.6	50.8	62.5	27.4
2030–40	0.7	12.1	45.1	53.2	26.2
2000–40	23.6	107.0	471.7	712.9	162.1

Sources: Derived by the authors from Texas Population Estimates and Projections
Program 2001; U.S. Census Bureau 2001b.

growth in households is expected to exceed the 67.9 percent
and 142.6 percent rates of growth projected for Texas' total
population. The faster growth in households than in population
is a reflection of the large number of non-Anglos who will

enter household-formation ages during this period. For example, under the 1.0 scenario, although the rate of increase in households from 2000 to 2040 exceeds that in the populations of all racial/ethnic groups, the percentage increase in households exceeds the rate of increase in the population by 13.2 percent for Anglos (23.6 percent rate of growth for households compared to 10.4 percent for the population) but by 42 percent for Blacks, 123 percent for Hispanics, and by 166.1 percent for the Other population group.

The diversity in the future population is reflected in the diversity of householders (see Table 3.5). By 2040 under the 1.0 scenario, 29 percent of all households would involve Anglo householders compared to 61.4 percent in 2000, 9 percent would involve Blacks compared to 11.4 percent in 2000, 52.8 percent would involve Hispanics compared to 24.2 percent in 2000, and 9.2 percent would involve persons from the Other racial/ethnic group compared to 3 percent in 2000.

Householders tend to have age structures older than the general population because one does not generally become a householder before one's late teens or early adult years. For this reason and because the non-Anglo population is younger than the Anglo population, the percentages of households that have a non-Anglo householder are lower than the non-Anglo proportion of the population. These data point, however, to a household structure in which a majority of households will have a non-Anglo householder by the second decade of this century. In fact, if one examines the net increase in the number of households between 2000 and 2040 under the 1.0 scenario, 91 percent is projected to be due to growth in the number of non-Anglo households with 7.5 percent due to Black, 70.4 percent due to Hispanic, and 13.1 percent due to increases in the number of households with a householder from the Other racial/ethnic group (see Table 3.6).

The age structure of Texas householders will become older in the coming years. In 2000 the median age of Texas householders was 45 (see Table 3.7), whereas the median age

Table 3.5

Percent of Households in Texas by Race/Ethnicity
in 2000 and Projections to 2040 Assuming Alternative
Projection Scenarios

Year	Anglo	Black	Hispanic	Other
2000	61.4	11.4	24.2	3.0
Assuming Rates of Net Migration Equal to One-Half of 1990–2000 (0.5 Scenario)				
2010	55.0	11.6	29.6	3.8
2020	49.2	11.6	34.7	4.5
2030	43.7	11.2	40.0	5.1
2040	38.2	10.6	45.5	5.7
Assuming Rates of Net Migration Equal to 1990–2000 (1.0 Scenario)				
2010	52.7	11.4	31.5	4.4
2020	44.2	11.0	38.8	6.0
2030	36.3	10.2	45.9	7.6
2040	29.0	9.0	52.8	9.2

Sources: Derived by the authors from Texas Population Estimates
and Projections Program 2001; U.S. Census Bureau 2001b.

Table 3.6

Number and Percent of Net Change in Texas Households Due
To Each Race/Ethnicity Group, Assuming Alternative
Projection Scenarios, 2000–40

Race/ Ethnicity	Number	Percent
Assuming Rates of Net Migration Equal to One-Half of 1990–2000 (0.5 Scenario)		
Anglo	663,784	10.7
Black	598,035	9.6
Hispanic	4,410,462	70.9
Other	550,624	8.8
Total	6,222,905	100.0
Assuming Rates of Net Migration Equal to 1990–2000 (1.0 Scenario)		
Anglo	1,070,244	9.0
Black	903,018	7.5
Hispanic	8,442,257	70.4
Other	1,567,924	13.1
Total	11,983,443	100.0

Sources: Derived by the authors from Texas Population Estimates
and Projections Program 2001; U.S. Census Bureau 2001b.

in the population was 32.3 (see Table 2.9). That trend will continue in the future. By 2040, under the 1.0 scenario, the median age of all householders would be 50.1 years. The faster growth scenario projects larger increases in the number of households because of faster growth in younger non-Anglo populations, and the 0.5 scenario shows a higher median age for householders with a median age of 51.7. What is particularly evident is that the number of households with elderly householders increases extensively such that by 2040, under the 1.0 scenario, 24.5 percent of all households would have a householder 65 years of age or older, compared to 17.6 percent in 2000.

The age of householders also varies by race/ethnicity. Reflecting their generally younger populations, the median age of non-Anglo households is younger and the proportion at older ages is smaller. For example, in 2000 the median age was 47.9 years for Anglo householders but 43.1 years for Blacks, 40.7 years for Hispanics, and 40.9 years for households headed by persons from the Other racial/ethnic group. Even in 2040, differentials remain: under the 1.0 scenario, the median age for Anglos would be 56.4 years, but it would be 51 years for Blacks, 46.5 years for Hispanics, and 55.2 years for the Other racial/ethnic group. Although the age of householders increases for all racial/ethnic groups, non-Anglo households remain younger.

The patterns projected for households indicate the expected patterns in that they show substantial growth, diversification, and an aging of the household base in Texas. These patterns were reflected in our previous projections (Murdock et al. 1997) and are ones that have been examined extensively.

The data in Table 3.8 provide projections of households by type. These projections were made using age-, race/ethnicity-, and household-type-specific rates for 2000. The data point to some reversal in household change patterns from those of the past. Because of the higher rates of family households among Hispanic and Other populations and the rapid growth expected

Table 3.7

Percent of Households in Texas by Age and Race/Ethnicity
of the Householder and Median Age of Householders by
Race/Ethnicity in 2000 and Projections to 2040 Assuming
Alternative Projection Scenarios

Age Group	Anglo	Black	Hispanic	Other	Total Percent
2000					
15–24	5.5	7.4	8.9	7.4	6.6
25–44	38.5	47.5	52.3	53.8	43.4
45–64	34.6	31.0	27.7	32.2	32.4
65+	21.4	14.1	11.1	6.6	17.6
Median Age	47.9	43.1	40.7	40.9	45.0
Assuming Rates of Net Migration Equal to One-Half of 1990–2000 (0.5 Scenario)					
2010					
15–24	5.3	7.2	7.4	5.4	6.2
25–44	31.7	40.1	48.8	43.5	38.1
45–64	40.4	39.1	32.7	39.4	37.9
65+	22.6	13.6	11.1	11.7	17.8
Median Age	51.1	46.2	42.5	45.5	47.7
2040					
15–24	4.1	4.6	5.5	3.4	4.7
25–44	27.5	32.5	38.7	28.5	33.2
45–64	32.2	37.4	35.1	33.3	34.2
65+	36.2	25.5	20.7	34.8	27.9
Median Age	56.3	51.4	48.0	55.9	51.7
Assuming Rates of Net Migration Equal to 1990–2000 (1.0 Scenario)					
2010					
15–24	5.3	7.4	7.7	5.5	6.3
25–44	31.8	40.2	51.3	44.7	39.5
45–64	40.2	38.8	30.8	38.6	37.0
65+	22.7	13.6	10.2	11.2	17.2
Median Age	51.0	46.1	41.5	44.9	47.0
2040					
15–24	4.1	4.7	5.3	3.2	4.7
25–44	27.3	33.0	41.6	28.3	35.4
45–64	32.3	37.2	36.5	35.9	35.4
65+	36.3	25.1	16.6	32.6	24.5
Median Age	56.4	51.0	46.5	55.2	50.1

Sources: Derived by the authors from Texas Population Estimates and
Projections Program 2001; U.S. Census Bureau 2001c.

Table 3.8

Number and Percent of Households in Texas by Type of Household and Race/Ethnicity of Householder in 2000 and Projections for 2040 Assuming Alternative Projection Scenarios

Family Type	Anglo Number	%	Black Number	%	Hispanic Number	%	Other Number	%	Total Number	%
2000										
Family households	3,047,023	67.1	576,324	68.3	1,463,353	81.8	161,094	73.2	5,247,794	71.0
Married-couple family	2,524,945	55.6	293,195	34.8	1,039,515	58.1	132,086	60.1	3,989,741	54.0
With own children	1,077,641	23.7	155,495	18.4	689,684	38.5	78,808	35.8	2,001,628	27.1
No own children	1,447,304	31.9	137,700	16.4	349,831	19.6	53,278	24.3	1,988,113	26.9
Other family	522,078	11.5	283,129	33.6	423,838	23.7	29,008	13.2	1,258,053	17.0
Male householder, spouse absent	138,641	3.1	44,957	5.3	126,459	7.1	10,407	4.7	320,464	4.3
With own children	72,840	1.6	22,560	2.7	58,594	3.3	3,420	1.6	157,414	2.1
No own children	65,801	1.5	22,397	2.6	67,865	3.8	6,987	3.1	163,050	2.2
Female householder, spouse absent	383,437	8.4	238,172	28.3	297,379	16.6	18,601	8.5	937,589	12.7
With own children	217,395	4.8	149,299	17.7	187,609	10.5	9,985	4.5	564,288	7.6
No own children	166,042	3.6	88,873	10.6	109,770	6.1	8,616	4.0	373,301	5.1
Nonfamily households	1,493,055	32.9	267,388	31.7	326,270	18.2	58,847	26.8	2,145,560	29.0
Male householder	1,236,907	27.2	228,911	27.1	241,493	13.5	44,830	20.4	1,752,141	23.7
Female householder	256,148	5.7	38,477	4.6	84,777	4.7	14,017	6.4	393,419	5.3
Total Households	4,540,078	100.0	843,712	100.0	1,789,623	100.0	219,941	100.0	7,393,354	100.0
Assuming Rates of Net Migration Equal to One-Half of 1990–2000 (0.5 Scenario)										
2040										
Family households	3,459,482	66.5	967,592	67.1	4,976,540	80.3	552,597	71.7	9,956,211	73.1
Married-couple family	2,896,800	55.7	503,628	34.9	3,540,823	57.1	452,371	58.7	7,393,622	54.3
With own children	1,056,499	20.3	242,221	16.8	2,186,445	35.3	199,283	25.9	3,684,448	27.1
No own children	1,840,301	35.4	261,407	18.1	1,354,378	21.8	253,088	32.8	3,709,174	27.2
Other family	562,682	10.8	463,964	32.2	1,435,717	23.2	100,226	13.0	2,562,589	18.8
Male householder, spouse absent	144,416	2.8	74,806	5.2	449,270	7.2	32,974	4.3	701,466	5.2
With own children	69,485	1.3	33,762	2.3	186,709	3.0	8,618	1.1	298,574	2.2
No own children	74,931	1.5	41,044	2.9	262,561	4.2	24,356	3.2	402,892	3.0
Female householder, spouse absent	418,266	8.0	389,158	27.0	986,447	16.0	67,252	8.7	1,861,123	13.6
With own children	201,259	3.9	217,024	15.1	549,510	8.9	24,278	3.2	992,071	7.3
No own children	217,007	4.1	172,134	11.9	436,937	7.1	42,974	5.5	869,052	6.3
Nonfamily households	1,744,380	33.5	474,155	32.9	1,223,545	19.7	217,968	28.3	3,660,048	26.9
Male householder	1,497,075	28.8	412,276	28.6	928,599	15.0	179,358	23.3	3,017,308	22.2
Female householder	247,305	4.7	61,879	4.3	294,946	4.7	38,610	5.0	642,740	4.7
Total Households	5,203,862	100.0	1,441,747	100.0	6,200,085	100.0	770,565	100.0	13,616,259	100.0
Assuming Rates of Net Migration Equal to 1990–2000 (1.0 Scenario)										
2040										
Family households	3,784,227	67.5	1,177,751	67.4	8,250,778	80.6	1,294,033	72.4	14,506,789	74.9
Married-couple family	3,194,833	56.9	634,783	36.3	5,924,365	57.9	1,064,991	59.6	10,818,972	55.8
With own children	1,179,309	21.0	314,001	18.0	3,821,479	37.3	482,045	27.0	5,796,834	29.9
No own children	2,015,524	35.9	320,782	18.3	2,102,886	20.6	582,946	32.6	5,022,138	25.9
Other family	589,394	10.5	542,968	31.1	2,326,413	22.7	229,042	12.8	3,687,817	19.0
Male householder, spouse absent	153,027	2.7	88,836	5.1	782,986	7.7	75,777	4.2	1,100,626	5.7
With own children	74,392	1.3	40,539	2.3	328,007	3.2	20,475	1.1	463,413	2.4
No own children	78,635	1.4	48,297	2.8	454,979	4.5	55,302	3.1	637,213	3.3
Female householder, spouse absent	436,367	7.8	454,132	26.0	1,543,427	15.0	153,265	8.6	2,587,191	13.3
With own children	211,848	3.8	253,646	14.5	906,561	8.9	58,239	3.3	1,430,294	7.4
No own children	224,519	4.0	200,486	11.5	636,866	6.1	95,026	5.3	1,156,897	5.9
Nonfamily households	1,826,095	32.5	568,979	32.6	1,981,102	19.4	493,832	27.6	4,870,008	25.1
Male householder	1,559,804	27.8	493,665	28.3	1,448,202	14.2	404,600	22.6	3,906,271	20.2
Female householder	266,291	4.7	75,314	4.3	532,900	5.2	89,232	5.0	963,737	4.9
Total Households	5,610,322	100.0	1,746,730	100.0	10,231,880	100.0	1,787,865	100.0	19,376,797	100.0

Sources: Derived by the authors from Texas Population Estimates and Projections Program 2001; U.S. Census Bureau 2001b.

to occur in these populations compared to Anglo and Black populations, the projections point to growth in the proportion of all households that would be family households and the proportion that would be married-couple families with children, thereby reversing the trends that have characterized change in Texas households during recent decades. Because of the faster growth of non-Anglo populations in the higher growth scenarios, the increase in family households and married-couple households is greater in these scenarios. For example, the percentage of family households in 2040 under the 0.5 scenario is 73.1 percent and increases to 74.9 percent under the 1.0 scenario. Similarly, the percentage of married-couple-with-children households increases from 27.1 percent in 2000 to 29.9 percent in 2040 under the 1.0 scenario but remains at 27.1 percent under the 0.5 scenario. These projections will not be correct, of course, if Hispanic and Other households come to display patterns more similar to Anglo or Black households.

Even if there is some closure in household patterns, however, it is evident that the projected demographic changes are likely to result in a larger number of family households and a larger number of households with children than would be the case if Anglo patterns were to prevail. Table 3.9 compares the total number of households by type in 2040 under the 1.0 scenario to the numbers that would result if Anglo rates were assumed for all racial/ethnic groups. The data show that there would be more than 1.7 million fewer family households and roughly 1.9 million fewer married-couple-with-children households if Anglo rates prevailed. What this suggests is that the large proportion of Texas growth that comes from Hispanic and Other population groups is also likely to result in issues involving families and children playing a larger role in Texas than in some other parts of the nation in the coming years.

Table 3.9

Total Number of Households by Type in 2040 under the 1.0 Projection
Scenario and Assuming That the Anglo Rates of Households by Type
Apply to All Race/Ethnicity Groups

Household Type	Assuming Race/Ethnicity-Specific Rates	Assuming Anglo Rates Apply to All Race/Ethnicity Groups	Difference between Projections
Family households	14,849,576	13,073,343	-1,776,233
Married couple	11,106,239	10,895,874	-210,365
With own children	6,710,020	4,768,772	-1,941,248
No own children	4,396,219	6,127,102	1,730,883
Other family	3,743,337	2,177,469	-1,565,868
Male householder, no spouse present	1,146,560	578,446	-568,114
With own children	524,116	303,943	-220,173
No own children	622,444	274,503	-347,941
Female householder, no spouse present	2,596,777	1,599,023	-997,754
With own children	1,645,731	910,422	-735,309
No own children	951,046	688,601	-262,445
Nonfamily households	4,527,221	6,303,454	1,776,233
Total Households	19,376,797	19,376,797	—

Sources: Derived by the authors from Texas Population Estimates and Projections Program 2001; U.S. Census Bureau 2001b.

SUMMARY

The data point to the following patterns:

1. The number of Texas households has increased rapidly in the last several decades as the population has grown and large numbers of persons from the baby-boom generation have entered household-formation ages. As a result, the state had 7,393,354 households by 2000.

2. Households have become increasingly diverse in form, with the percentages of married-couple and married-couple-with-children households declining and the percentage of single-parent families and nonfamily and unmarried-partner households increasing.

3. Because of the rapid growth of non-Anglo populations in the 1990s, and the fact that they are more likely to have larger households and higher proportions of family households, the 1990s witnessed slower growth in households than in the population—a pattern not seen for several decades—and the diversification toward fewer married-couple and nonfamily households slowed compared to earlier decades.

4. Although the diversity in patterns of household change was abated somewhat in the 1990s, the historical trends in Texas households can be characterized as ones of rapid growth and diversification in form toward larger proportions of single-parent, nonfamily, and unmarried-partner households.

5. Projections of households suggest that the patterns of the past will continue. Under the 1.0 scenario, the number of Texas households would increase to 19.4 million by 2040 compared to 7.4 million in 2000, an increase of 162.1 percent. The percentage of households with an Anglo householder would decline from 61.4 percent in 2000 to 29 percent of all households by 2040, while the percentage of householders who are Black would decrease from 11.4 to 9 percent of all households, the percentage of all households with a Hispanic householder would increase from 24.2 to 52.8 percent, and the percentage of all households with an Other householder would increase from 3 percent to 9.2 percent. The median age of householders would increase under the 1.0 scenario from forty-five in 2000 to 50.1 years of age in 2040.

6. Because of the rapid growth projected in the Hispanic and Other populations with larger household sizes and larger proportions of family and married-couple households, future patterns of change in household composition could differ from those in the past, resulting in larger proportions of married-couple and married-couple-with-children households.

Texas can expect to have an increasing number of households that are ever more racially/ethnically diverse and older. Issues impacting older householders will be of increasing importance, as will issues of concern to non-Anglo households. Coupled with such previously projected changes may be an unanticipated increase in concerns related to non-Anglo families, including families with children. The growth and the diversity of Texas households may thus provide substantial challenges and opportunities for the state in the coming decades.

CHAPTER 4

Population Change and Income in Texas

In the introduction we noted that demographic change may lead
to socioeconomic change; that is, to change in income, poverty,
wealth, and related factors. As the age, sex, race/ethnicity, and
other characteristics of populations change, socioeconomic
characteristics associated with them may also change (Murdock
et al. 1997). For example, because middle-aged populations
tend to have higher incomes, all other things being the same, a
population with a larger proportion of middle-age householders
will have more resources. Similarly, because non-Anglo
populations tend to have lower incomes, larger proportionate
increases in non-Anglo populations may lead to lower average
household incomes for the total (aggregate) population. Such
changes may, in turn, affect both the markets for private-sector
goods and services and the revenues collected in the public
sector.

The relationships that exist between demographic and
socioeconomic characteristics are a product of a variety of
historical, discriminatory, and other factors. Although such
relationships may change over time, much can be learned about
how population change may affect Texas' future socioeconomic
characteristics by examining projected demographic change in
conjunction with existing differences in the socioeconomic
characteristics of population subgroups. In this chapter we
examine the implications of the relationships between
demographic change and socioeconomic change for Texas'
future by concentrating on the effects of demographic change

on income, poverty, and tax revenues. Specifically, we use projections of the population and households as shown in Chapters 2 and 3 together with data on the income, poverty, and tax levels of persons and households with different demographic characteristics to examine how changes in Texas' population may impact future levels of income, poverty, and state tax revenues. This examination is done primarily by assuming that socioeconomic differences among key demographic groups remain as they were in 2000 and that populations and households change in the manner projected in Chapters 2 and 3. In some instances, however, we also examine the implications of changes in the relationships between demographic and socioeconomic characteristics on trends in socioeconomic characteristics, assuming that these relationships change in specific manners. In Chapter 5 we examine the implications of demographic change for Texas' private sector.

Through such analyses we attempt to examine how the state's socioeconomic future is likely to change depending on what does or does not change in Texas' population and in the relationships between demographic and socioeconomic characteristics. Since socioeconomic characteristics are strongly associated with the level of use of state services, this chapter provides a basis for the analyses and discussion provided in subsequent chapters devoted to future demand for specific services.

RECENT SOCIOECONOMIC TRENDS

In the last two decades, Texas has experienced periods of economic recession and expansion relative to the nation as a whole. By the time of the 2000 Census, however, it had still failed to achieve economic parity with the nation on many socioeconomic indicators (see Table 4.1).

In constant dollars, median household income in Texas declined by 1.3 percent from 1979 to 1989 (the reference year for income data for decennial censuses is the calendar year

Table 4.1

Median Household Income, Per Capita Income, Percent of Persons in Poverty in Texas and
the United States, and Texas Values as a Percentage of United States Values, 1979–99

				Percent Change		
Income/Poverty	1979	1989	1999	1979–89	1989–99	1979–99
TEXAS	**Panel A: Constant Dollars**					
Median Household Income	$ 35,539	$ 35,063	$ 39,927	-1.3	13.9	12.3
Per Capita Income	$ 15,326	$ 16,748	$ 19,617	9.3	17.1	28.0
Percent of Persons in Poverty	14.7	18.1	15.4	23.1	-14.9	4.8
	Panel B: Current Dollars					
Median Household Income	$ 16,708	$ 27,016	$ 39,927	61.7	47.8	139.0
Per Capita Income	$ 7,205	$ 12,904	$ 19,617	79.1	52.0	172.3
Percent of Persons in Poverty	14.7	18.1	15.4	23.1	-14.9	4.8
UNITED STATES	**Panel A: Constant Dollars**					
Median Household Income	$ 35,822	$ 39,009	$ 41,994	8.9	7.7	17.2
Per Capita Income	$ 15,555	$ 18,715	$ 21,587	20.3	15.3	38.8
Percent of Persons in Poverty	12.4	13.1	12.4	5.6	-5.3	0.0
	Panel B: Current Dollars					
Median Household Income	$ 16,841	$ 30,056	$ 41,994	78.5	39.7	149.4
Per Capita Income	$ 7,313	$ 14,420	$ 21,587	97.2	49.7	195.2
Percent of Persons in Poverty	12.4	13.1	12.4	5.6	-5.3	0.0
Texas Values As A Percentage of United States Values						
Median Household Income	99.2	89.9	95.1	-9.4	5.8	-4.2
Per Capita Income	98.5	89.5	90.9	-9.2	1.6	-7.8
Percent of Persons in Poverty	118.5	138.2	124.2	16.5	-10.1	4.8

Sources: Derived by the authors from U.S. Census Bureau 2002a and 1991c.

prior to the census year) and per capita income increased by 9.3
percent, while in the nation as a whole median household
income increased by 8.9 percent and per capita income
increased by 20.3 percent. Similarly, whereas Texas' poverty
rate increased by 23.1 percent from 14.7 percent in 1979 to
18.1 percent in 1989, the national rate increased by only 5.6
percent from 12.4 percent to 13.1 percent. As a result, the
differences in income levels in Texas and the United States that
had virtually disappeared by 1979 reemerged, such that Texas'
income levels were less than 90 percent of, and its poverty rate
38 percent greater than, those for the nation by 1989.

The 1989–99 data show the 1990s to be a period of
substantial economic expansion in Texas. In constant dollars,
the state's median household income increased by 13.9 percent
compared to only 7.7 percent in the nation and per capita
income increased by 17.1 percent compared to 15.3 percent

nationwide. Poverty rates for persons fell by 14.9 percent in Texas compared to a decline of only 5.3 percent nationally. However, Texas' 1999 median and per capita income levels remained lower than those in the nation, with a median household income of $39,927 in Texas compared to $41,994 nationally and per capita income in Texas being $19,617 compared to $21,587 for the nation. Poverty levels remained higher at 15.4 percent for Texas in 1999 compared to 12.4 percent for the nation, but the differences between Texas and U.S. values decreased in the 1990s, such that Texas' median household income levels were 95.1 percent of U.S. levels, Texas' per capita income levels were 90.9 percent of U.S. levels, and Texas' poverty rate was 124.2 percent of that for the nation in 1999.

Despite the rapid growth of the 1990s, the disparities among groups in Texas remained large (Table 4.2). Although the percentage increases in income and declines in poverty rates were generally larger for Hispanics and Blacks than for Anglos from 1989 to 1999, large differences in income and poverty remained, and in some cases, differentials between Anglos and non-Anglos increased in absolute terms. For example, median household incomes (in current dollars) for Anglos increased by 49.8 percent from 1989 to 1999, for Blacks 64 percent, and for Hispanics 55.3 percent. As a result, Black and Hispanic median household incomes increased as a proportion of Anglo incomes (from 56.8 percent in 1989 to 62.1 percent in 1999 for Blacks and from 61.1 percent in 1989 to 63.3 percent in 1999 for Hispanics). However, the absolute difference in Anglo-Black median household income levels was $13,602 in 1989 but $17,857 in 1999 and the Anglo-Hispanic difference was $12,242 in 1989 but $17,289 in 1999. Similarly, the Anglo poverty rate for persons decreased by 17.9 percent, the Black poverty rate decreased by 24.5 percent, and the Hispanic rate decreased by 23 percent. Nevertheless, the poverty rates of Blacks (23.4 percent) and Hispanics (25.4

Table 4.2

Income and Poverty Characteristics of the Population in Texas by Race/Ethnicity, 1989–99

Race/ Ethnicity	Median Household Income	Median Family Income	Per Capita Income	Number (in thousands of persons) and Percent in Poverty							
				Persons		Families		Children		Elderly	
				Number	%	Number	%	Number	%	Number	%
1989											
Anglo	$ 31,475	$ 38,051	$ 16,469	953.7	9.5	188.7	6.6	244.5	10.1	158.8	12.8
Black	17,873	20,630	8,137	590.6	31.0	132.6	27.6	247.1	39.2	58.7	39.6
Hispanic	19,233	20,121	6,633	1,395.0	33.0	284.1	29.7	631.1	40.0	76.5	36.3
Total	27,016	31,553	12,904	3,000.5	18.1	618.0	14.1	1,140.4	24.0	296.7	18.4
1999											
Anglo	$ 47,162	$ 57,194	$ 26,197	826.5	7.8	156.2	5.2	205.7	8.3	113.6	8.0
Black	29,305	33,276	14,253	525.1	23.4	118.0	20.4	218.1	30.0	45.4	27.3
Hispanic	29,873	30,840	10,770	1,658.4	25.4	338.1	22.8	734.3	31.2	85.3	25.7
Total	39,927	45,861	19,617	3,117.6	15.4	632.7	12.0	1,189.9	20.5	251.2	12.8
Percent Change 1989–99*											
Anglo	49.8	50.3	59.1	-13.3	-17.9	-17.2	-21.2	-15.9	-17.8	-28.5	-37.5
Black	64.0	61.3	75.2	-11.1	-24.5	-11.0	-26.1	-11.8	-23.5	-22.7	-31.1
Hispanic	55.3	53.3	62.4	18.9	-23.0	19.0	-23.2	16.3	-22.0	11.5	-29.2
Total	47.8	45.3	52.0	3.9	-14.9	2.4	-14.9	4.3	-14.6	-15.3	-30.4

Sources: Derived by the authors from U.S. Census Bureau 2002a and 1991c.

* Changes in values by race/ethnicity are only approximate because exact comparability cannot be obtained given 1990 and 2000 census differences in race/ethnicity classification procedures. For purposes of these comparisons, Hispanics of all races and non-Hispanic Whites in 1990 are compared to the same groups in 2000. Black non-Hispanics in 1990 are compared to Black alone in 2000.

percent) were still roughly three times as high as the poverty rate among Anglos (7.8 percent).

The state's revenues and expenditures have also shown substantial increases in several key areas (see Tables 4.3 and 4.4). State tax revenues (in current dollars) increased from roughly $13.6 billion in 1990 to nearly $25.3 billion by 2000 and net expenditures by function increased from $22.7 billion to $49.7 billion (the expenditures shown include expenditures from all sources, including nonstate sources). These represent increases of approximately 43 and 70 percent, respectively, in constant dollar terms. Particularly noticeable are the real (constant) dollar increases in expenditures for health and human services, public safety, and education. Of the increase in net expenditures of $20.5 billion (in real dollar terms), approximately $16.9 billion or 82.4 percent occurred in these three areas. Overall, Texas' population growth has been accompanied by increasing revenues and costs.

Table 4.3

Total State Tax Collections and Per Capita Collections in Texas, 1971–2000

Fiscal Year	State Tax Collections	Resident Population*	Per Capita Tax Collections	Percent Change	Taxes as a Percent Personal Income
1971	$ 1,992,055,564	11,475,893	$ 173.59	8.7	4.6
1972	2,341,326,235	11,727,295	199.65	15.0	5.0
1973	2,582,903,255	11,984,910	215.51	7.9	4.8
1974	3,026,705,043	12,238,925	247.30	14.8	4.9
1975	3,367,751,883	12,532,443	268.72	8.6	4.9
1976	3,913,827,072	12,857,805	304.39	13.2	5.0
1977	4,419,881,616	13,156,205	335.95	10.5	5.0
1978	5,032,274,299	13,464,130$_r$	373.75$_r$	11.3	5.0$_r$
1979	5,390,313,009	13,842,213$_r$	389.41$_r$	4.2	4.5$_r$
1980	6,343,785,161	14,280,510$_r$	444.23$_r$	14.1	4.6
1981	7,742,032,894	14,705,060$_r$	526.49	18.5$_r$	4.8
1982	8,650,025,743	15,246,820$_r$	567.33	7.8	4.8
1983	8,497,817,125	15,689,250$_r$	541.63	-4.5	4.5$_r$
1984	9,305,839,492	15,977,270$_r$	582.44	7.5	4.5$_r$
1985	10,721,208,262	16,242,810$_r$	660.06	13.3	4.8$_r$
1986	10,231,670,211	16,512,640$_r$	619.63	-6.1	4.4$_r$
1987	10,266,162,781	16,615,480$_r$	617.87$_r$	-0.3	4.4$_r$
1988	12,364,618,924	16,669,270$_r$	741.76$_r$	20.1	5.0$_r$
1989	12,905,940,817	16,796,030$_r$	768.39$_r$	3.6	4.8$_r$
1990	13,632,640,459	17,019,370$_r$	801.01$_r$	4.2$_r$	4.7$_r$
1991	14,922,113,980	17,310,680$_r$	862.02$_r$	7.6$_r$	4.8$_r$
1992	15,848,915,148	17,624,370$_r$	899.26$_r$	4.3$_r$	4.8
1993	17,010,737,258	17,964,540$_r$	946.91$_r$	5.3$_r$	4.9$_r$
1994	18,105,950,594	18,305,230$_r$	989.11$_r$	4.5$_r$	4.9
1995	18,858,790,042	18,649,930$_r$	1,011.20$_r$	2.2$_r$	4.8$_r$
1996	19,762,504,350	18,966,000$_r$	1,042.00$_r$	3.0$_r$	4.7$_r$
1997	21,187,868,237	19,312,000$_r$	1,097.13$_r$	5.3$_r$	4.7$_r$
1998	22,634,019,740	19,666,000$_r$	1,150.92$_r$	4.9$_r$	4.6$_r$
1999	23,614,611,235	20,003,000	1,180.55	2.6	4.5
2000	25,283,768,842	20,342,000	1,242.93	5.3	4.5

Sources: Texas Comptroller of Public Accounts, 2002a, 2002b, and 1995.

* Population figures are for fiscal years.

r = Revised

Recent changes in socioeconomic factors in the state have brought about substantial real dollar increases in the incomes of Texans from all racial and ethnic groups. Substantial gaps remain between groups, however, and absolute differences have increased in some cases. The impact of demographic change on socioeconomic change thus requires further analysis.

PROJECTING THE SOCIOECONOMIC EFFECTS OF POPULATION CHANGE

As noted above, the socioeconomic characteristics resulting from demographic change are projected assuming that the

Table 4.4

Net Expenditures* for State Government in Texas by Function in Constant (2000) and Current (Millions of) Dollars, and Percent Change, 1990–2000

| Function | Fiscal Year (ending August 31) | | | | | |
| | 1990 | 2000 | Percent Change 1990– 2000 | 1990 | 2000 | Percent Change 1990– 2000 |
	Constant Dollars			Current Dollars		
General Government						
Executive	$ 1,227.2	$ 1,505.1	22.6	$ 953.5	$ 1,505.1	57.9
Legislative	69.8	96.9	38.9	54.2	96.9	78.7
Judicial	93.2	149.1	59.9	72.4	149.1	105.8
Total	1,390.2	1,751.1	26.0	1,080.1	1,751.1	62.1
Services						
Health & Human Services	$ 7,281.7	$ 16,332.2	124.3	$ 5,657.5	$ 16,332.2	188.7
Public Safety and Corrections	1,333.8	3,012.3	125.8	1,036.3	3,012.3	190.7
Transportation	3,322.9	4,459.4	34.2	2,581.7	4,459.4	72.7
Natural Resources/ Recreational Services	321.6	1,349.1	319.4	249.9	1,349.1	439.9
Education	12,944.2	19,104.7	47.6	10,056.9	19,104.7	90.0
Regulatory Agencies	202.4	196.3	-3.0	157.2	196.3	24.9
Employee Benefits	1,455.5	1,961.9	34.8	1,130.8	1,961.9	73.5
Debt Service	406.0	598.0	47.3	315.5	598.0	89.6
Capital Outlay	533.3	693.1	30.0	414.3	693.1	67.3
Lottery Winnings Paid	—	249.7	—	—	249.7	—
Total	29,191.7	49,707.8	70.3	22,680.3	49,707.8	119.2

Sources: Texas Comptroller of Public Accounts 2002a and 2002b.

*Funds 1-849, excluding Fund 021 as it is a trust account.

Note: Totals may not add due to rounding.

socioeconomic differences that existed among age, sex, race/ethnicity, and other population and household groups in 2000 will continue throughout the projection period or change in a specified assumed manner.

In most cases, the analysis was completed by simply multiplying the value of a socioeconomic factor in 2000 by its associated population for a specific projection period for a specific projection scenario (for example, multiplying the average annual household incomes for Anglo householders of a given age in 2000 by the projected number of Anglo householders in 2010 in that age group under the 1.0 scenario). This same value for the socioeconomic factor is applied to the same age, sex, and race/ethnicity group for each projection year and scenario across time to provide values in 2000 constant dollars and to assess what the future will hold if socioeconomic differences among demographic groups do not change from those that existed in 2000. These projections—assuming that differences existing in 2000 do not change—are used as base values for comparisons throughout this chapter. Given this base, we simulate the implications of alternative socioeconomic characteristics by completing projections based on alternative assumptions about socioeconomic differences among racial/ethnic groups and/or assumptions about the applicability of recent patterns of change to the future. Due to space limitations we present data for only the 1.0 scenario.

In presenting these projections, we wish to make it clear that numerous economic and market factors, the overall state of the economy, political and policy factors, and numerous other factors may be as important, and in many instances perhaps more important, than population change in altering the state's socioeconomic conditions. We recognize that actual future socioeconomic conditions in Texas will likely be different from those projected here and that the determinants of socioeconomic conditions and change in such conditions are numerous and complex.

IMPACT ON INCOME AND POVERTY
Household Income
The data in Tables 4.5 and 4.6 show the 2000 income distributions of Texas' population and projections under the 1.0 scenario for 2040. An increasing number of non-Anglo households will be included at all income levels. For example, although Anglos make up a majority of households with an income above $20,000 in 2000, they represent a majority of households at only the $125,000 or more income level by 2040 (see Table 4.5). As this suggests, Anglos are projected to continue to have higher income levels than Blacks or Hispanics. Anglos, who are projected to make up only 29 percent of households by 2040, would hold a share of households of more than 29 percent for all households with incomes of $40,000 or more in 2040. By comparison, Blacks,

Table 4.5

Household Income in Texas by Income Category and Race/Ethnicity of Householder in 2000 and Projections for 2040 Using the Population Projection That Assumes 1990–2000 Rates of Net Migration (1.0 Scenario) (Percentaged within Income Group)

Household Income	Anglo Number	%	Black Number	%	Hispanic Number	%	Other Number	%	Total Number
2000									
$ < 10,000	341,684	44.6	149,514	19.5	251,625	32.8	23,995	3.1	766,818
10,000–14,999	242,608	49.4	70,966	14.5	165,395	33.7	11,714	2.4	490,683
15,000–19,999	242,784	49.9	66,404	13.7	165,277	34.0	11,702	2.4	486,167
20,000–24,999	269,952	52.2	67,047	13.0	167,064	32.3	13,167	2.5	517,230
25,000–29,999	272,946	54.3	63,339	12.6	154,110	30.7	12,152	2.4	502,547
30,000–34,999	285,102	57.8	55,869	11.3	139,362	28.3	12,711	2.6	493,044
35,000–39,999	267,306	60.0	48,014	10.8	118,350	26.6	11,541	2.6	445,211
40,000–44,999	257,415	61.8	43,160	10.4	104,374	25.1	11,327	2.7	416,276
45,000–49,999	226,205	63.3	35,376	9.9	85,512	23.9	10,219	2.9	357,312
50,000–59,999	422,419	66.4	59,528	9.3	134,970	21.2	19,999	3.1	636,916
60,000–74,999	506,652	70.1	62,038	8.6	129,151	17.9	24,202	3.4	722,043
75,000–99,999	530,742	75.2	51,636	7.3	98,607	14.0	24,495	3.5	705,480
100,000–124,999	263,225	72.7	50,412	13.9	35,631	9.8	13,145	3.6	362,413
125,000–149,999	142,048	81.8	8,489	4.9	15,018	8.7	7,899	4.6	173,454
150,000–199,999	129,469	84.4	5,723	3.7	11,771	7.7	6,481	4.2	153,444
200,000+	139,521	84.8	6,197	3.8	13,406	8.2	5,192	3.2	164,316
Total	4,540,078	61.4	843,712	11.4	1,789,623	24.2	219,941	3.0	7,393,354
2040									
$ < 10,000	479,999	18.4	345,355	13.1	1,540,524	58.6	261,203	9.9	2,627,081
10,000–14,999	361,915	22.3	161,709	10.0	979,973	60.5	116,647	7.2	1,620,244
15,000–19,999	346,318	22.2	142,557	9.1	954,754	61.3	115,100	7.4	1,558,729
20,000–24,999	363,863	23.2	137,322	8.8	949,951	60.7	113,497	7.3	1,564,633
25,000–29,999	356,443	24.6	127,449	8.8	868,319	59.8	98,960	6.8	1,451,171
30,000–34,999	360,076	26.6	111,475	8.2	779,413	57.4	106,393	7.8	1,357,357
35,000–39,999	331,945	28.1	95,017	8.1	663,002	56.2	90,019	7.6	1,179,983
40,000–44,999	312,427	29.3	84,978	8.0	583,013	54.6	86,739	8.1	1,067,157
45,000–49,999	271,793	30.4	69,708	7.8	475,753	53.3	76,016	8.5	893,270
50,000–59,999	495,547	32.9	116,574	7.7	750,555	49.7	146,538	9.7	1,509,214
60,000–74,999	577,848	36.4	119,819	7.6	715,510	45.1	172,258	10.9	1,585,435
75,000–99,999	592,918	42.0	99,976	7.1	547,548	38.8	170,647	12.1	1,411,089
100,000–124,999	294,570	43.3	93,514	13.8	197,864	29.1	93,764	13.8	679,712
125,000–149,999	158,617	50.4	16,318	5.2	83,926	26.7	55,573	17.7	314,434
150,000–199,999	145,232	53.9	11,492	4.3	65,928	24.4	47,049	17.4	269,701
200,000+	160,811	55.9	13,467	4.7	75,847	26.4	37,462	13.0	287,587
Total	5,610,322	29.0	1,746,730	9.0	10,231,880	52.8	1,787,865	9.2	19,376,797

Sources: Derived from Texas Population Estimates and Projections Program 2001; U.S. Census 2002a.

who would be 9 percent of households, would be 9 percent or more of households in only four income groups—with three of the four being the three lowest categories. Hispanics, would be 52.8 percent of households, more than 52.8 percent in all income categories below $50,000, but less than that in all income categories of $50,000 or more. Persons from the Other racial/ethnic group would account for 9.2 percent of households and would represent at least that percentage in all categories of $50,000 or more and in the lowest category.

Table 4.6

Household Income in Texas by Income Category and Race/Ethnicity of Householder in 2000
and Projections for 2040 Using the Population Projection That Assumes 1990–2000
Rates of Net Migration (1.0 Scenario) (Percentaged within Race/Ethnicity Group)

Household Income	Anglo		Black		Hispanic		Other		Total	
	Number	%	Number	%	Number	%	Number	%	Number	%
2000										
$ < 10,000	341,684	7.5	149,514	17.7	251,625	14.3	23,995	11.0	766,818	10.5
10,000–14,999	242,608	5.3	70,966	8.4	165,395	9.2	11,714	5.3	490,683	6.6
15,000–19,999	242,784	5.3	66,404	7.9	165,277	9.2	11,702	5.3	486,167	6.6
20,000–24,999	269,952	5.9	67,047	7.9	167,064	9.3	13,167	6.0	517,230	7.0
25,000–29,999	272,946	6.0	63,339	7.5	154,110	8.6	12,152	5.5	502,547	6.8
30,000–34,999	285,102	6.3	55,869	6.6	139,362	7.8	12,711	5.8	493,044	6.7
35,000–39,999	267,306	5.9	48,014	5.7	118,350	6.6	11,541	5.2	445,211	6.0
40,000–44,999	257,415	5.7	43,160	5.1	104,374	5.8	11,327	5.2	416,276	5.6
45,000–49,999	226,205	5.0	35,376	4.2	85,512	4.8	10,219	4.6	357,312	4.8
50,000–59,999	422,419	9.3	59,528	7.1	134,970	7.5	19,999	9.1	636,916	8.6
60,000–74,999	506,652	11.2	62,038	7.4	129,151	7.2	24,202	11.0	722,043	9.8
75,000–99,999	530,742	11.7	51,636	6.1	98,607	5.5	24,495	11.1	705,480	9.5
100,000–124,999	263,225	5.8	50,412	6.0	35,631	2.0	13,145	6.0	362,413	4.9
125,000–149,999	142,048	3.1	8,489	1.0	15,018	0.8	7,899	3.6	173,454	2.3
150,000–199,999	129,469	2.9	5,723	0.7	11,771	0.7	6,481	2.9	153,444	2.1
200,000+	139,521	3.1	6,197	0.7	13,406	0.7	5,192	2.4	164,316	2.2
Total	4,540,078	100.0	843,712	100.0	1,789,623	100.0	219,941	100.0	7,393,354	100.0
2040										
$ < 10,000	479,999	8.4	345,355	19.5	1,540,524	15.2	261,203	14.8	2,627,081	13.5
10,000–14,999	361,915	6.5	161,709	9.3	979,973	9.6	116,647	6.5	1,620,244	8.4
15,000–19,999	346,318	6.2	142,557	8.2	954,754	9.3	115,100	6.4	1,558,729	8.0
20,000–24,999	363,863	6.5	137,322	7.9	949,951	9.3	113,497	6.3	1,564,633	8.1
25,000–29,999	356,443	6.4	127,449	7.3	868,319	8.5	98,960	5.5	1,451,171	7.5
30,000–34,999	360,076	6.4	111,475	6.4	779,413	7.6	106,393	6.0	1,357,357	7.0
35,000–39,999	331,945	5.9	95,017	5.4	663,002	6.5	90,019	5.0	1,179,983	6.1
40,000–44,999	312,427	5.6	84,978	4.9	583,013	5.7	86,739	4.9	1,067,157	5.5
45,000–49,999	271,793	4.8	69,708	4.0	475,753	4.6	76,016	4.3	893,270	4.6
50,000–59,999	495,547	8.8	116,574	6.7	750,555	7.3	146,538	8.2	1,509,214	7.8
60,000–74,999	577,848	10.3	119,819	6.9	715,510	7.0	172,258	9.6	1,585,435	8.2
75,000–99,999	592,918	10.6	99,976	5.7	547,548	5.4	170,647	9.5	1,411,089	7.3
100,000–124,999	294,570	5.3	93,514	5.4	197,864	1.9	93,764	5.2	679,712	3.5
125,000–149,999	158,617	2.8	16,318	0.9	83,926	0.8	55,573	3.1	314,434	1.6
150,000–199,999	145,232	2.6	11,492	0.7	65,928	0.6	47,049	2.6	269,701	1.4
200,000+	160,811	2.9	13,467	0.8	75,847	0.7	37,462	2.1	287,587	1.5
Total	5,610,322	100.0	1,746,730	100.0	10,231,880	100.0	1,787,865	100.0	19,376,797	100.0

Sources: Derived from Texas Population Estimates and Projections Program 2001; U.S. Census Bureau 2002a.

What is also apparent is that if the income distributions of non-Anglo populations were not to change, the income levels of the average household in the state would decrease as well. The distributions of households would generally shift toward the lower income categories because of the more rapid growth of Hispanic and Black populations, which have lower incomes (see Table 4.6 and Figure 4.1). In 2000, 37.5 percent of all households had an income of less than $30,000, but by 2040 (under the 1.0 scenario and in 2000 constant dollars) 45.5 percent of all households would have incomes of less than $30,000 per year. On the other hand, although 11.5 percent of all households had incomes of $100,000 or more in 2000, only

Figure 4.1

Percent of Households by Income Category for the
State of Texas in 2000 and Projections for 2040*

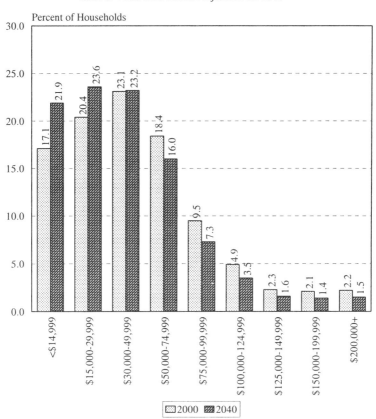

* Projections are shown for the 1.0 scenario

8.0 percent would have such incomes by 2040. Overall, the
median income level (not shown but computed from Table
4.6), which was $39,927 in 2000, would drop to $33,191 in
2000 constant dollars. It is clear that the median income of all
Texas households would decline in 2000 constant dollars as a
result of the projected demographic changes and the existent
differentials in income among racial/ethnic groups. Such data
suggest that, in the absence of change in the incomes of Black
and Hispanic households, Texas households would, on average,

be poorer in 2000 constant dollars in 2040 than they were in 2000.

Aggregate Income

Another means of examining the effects of demographic change on socioeconomic change can be obtained by projecting age, sex, and race/ethnicity effects on aggregate income (see Table 4.7). The effect of the projected demographic changes would be to increase total aggregate income from $402.5 billion in 2000 to $927.8 billion under the 1.0 scenario, an increase of 130.5 percent. Since this rate of growth is slower than the projected change in households of 162.1 percent, it suggests a decline in average income over time. As shown in the last column of Table 4.7, the average income of Texas households (in 2000 constant dollars) would decline from $54,441 in 2000 to $47,883 in 2040. This value represents an absolute constant dollar decline of $6,558 or 12.1 percent.

Whether examined from the standpoint of mean incomes or proportions of households by income category, the projections of income shown here point to real dollar declines in the total incomes and in the average incomes (both median and mean) of Texas households, given projected demographic changes and 2000 socioeconomic differentials.

Table 4.7

Aggregate Household Income in Texas (in Billions of 2000 Dollars) by Race/Ethnicity and Mean Household Income in Texas in 2000 and Projections to 2040 Using the Population Projection That Assumes 1990–2000 Rates of Net Migration (1.0 Scenario)

Year	Aggregate of Household Income (Billions)					Mean Household Income
	Anglo	Black	Hispanic	Other	Total	
2000	$ 286.6	$ 33.2	$ 69.5	$ 13.2	$ 402.5	$ 54,441
2010	312.5	42.1	114.8	24.9	494.3	52,639
2020	336.2	52.1	181.7	43.2	613.2	50,903
2030	351.7	61.3	274.0	70.1	757.1	49,326
2040	354.1	68.7	397.5	107.5	927.8	47,883

Sources: Derived by the authors from Texas Population Estimates and Projections Program 2001; U.S. Census Bureau 2002a.

Poverty Rates

A third way of examining socioeconomic change related to change in race/ethnicity and household composition is to consider the likely impacts of such changes on family poverty levels (see Table 4.8). The number of families in poverty and the poverty rate for such families will increase as a result of the projected demographic change if socioeconomic differentials do not change. A comparison of the 2000 data to that projected for 2040 under the 1.0 scenario shows that the number of families in poverty would increase by 274.0 percent, and the poverty rate for all family households would increase from 11.4 percent in 2000 to 15.4 percent in 2040. Increases in poverty would be pervasive across family types. For example, the poverty rate for married couples would increase from 7.5

Table 4.8

Number and Rate of Families in Poverty in Texas by Type and Race/Ethnicity in 2000 and Projections for 2040 Using the Population Projection That Assumes 1990–2000 Rates of Net Migration (1.0 Scenario)

Family Type	Anglo		Black		Hispanic		Other		Total	
	Number	%	Number	%	Number	%	Number	%	Number	%
2000										
Family households	155,348	5.1	109,693	19.0	316,590	21.6	16,694	10.4	598,325	11.4
Married couple	80,583	3.2	24,876	8.5	183,992	17.7	10,787	8.2	300,238	7.5
With own children	40,388	3.7	13,885	8.9	145,613	21.1	7,207	9.1	207,093	10.3
No own children	40,195	2.8	10,991	8.0	38,379	11.0	3,580	6.7	93,145	4.7
Other family	74,765	14.3	84,817	30.0	132,598	31.3	5,907	20.4	298,087	23.7
Male householder,										
spouse absent	12,920	9.3	9,225	20.5	24,480	19.4	1,306	12.5	47,931	15.0
With own children	8,684	11.9	5,515	24.4	16,315	27.8	620	18.1	31,134	19.8
No own children	4,236	6.4	3,710	16.6	8,165	12.0	686	9.8	16,797	10.3
Female householder,										
spouse absent	61,845	16.1	75,592	31.7	108,118	36.4	4,601	24.7	250,156	26.7
With own children	49,968	23.0	59,600	39.9	88,414	47.1	3,493	35.0	201,475	35.7
No own children	11,877	7.2	15,992	18.0	19,704	18.0	1,108	12.9	48,681	13.0
2040										
Family households	178,858	4.7	208,886	17.7	1,725,148	20.9	124,988	9.7	2,237,880	15.4
Married couple	100,174	3.1	53,644	8.5	1,037,529	17.5	83,248	7.8	1,274,595	11.8
With own children	44,198	3.7	28,039	8.9	806,828	21.1	44,082	9.1	923,147	15.9
No own children	55,976	2.8	25,605	8.0	230,701	11.0	39,166	6.7	351,448	7.0
Other family	78,684	13.3	155,242	28.6	687,619	29.6	41,740	18.2	963,285	26.1
Male householder,										
spouse absent	13,932	9.1	17,911	20.2	146,069	18.7	9,141	12.1	187,053	17.0
With own children	8,869	11.9	9,911	24.4	91,330	27.8	3,713	18.1	113,823	24.6
No own children	5,063	6.4	8,000	16.6	54,739	12.0	5,428	9.8	73,230	11.5
Female householder,										
spouse absent	64,752	14.8	137,331	30.2	541,550	35.1	32,599	21.3	776,232	30.0
With own children	48,693	23.0	101,255	39.9	427,232	47.1	20,374	35.0	597,554	41.8
No own children	16,059	7.2	36,076	18.0	114,318	18.0	12,225	12.9	178,678	15.4

Sources: Derived from Texas Population Estimates and Projections Program 2001; U.S. Census 2002a.

percent in 2000 to 11.8 percent in 2040, the rate for married couples with children would increase from 10.3 to 15.9 percent, and the rate for family households without children would increase from 4.7 to 7 percent. For female-householder families with children, the percent in poverty would increase from 35.7 percent in 2000 to 41.8 percent in 2040. Unless the socioeconomic differentials among racial/ethnic groups change substantially, the number of families in poverty will also increase substantially.

ALTERNATIVE SIMULATIONS

How would changes in socioeconomic characteristics affect the future incomes of Texas households? To examine this question, we simulate two alternative income distributions (see Table 4.9) to compare with the baseline scenario (which assumes that 2000 income differentials continue throughout the projection period). First, we simulate the change that would be produced if the change in the percentage of Black to Anglo and of Hispanic to Anglo incomes that occurred from 1990 to 2000 were to continue during each decade from 2000 to 2040. Specifically, we simulate what the effects would be if the increases in the ratios of Black and Hispanic incomes to Anglo incomes from 1989 to 1999 (these ratios were .568 for Anglo-Black and .611 for Anglo-Hispanic differences in 1989 and increased to .621 and .633, respectively, in 1999) continue during each decade of the projection period and if the incomes of Anglos and persons in the Other category remain as they were in 2000. This assumption would reduce the gap in income so that by 2040 the income of Blacks would be .836 (83.6 percent) of Anglo income and the income of Hispanics would be .723 (72.3 percent) of Anglo income.

In the second simulation, we examine the effects of a complete closure between Anglo and all other racial/ethnic groups. The effects of significant closures in socioeconomic differentials would be to substantially increase aggregate income in the state and to close the gap in average incomes (see Table 4.9 and Figure 4.2). Assuming the 1.0 scenario and rates

Table 4.9

Projected Total Annual Aggregate (in Billions of 2000 Dollars) and
Mean Household Income in 2040 by Race/Ethnicity Assuming 2000
Aggregate Household Income Differentials by Race/Ethnicity, 1990–
2000 Rates of Closure in Anglo-Black and Anglo-Hispanic Household
Incomes, and Anglo Income Levels Obtained by All Race/Ethnicity
Groups and Using the Population Projection That Assumes 1990–2000
Rates of Net Migration (1.0 Scenario)

Race/ Ethnicity	Assuming 2000 Income Differentials		Assuming 1990–2000 Closure in Differentials		Assuming Anglo Incomes for All Groups	
	Aggregate	Mean	Aggregate	Mean	Aggregate	Mean
Anglo	$ 354.1	$ 63,116	$ 354.1	$ 63,116	$ 354.1	$ 63,116
Black	68.7	39,354	92.1	52,753	110.2	63,116
Hispanic	397.5	38,850	466.7	45,608	645.8	63,116
Other	107.5	60,111	107.5	60,111	112.8	63,116
Total	927.8	47,883	1,020.4	52,659	1,223.0	63,116

Sources: Derived by the authors from Texas Population Estimates and
Projections Program 2001; U.S. Census Bureau 2002a.

of closure between Anglo and Black and Anglo and Hispanic
incomes experienced during the 1990s, the total level of
aggregate income increases to $1 trillion by 2040, an increase
of approximately $93 billion compared to that projected for
2040 assuming 2000 income differentials, and the difference
between the mean household income in 2000 (of $54,441) and
that projected for 2040 ($52,659) decreases to $1,782, instead
of the $6,558 decrease that would occur if 2000 differentials
continue. Assuming that Blacks and Hispanics achieve Anglo
income levels, the level of aggregate income increases to
$1.223 trillion, an increase of $295 billion compared to the
2040 value projected assuming 2000 income differentials, and
the average household income increases to the Anglo level of
$63,116 for all groups. Under these assumptions, the mean
income for all households in 2040 would be $8,675 (15.9
percent) higher than the average income level of $54,441 in
2000 and $15,233 (31.8 percent) higher than the average
income projected for 2040 under the scenario assuming 2000
differentials. Maintaining the declines in the differentials that
occurred in the 1990s during the coming decades would

Figure 4.2

Mean Household Income in Texas in 2000 and Projections for 2040*
Assuming 2000 Rates in 2040, 1990–2000 Rates of Closure between
Anglo-Black and Anglo-Hispanic Incomes, and Anglo Income Levels for
All Race/Ethnicity Groups

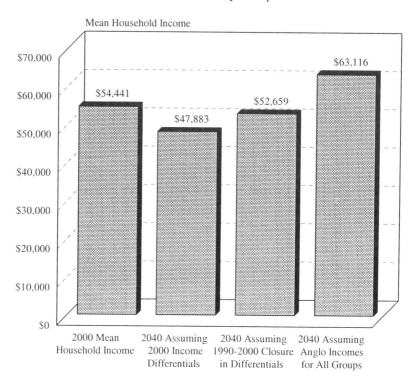

* Projections are shown for the 1.0 scenario

substantially impact the state's aggregate wealth, whereas
attaining complete closure among racial/ethnic groups would
mean that household change would be accompanied by similar
changes in socioeconomic conditions—that is, Texas' wealth
would increase as rapidly as its number of households.

The projections of income and poverty clearly show that
incomes will decline and poverty increase as a result of
demographic change if the 2000 differentials in the
socioeconomic characteristics of Black and Hispanic
households do not change. If they do change, as shown in Table

4.9, the socioeconomic picture could be substantially more positive. Much will depend on the state of the economy and other economic factors in the coming years. Under any foreseeable set of conditions, however, it seems likely that increasing the income and reducing the poverty of Texans in light of the projected demographic changes will represent a formidable challenge.

IMPLICATIONS FOR TAX REVENUES

One of the major implications of change in Texas' socioeconomic characteristics is the effect on tax revenues. In this section we examine such change by using data on the percentage of income paid in taxes in each decile of households (from the Texas Comptroller of Public Accounts 2001) and projections of aggregate income (as presented in Tables 4.7 and 4.9) adjusted for proportions of total aggregate income subject to taxation. Our figures are purely exemplary and should not be confused with the much more sophisticated values produced by the comptroller's office for revenue forecasting. The projections presented here provide an indication only of the effects of demographic change on tax revenues and are thus inclusive of only some of the factors impacting tax revenues.

Table 4.10 shows the overall projections of state tax revenues that would be collected assuming that the aggregate household income rates of 2000 prevail throughout the projection period, that total aggregate income is distributed among racial/ethnic groups as in the projections of such income noted in Table 4.7, and that the level of taxation per income decile remains as it was in 2000 data reported by the comptroller (Texas Comptroller of Public Accounts 2001). The data in this table suggest that tax revenues will increase substantially from 2000 to 2040. Revenues would increase from $29.5 billion in 2000 to $68 billion by 2040 (see Table 4.10). This value represents an increase of 130.5 percent.

The effects of the diversification of the state's population are clearly evident in the revenue data shown in Table 4.10.

Table 4.10

State Tax Revenues in Texas (in Billions of 2000
Dollars) by Race/Ethnicity in 2000 and Projections to
2040 Assuming 2000 Decile Tax Rates and Using the
Population Projection That Assumes 1990–2000
Rates of Net Migration (1.0 Scenario)

Year	Anglo	Black	Hispanic	Other	Total
2000	$ 21.0	$ 2.4	$ 5.1	$ 1.0	$ 29.5
2010	22.9	3.1	8.4	1.8	36.2
2020	24.7	3.8	13.3	3.2	45.0
2030	25.8	4.5	20.1	5.1	55.5
2040	26.0	5.0	29.1	7.9	68.0

Sources: Derived by the authors from Texas Population
Estimates and Projections Program, Projections of the
Population of Texas and Counties in Texas by Age, Sex, and
Race/Ethnicity for 2000-2040, 2001. Texas Comptroller of
Public Accounts, Tax Exemptions and Tax Incidence [online],
2001.

Under the 1.0 scenario, tax revenues for Anglo, Black,
Hispanic, and Other households increase by 23.6, 107, 471.7
and 712.9 percent, respectively. As a result of such changes,
the percentage of all tax revenues from Anglo households
declines from 71.2 percent in 2000 to only 38.2 percent.
Revenues from Black households decrease from 8.2 percent in
2000 to 7.4 percent of all revenues (the absolute dollars of
revenues from Anglo and Black households continue to
increase, but the proportion of all revenues accounted for by
these households declines because of faster growth in
households in the Hispanic and Other racial/ethnic groups).
The percentage of taxes from Hispanic households increases
from 17.3 percent in 2000 to 42.8 percent, while the percentage
from households with a householder from the Other
racial/ethnic group increases from 3.3 in 2000 to 11.6 percent
in 2040 (see Figure 4.3). Thus, by 2040, 61.8 percent of total
revenues would come from non-Anglo households compared to
28.8 percent in 2000. Of the net change in tax revenues
between 2000 and 2040, only 12.9 percent would come from

Figure 4.3

Proportion of State Tax Revenues Due To Households
from Each Race/Ethnicity Group, 2000 and 2040*

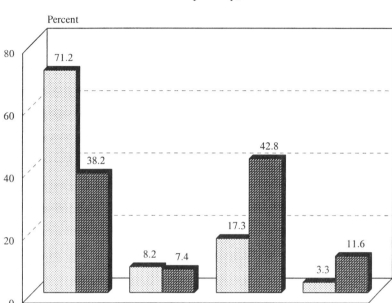

* Projections are shown for the 1.0 scenario

Anglo households. Texas state tax revenues will be increasingly dependent on the incomes and expenditures of non-Anglo households.

The data also suggest that, in the absence of changes in 2000 race/ethnicity income differentials, the average amount of revenue collected per household in Texas will decline because the number of households increases faster than revenues. The number of Texas households is projected to increase by 162.1 percent, while revenues increase by 130.5 percent. As a result, tax revenues per household decrease from $3,992 in 2000 to $3,511 in 2040, a decrease of 12 percent. In the absence of change in socioeconomic differentials, population change in

Texas will lead to decreased levels of per-household taxes to address the state's service needs.

As noted above, changes in the socioeconomic differentials among racial/ethnic groups could significantly affect incomes and, as a result, tax revenues. In Table 4.11 we examine the same three scenarios for tax revenues that we examined in Table 4.9 for income. That is, we examine the revenues as shown in Table 4.10 and compare them to what would be collected if the 1990–2000 levels of closure between Anglo and Black and Anglo and Hispanic incomes continued throughout the projection period and to those that would be generated as a result of total closure between Anglo incomes and the incomes of all Other racial/ethnic groups. The data in Table 4.11 show that changes in income would have a substantial impact on tax revenues. If the relative increases in Black and Hispanic incomes that occurred from 1990 to 2000 could be maintained from 2000 to 2040, an additional $6.8 billion (more than that projected for 2040 assuming 2000 income differentials) would be generated annually by 2040, and if Blacks and Hispanics were to come to have the incomes of Anglos, more than $21.6

Table 4.11

Projected Annual State Tax Revenues (in Millions of 2000 Dollars) in 2040 by Race/Ethnicity Assuming 2000 Aggregate Household Income Differentials by Race/Ethnicity, 1990–2000 Rates of Closure in Anglo-Black and Anglo-Hispanic Household Incomes, and Anglo Income Levels Obtained by All Race/Ethnicity Groups and Using the Population Projection That Assumes 1990–2000 Rates of Net Migration (1.0 Scenario)

Race/ Ethnicity	Assuming 2000 Income Differentials	Assuming 1990–2000 Closure in Differentials	Assuming Anglo Incomes for All Groups
Anglo	$ 25,962.3	$ 25,962.3	$ 25,962.3
Black	5,040.0	6,755.9	8,083.1
Hispanic	29,144.4	34,214.3	47,348.9
Other	7,879.6	7,879.6	8,273.5
Total	68,026.2	74,812.0	89,667.8

Sources: Derived from Texas Population Estimates and Projections Program, Projections of the Population of Texas and Counties in Texas by Age, Sex, and Race/Ethnicity for 2000-2040, 2001. U.S. Census Bureau, Census 2000 Summary File 3, [machine-readable data files], 2002a.

billion in additional revenue would be generated each year. In addition (see Figure 4.4) per-household revenues would increase by $636 from 2000 to 2040 rather than decline by $481. State revenues would be enhanced by increases in non-Anglo incomes.

Figure 4.4

Mean Per-Household State Tax Revenues in Texas in 2000 and Projections for 2040* Assuming 2000 Rates in 2040, 1990–2000 Rates of Closure between Anglo-Black and Anglo-Hispanic Incomes, and Anglo Income Levels for All Groups

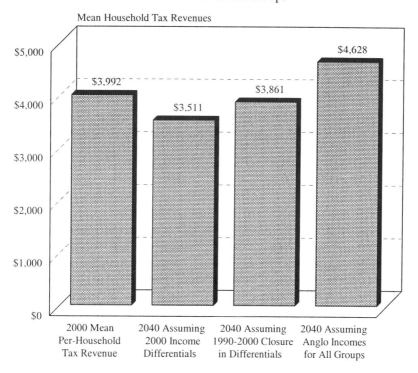

* Projections are shown for the 1.0 scenario

SUMMARY

In this chapter we have examined the implications of demographic change for the socioeconomic characteristics of Texas' population. The results point to substantial shifts in the overall level of socioeconomic resources. Specifically:

1. Texas has displayed patterns of both economic stagnation and economic expansion in recent decades. During the 1980s, the state's median household income and per capita income levels failed to keep pace with national increases, while poverty levels increased more rapidly than those in the nation. In the 1990s, Texas' income levels increased faster than those in the nation, the state's poverty rate decreased more rapidly, and differentials in Anglo-Black and Anglo-Hispanic incomes decreased while the ratio of Black and Hispanic incomes to those for Anglos increased. Despite these changes, Black and Hispanic incomes were less than two-thirds the level for Anglos and their poverty rates roughly three times those for Anglos. The 1990s brought socioeconomic progress to the state, but the differentials remain substantial.

2. If 2000 differentials among age and race/ethnicity groups were to prevail, the average income for all Texas households would decline by $6,558 from 2000 to 2040 (in 2000 constant dollars) under the 1.0 scenario. Total aggregate income would increase by 130.5 percent under the 1.0 scenario compared to the 162.1 percent increase in the number of households, suggesting a decline in the overall level of per-household aggregate income in the state. The distributions of households by income level would also show a general shift toward lower income categories. Under the 1.0 scenario, the 37.5 percent of households with incomes below $30,000 in 2000 would increase to 45.5 percent in 2040 (in 2000 constant dollars), while the percentage with incomes of $100,000 or more would decrease from 11.5 percent to 8 percent. Similarly, poverty rates would increase by 4 percent for families if the

demographic trends projected under the 1.0 scenario were to occur. Overall, if 2000 socioeconomic differentials do not change and if the population does change as projected, Texas will be poorer in the future.

3. If Texas could close the gap among racial/ethnic groups, the socioeconomic implications could be dramatic. A simulation assuming that 1990–2000 increases in relative income between Anglos and Blacks and Anglos and Hispanics continued to 2040 suggests that, under the 1.0 scenario, total aggregate income by 2040 would increase by $93 billion and average household income (in 2000 constant dollars) would decline by only $1,782 rather than by the more than $6,500 projected to occur if 2000 differentials continue. Under the simulation assuming that Blacks and Hispanics come to have Anglo levels of income and that household growth is at the level of the 1.0 population projection scenario, aggregate income in Texas would increase by $295 billion and average household incomes would be $63,116 rather than the $54,441 that they were in 2000 or the $47,883 that they are projected to be in 2040 under the assumption of continuing 2000 differentials. Changing the socioeconomic differentials existent in Texas society is of clear significance for changing the economic future of the state.

4. Demographic changes will also affect tax revenues through their impact on socioeconomic resources. Although tax revenues are projected to increase by 130.5 percent under the 1.0 scenario, this rate of increase would be slower than the 162.1 percent rate of growth in households. As a result, in the absence of changes in the 2000 socioeconomic income differentials, per-household revenues would decline by 12 percent from 2000 to 2040. Revenue sources would also change. The percentage of revenues from non-Anglo households would increase to 61.8 percent (under the 1.0 scenario) of all revenues by 2040, compared to only 28.8

percent in 2000. If income differentials were to decline as a result of increases in Black and Hispanic incomes, then revenues would also be affected. If 1990–2000 declines in differentials were to continue through 2040, annual tax revenues would be $6.8 billion higher in 2040, and if Black and Hispanic incomes were to reach the levels of Anglos in 2000, annual revenues would (under the 1.0 projection scenario) be $21.6 billion higher by 2040.

The analysis in this chapter points to a Texas that will be poorer in the future if the 2000 income differentials and related socioeconomic resources among population subgroups do not change. The result would be reduced aggregate income, increased poverty, and decreased per-household tax revenues. If these differentials change, the state's socioeconomic resources could be increased significantly. Changes in the economy and other factors likely will drive much of the change that actually does occur, but altering socioeconomic differentials is clearly of importance to Texas' private and public sectors.

CHAPTER 5

Implications of Population Change for the Private Sector in Texas

The data discussed in the preceding chapter indicate that population change may affect the total level of resources available in Texas and the ability of state government to pay for service needs in the coming years. The results point to substantial declines in per-household resources and tax revenues if 2000 differentials do not change, but also to more positive effects if closure in differentials among racial/ethnic groups occurs.

In this chapter we examine the effects of population change on private-sector markets for goods and services. We examine the effects of changes in the population on two key factors impacting Texas businesses: consumer expenditures and the net worth and assets of households. We then examine specific effects within two broad sectors of the economy: housing and health care.

The items and sectors examined are only some of those relevant to businesses; a large number of other factors are equally deserving of attention (Pol 1987; Pol and Thomas 1992; Kintner et al. 1994). The intent here is to demonstrate how the private sector may be impacted by population change in Texas. It is obvious that demography is only one of the many factors affecting future markets for goods and services and that the overall state of the economy, technological developments, regulatory and policy considerations, and numerous other factors also will affect Texas markets and the private sector. The analysis presented here is not exhaustive, but it is one that should indicate the relevance of population change for Texas markets and businesses. Due to space limitations, all results are shown only for the 1.0 population projection scenario.

HISTORICAL PATTERNS OF ECONOMIC AND BUSINESS EXPANSION

Texas has shown extensive economic expansion in the last two decades (Texas Comptroller of Public Accounts 2002c). The gross state product of Texas increased by 100.5 percent from 1980 to 2000 (in 1992 constant dollars), employment increased by 60.4 percent, and retail sales increased by 68.5 percent (see Table 5.1), outpacing the state's 46.5 percent rate of population growth. As with income (see Chapter 4), the data on gross state product, employment, and retail sales for the 1990s revealed different patterns from those for the 1980s. In the 1980s, the gross state product increased by 26.1 percent, employment by 21.3 percent, and retail sales by 29.9 percent, but in the 1990s the gross state product increased by 59.1 percent, employment by 32.3 percent, and retail sales by 29.7 percent. The generally faster growth in the economy in the 1990s is evident in these data.

The growth in economic activity was only partially due to population growth. Percentage changes in all three indicators were greater than the 19.4 percent rate of population increase from 1980 to 1990 or the 22.8 percent growth in population from 1990 to 2000, and both per capita gross state product and retail sales values increased during the 1980s and 1990s. Texas exports increased by 169.1 percent from 1980 to 2000 compared to a 46.5 percent increase in population, further indicating that the state's businesses were producing products and services beyond those needed by its own population. The Texas economy is driven by numerous factors in addition to those related to the population. Population change, however, plays a role in changing markets.

Table 5.1

Gross State Product, Nonfarm Employment, and Total Retail
Sales in Texas and Texas Exports, 1980–2000

				Percent Change		
Economic Indicator	1980	1990	2000	1980–90	1990–2000	1980–2000
Gross State Product (Billions of 1992 Constant Dollars)	$ 320.9	$ 404.5	$ 643.4	26.1	59.1	100.5
Per Capita Gross State Product	$ 23,552	$ 23,813	$ 30,856	1.1	29.6	31.0
Nonfarm Employment (in thousands)	5,852.2	7,096.8	9,388.3	21.3	32.3	60.4
Retail Sales (Millions of 1992 Constant Dollars)	$ 109,378	$ 142,039	$ 184,271	29.9	29.7	68.5
Per Capita Sales	$ 7,687	$ 8,362	$ 8,837	8.8	5.7	15.0
Texas Exports (Billions of 1992 Constant Dollars)	$ 24.6	$ 43.4	$ 66.2	76.4	52.5	169.1

Source: Texas Comptroller of Public Accounts 2002c. Per capita figures derived by the authors.

PROJECTIONS OF CONSUMER EXPENDITURES

In this section we examine the effects of projected demographic changes on expenditures for goods and services. To complete projections of expenditures, data on consumer expenditures from the 2000 Consumer Expenditure Survey (Bureau of Labor Statistics 2002) for households differentiated by age, race/ethnicity, tenure, and income category of the householder and also the household type of the householder were used in various combinations to compute average expenditures by age, race/ethnicity, tenure, and income level as well as by household type for each expenditure category. These average expenditures were then multiplied by the projections of households by age, race/ethnicity, tenure of the householder, and household type and summed across household and income categories to obtain the projected expenditures by categories shown in the tables presented below. The expenditure data used are national-level data because data on expenditure patterns for persons with specific age and race/ethnicity characteristics were not available for Texas. We believe, however, that patterns of expenditures within age, sex, race/ethnicity, and household types are likely to be sufficiently similar across the United States to make the results of the analysis useful for examining the effects of population change on expenditures in Texas households.

Substantial increases are projected to occur in the level of consumer expenditures over time, from $274.3 billion in 2000 to $656.3 billion in 2040 under the 1.0 scenario, an increase of 139.3 percent (see Tables 5.2 and 5.3). This rate of growth would be less than projected household growth, which is projected to be 162.1 percent (see Table 3.4), suggesting that reduced income levels associated with socioeconomic differentials among racial/ ethnic groups would reduce relative growth in expenditures.

Total expenditures will increase more for non-Anglos than for Anglos because of the faster growth in the number of non-Anglo households (see Table 5.3). For example, under this (the

Table 5.2

Consumer Expenditures in Texas (in Billions of 2000 Dollars) by Category in 2000 and Projections to 2040 Using the Population Projection That Assumes 1990–2000 Rates of Net Migration (1.0 Scenario)

Year	Total	Food	Alcohol	Housing	Apparel	Trans-portation	Health	Enter-tainment
2000	$ 274.3	$ 38.1	$ 2.1	$ 85.3	$ 10.4	$ 55.8	$ 13.7	$ 13.0
2010	342.4	48.0	2.6	106.7	12.9	70.3	17.1	15.7
2020	428.2	61.1	3.1	134.2	16.2	88.6	21.7	19.1
2030	530.9	77.1	3.7	167.2	20.0	110.5	27.2	22.8
2040	656.3	96.6	4.4	207.8	24.7	137.5	33.5	27.5

	Personal	Reading	Edu-cation	Tobacco	Miscel-laneous	Cash	Insurance
2000	$ 2.3	$ 1.1	$ 4.0	$ 2.3	$ 5.5	$ 9.2	$ 31.5
2010	2.9	1.3	4.8	2.8	6.8	11.4	39.0
2020	3.7	1.5	5.6	3.3	8.6	14.2	47.4
2030	4.7	1.8	6.7	3.9	10.6	17.4	57.3
2040	5.8	2.1	8.1	4.6	13.0	20.6	70.3

Sources: Derived by the authors from Texas Population Estimates and Projections Program 2001. Bureau of Labor Statistics 2002.

Table 5.3

Percent Change in Projected Consumer Expenditures in Texas by Expenditure Category
and Race/Ethnicity Using the Population Projection That Assumes 1990–2000 Rates of Net
Migration (1.0 Scenario), 2000–40

Time Period	Total	Food	Alcohol	Housing	Apparel	Trans-portation	Health	Enter-tainment
Total								
2000–10	24.8	26.2	20.4	25.0	24.9	26.0	24.8	20.7
2010–20	25.1	27.2	20.1	25.8	25.0	26.0	26.9	21.1
2020–30	24.0	26.2	18.3	24.6	23.8	24.6	25.7	19.7
2030–40	23.6	25.3	19.3	24.3	23.3	24.5	22.9	20.4
2000–40	139.3	153.9	104.0	143.6	138.2	146.3	144.8	110.5

	Personal	Reading	Edu-cation	Tobacco	Miscel-laneous	Cash	Insurance
2000–10	26.2	20.7	21.4	19.1	25.1	24.0	23.7
2010–20	26.7	20.5	16.8	19.1	25.6	24.6	21.6
2020–30	25.5	18.8	19.7	17.7	23.7	22.6	20.9
2030–40	24.0	17.7	20.1	18.7	23.1	17.8	22.6
2000–40	148.8	103.2	103.7	97.9	139.3	123.1	122.9

Time Period	Total	Food	Alcohol	Housing	Apparel	Trans-portation	Health	Enter-tainment
Anglo								
2000–10	8.1	7.8	7.2	7.5	7.0	7.8	12.6	7.3
2010–20	5.0	5.6	4.2	4.9	3.4	4.6	11.7	4.4
2020–30	1.8	2.5	-0.2	2.1	0.7	0.8	7.9	0.3
2030–40	-0.5	-0.5	-1.6	-0.3	-1.2	-1.2	1.7	-1.4
2000–40	15.0	16.0	9.8	14.9	10.2	12.3	38.1	10.7

	Personal	Reading	Edu-cation	Tobacco	Miscel-laneous	Cash	Insurance
2000–10	9.3	10.6	6.8	6.5	8.0	13.3	7.4
2010–20	7.0	7.3	-4.4	3.4	5.7	12.6	0.9
2020–30	4.2	3.4	-1.4	-0.1	2.7	8.4	-2.4
2030–40	0.3	0.0	-0.3	-1.6	-0.4	0.8	-1.1
2000–40	22.4	22.8	0.3	8.1	16.8	39.3	4.6

Time Period	Total	Food	Alcohol	Housing	Apparel	Trans-portation	Health	Enter-tainment
Black								
2000–10	25.8	26.1	25.3	25.2	23.9	25.3	28.8	23.5
2010–20	22.4	23.0	21.6	22.2	21.1	22.1	28.1	20.8
2020–30	15.6	16.4	12.2	15.6	14.3	15.5	23.3	14.7
2030–40	10.6	11.3	8.7	10.7	9.0	10.0	14.7	9.9
2000–40	97.0	100.9	85.8	95.8	86.9	94.3	133.1	88.0

	Personal	Reading	Edu-cation	Tobacco	Miscel-laneous	Cash	Insurance
2000–10	25.4	29.1	25.0	30.0	32.0	28.4	27.0
2010–20	21.9	25.1	17.0	24.3	27.6	24.6	21.0
2020–30	15.5	16.8	8.9	15.6	15.8	15.7	13.4
2030–40	10.4	11.9	9.5	10.1	11.1	11.0	10.1
2000–40	94.8	111.1	74.6	105.8	116.8	105.5	91.7

Table 5.3, continued

Time Period	Total	Food	Alcohol	Housing	Apparel	Trans-portation	Health	Enter-tainment
				Hispanic				
2000–10	66.7	66.1	65.7	66.4	65.4	66.4	68.0	67.0
2010–20	58.3	58.6	56.0	58.3	57.3	57.2	62.7	58.9
2020–30	49.2	49.8	47.1	48.9	47.8	48.4	54.8	49.2
2030–40	43.1	43.6	42.2	43.1	42.0	42.8	47.6	43.5
2000–40	463.7	466.9	440.8	461.3	446.1	454.3	524.7	468.1

	Personal	Reading	Edu-cation	Tobacco	Miscel-laneous	Cash	Insurance
2000–10	66.4	66.7	64.7	67.3	66.9	70.6	68.2
2010–20	59.3	61.0	57.3	59.5	58.6	59.7	58.8
2020–30	50.8	51.1	48.9	49.6	49.1	54.1	48.7
2030–40	44.2	43.9	37.7	43.9	43.5	43.6	42.1
2000–40	476.2	483.1	431.3	474.4	466.1	502.9	464.3

Time Period	Total	Food	Alcohol	Housing	Apparel	Trans-portation	Health	Enter-tainment
				Other				
2000–10	86.0	89.1	76.4	83.6	85.3	88.5	103.8	86.4
2010–20	70.0	72.1	63.6	68.2	68.4	70.9	86.1	70.3
2020–30	56.9	60.2	54.8	55.7	53.8	57.6	71.3	56.8
2030–40	48.0	50.2	45.8	48.1	43.4	47.2	60.0	47.8
2000–40	634.0	682.7	551.0	612.4	588.4	647.3	939.8	635.8

	Personal	Reading	Edu-cation	Tobacco	Miscel-laneous	Cash	Insurance
2000–10	89.9	85.4	72.0	98.0	86.6	80.6	83.3
2010–20	71.9	73.6	67.5	76.8	66.1	71.0	66.3
2020–30	59.5	61.9	43.1	60.2	52.2	58.6	53.6
2030–40	51.5	49.3	39.3	54.3	43.7	50.8	44.7
2000–40	688.8	678.0	474.0	765.0	578.0	638.8	577.3

Sources: Derived by the authors from Texas Population Estimates and Projections Program 2001; Bureau of Labor Statistics 2002.

1.0) scenario, the increase in expenditures among Anglos would be 15 percent, the increase among Blacks 97 percent, the increase among Hispanics 463.7 percent, and the increase among persons from the Other racial/ethnic group would be 634 percent from 2000 to 2040. Because of the faster growth in expenditures among non-Anglo populations, the proportion of total expenditures accounted for by Anglos decreases from 66.4 percent in 2000 to 31.9 percent in 2040, the proportion accounted for by Blacks decreases from 8.7 in 2000 to 7.1 percent in 2040, the proportion due to the Hispanic population increases from 21.9 percent to 51.7 percent, and the proportion accounted for by the Other population increases from 3 percent to 9.3 percent (see Table 5.4 and Figure 5.1). Since Anglo households are projected to be approximately 29 percent of all households, Black households to account for about 9 percent, Hispanic households for about 53 percent, and the Other population for about 9 percent of households by 2040, Anglo households and households with householders from the Other racial/ethnic group will account for larger proportions of expenditures than their proportions of households while Blacks and Hispanics in particular, will account for lower proportions of all expenditures than their proportions of households. Nevertheless, it is evident that a majority of the increase in consumer expenditures will involve non-Anglo populations, with 92.8 percent of the net change in expenditures being due to non-Anglo households (see Table 5.5).

The projections of expenditures within individual categories also show the effects of demographic and socioeconomic characteristics. For example, if one examines the proportion of expenditures accounted for by each racial/ethnic group (see Table 5.4), one finds that Hispanics tend to account for proportions of such basic categories as food, apparel, housing, and transportation that are larger than their proportion of all expenditures, while Anglos show larger proportionate expenditures in areas such as health. In fact, reflecting the relative age differences in the populations in different racial/ethnic groups, Anglos (who would account for only 7.2 percent of the net change in all expenditures) would account for 19.6 percent of the net change in expenditures for health from 2000 to 2040, while Hispanics (who account for 73 percent of the net change in expenditures) would account for only 60.9 percent of the net change in expenditures for health (see Table 5.5). Age and race/ethnicity will affect the types as well as the levels of consumer expenditures in the state.

Consumer expenditures will also vary across different types of households (see Tables 5.6 and 5.7). Because data were not

Table 5.4

Percent of Consumer Expenditures in Texas by Expenditure Category and
Race/Ethnicity in 2000 and Projections for 2040 Using the Population Projection
That Assumes 1990–2000 Rates of Net Migration (1.0 Scenario)

Race/ Ethnicity	Total	Food	Alcohol	Housing	Apparel	Trans- portation	Health	Enter- tainment
			2000					
Anglo	66.4	63.2	73.7	64.5	62.2	64.5	74.6	73.6
Black	8.7	9.3	6.0	9.4	11.4	8.0	6.5	6.6
Hispanic	21.9	24.5	18.2	22.9	23.5	24.2	16.8	17.4
Other	3.0	3.0	2.1	3.2	2.9	3.3	2.1	2.4

	Personal	Reading	Edu- cation	Tobacco	Miscel- laneous	Cash	Insurance
Anglo	60.2	78.8	70.2	74.4	66.8	76.2	68.5
Black	15.6	6.2	7.6	9.6	8.5	7.5	8.1
Hispanic	21.8	12.0	16.7	13.9	22.0	14.1	20.1
Other	2.4	3.0	5.5	2.1	2.7	2.2	3.3

Race/ Ethnicity	Total	Food	Alcohol	Housing	Apparel	Trans- portation	Health	Enter- tainment
			2040					
Anglo	31.9	29.0	39.6	30.4	28.7	29.4	42.1	38.7
Black	7.1	7.3	5.5	7.6	9.0	6.3	6.2	5.9
Hispanic	51.7	54.6	48.2	52.8	53.8	54.4	42.9	47.0
Other	9.3	9.1	6.7	9.2	8.5	9.9	8.8	8.4

	Personal	Reading	Edu- cation	Tobacco	Miscel- laneous	Cash	Insurance
Anglo	29.6	47.6	34.6	40.6	32.6	47.5	32.1
Black	12.3	6.4	6.5	10.0	7.7	6.9	7.0
Hispanic	50.4	34.5	43.5	40.4	52.0	38.2	50.9
Other	7.7	11.5	15.4	9.0	7.7	7.4	10.0

Sources: Derived by the authors from Texas Population Estimates and Projections Program
2001; Bureau of Labor Statistics 2002.

available by age, sex, race/ethnicity, and household type, these
values were computed using data on only household-type
differences, and total values will vary somewhat from those
presented above. Married-couple families are clearly dominant
among purchasers of goods and services. This finding reflects
their greater numbers and the differences in average size
between married-couple and other households. The household
change noted in Chapter 3, however, points out that the
diversity of households is expected to increase, with single-

Figure 5.1

Percent of Total Consumer Expenditures in Texas by
Race/Ethnicity for 2000 and Projections for 2040*

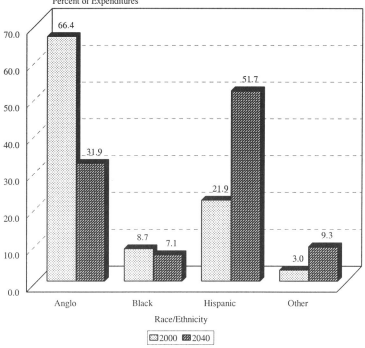

* Projections are shown for the 1.0 scenario

parent householder families increasing rapidly. The increase in
total expenditures as well as virtually all categories of
expenditures will increase faster for single-parent families than
for married-couple households. For example, whereas total
household expenditures would increase by 136.9 percent from
2000 to 2040, the increase for married-couple families is 141.5
percent, while that for male-householder families is 200.5
percent and that for female-householder families is 151.3
percent. The higher proportion of family households among the
most rapidly growing segments of Texas' population results in
slower growth in expenditures among nonfamily households, in
which expenditures increase by 111.7 percent. Changes in

Table 5.5

Percent of Net Change in Consumer Expenditures in Texas by Expenditure
Category and Race/Ethnicity Using the Population Projection That Assumes
1990–2000 Rates of Net Migration (1.0 Scenario), 2000–40

Race/ Ethnicity	Total	Food	Alcohol	Housing	Apparel	Trans- portation	Health	Enter- tainment
Anglo	7.2	6.6	6.9	6.6	4.5	5.4	19.6	7.1
Black	6.0	6.1	5.0	6.3	7.2	5.2	6.0	5.3
Hispanic	73.0	74.2	77.0	73.6	75.8	75.0	60.9	73.8
Other	13.8	13.1	11.1	13.5	12.5	14.4	13.5	13.8
Total	100.0	100.0	100.0	100.0	100.0	100.0	100.0	100.0

	Personal	Reading	Edu- cation	Tobacco	Miscel- laneous	Cash	Insurance
Anglo	9.0	17.4	0.2	6.2	8.1	24.3	2.5
Black	10.0	6.6	5.4	10.4	7.1	6.4	6.1
Hispanic	69.7	56.2	69.4	67.4	73.6	57.7	76.0
Other	11.3	19.8	25.0	16.0	11.2	11.6	15.4
Total	100.0	100.0	100.0	100.0	100.0	100.0	100.0

Sources: Derived by the authors from Texas Population Estimates and Projections Program
2001; Bureau of Labor Statistics 2002.

household type will alter the type of consuming unit in Texas in the coming years with clear implications for the state's businesses.

Overall, the data show that consumer expenditures for goods and services will increase substantially—but less than would be expected given the projected increase in the number of households. This finding suggests that although the absolute volume of future expenditures will increase, the expenditures per household will decline, given the projected change in household composition and the existent differentials in household incomes. The increase in expenditures will largely be due to non-Anglo households, particularly to Hispanic household growth. Of the total net change in expenditures between 2000 and 2040, nearly 93 percent will be due to non-Anglo households, and by 2040 more than 68 percent of all household expenditures in Texas will involve non-Anglo households. Similarly, expenditures will increasingly involve male- and female-householder households. Such data point to rapidly changing household markets and market segments for Texas businesses.

Table 5.6

Consumer Expenditures by Household Type and Expenditure Category
in 2000 (in Millions of 2000 Dollars) and Projections for 2040 Using
the Population Projection That Assumes 1990–2000 Rates of Net
Migration (1.0 Scenario)

Expenditure Category	All House-holds	Married-Couple Families	Male-House-holder Families	Female-House-holder Families	Non-family House-holds
2000					
Food	$ 39,590.9	$ 25,248.3	$ 1,146.1	$ 3,180.0	$ 10,016.5
Alcohol	2,164.0	1,189.4	128.5	132.2	713.8
Housing	87,379.4	55,779.8	2,465.4	8,169.8	20,964.4
Apparel	10,792.6	6,937.7	258.9	1,002.0	2,594.0
Transportation	58,640.1	39,500.2	1,375.4	3,550.1	14,214.5
Health	13,973.4	9,470.2	291.1	930.2	3,281.9
Entertainment	13,512.1	9,214.9	359.7	920.0	3,017.5
Personal	2,410.2	1,508.3	51.9	241.7	608.3
Reading	1,076.9	689.5	29.2	87.5	270.6
Education	4,337.8	2,740.8	115.9	254.0	1,227.2
Tobacco	2,579.3	1,364.1	80.8	162.1	972.3
Miscellaneous	5,475.1	3,468.8	223.2	481.4	1,301.7
Cash	8,402.5	6,300.3	343.2	465.6	1,293.4
Insurance	32,159.5	23,129.9	839.3	1,986.7	6,203.5
Total	282,493.8	186,542.2	7,708.7	21,563.3	66,679.6
2040					
Food	$ 99,574.8	$ 65,048.8	$ 3,766.8	$ 8,323.5	$ 22,435.8
Alcohol	4,460.5	2,492.9	378.3	269.7	1,319.6
Housing	211,875.3	138,457.7	7,669.4	21,225.4	44,522.8
Apparel	25,918.9	16,996.0	901.1	2,423.4	5,598.4
Transportation	142,715.0	98,745.0	3,831.7	8,737.6	31,400.7
Health	32,562.4	22,393.4	900.1	2,333.9	6,935.0
Entertainment	28,331.1	19,351.9	1,015.4	2,180.9	5,782.9
Personal	5,893.4	3,773.8	186.4	560.3	1,372.9
Reading	2,173.2	1,392.6	76.0	195.4	509.1
Education	8,830.5	5,949.0	272.5	500.7	2,108.3
Tobacco	4,977.6	2,760.1	220.8	331.3	1,665.4
Miscellaneous	12,992.0	8,078.2	823.4	1,313.3	2,777.1
Cash	18,233.2	13,680.7	925.5	1,166.3	2,460.8
Insurance	70,567.2	51,469.0	2,198.8	4,631.6	12,267.8
Total	669,105.3	450,589.1	23,166.4	54,193.2	141,156.5

Sources: Derived by the authors from Texas Population Estimates and Projections
Program 2001; Bureau of Labor Statistics 2002.

PROJECTIONS OF ASSET ACCUMULATION

Although there are marked differences in the incomes and
expenditures of Anglo and non-Anglo households, racial/ethnic

Table 5.7

Percent Change in Consumer Expenditures in Texas by Household Type
and Expenditure Category Using the Population Projection That Assumes
1990–2000 Rates of Net Migration (1.0 Scenario), 2000–40

Expenditure Category	All House-holds	Married-Couple Families	Male-House-holder Families	Female-House-holder Families	Non-family House-holds
Food	151.5	157.6	228.7	161.7	124.0
Alcohol	106.1	109.6	194.4	103.9	84.9
Housing	142.5	148.2	211.1	159.8	112.4
Apparel	140.2	145.0	248.1	141.9	115.8
Transportation	143.4	150.0	178.6	146.1	120.9
Health	133.0	136.5	209.2	150.9	111.3
Entertainment	109.7	110.0	182.3	137.0	91.6
Personal	144.5	150.2	258.9	131.9	125.7
Reading	101.8	102.0	160.0	123.3	88.1
Education	103.6	117.1	135.2	97.1	71.8
Tobacco	93.0	102.3	173.2	104.4	71.3
Miscellaneous	137.3	132.9	268.9	172.8	113.3
Cash	117.0	117.1	169.6	150.5	90.3
Insurance	119.4	122.5	162.0	133.1	97.8
Total	136.9	141.5	200.5	151.3	111.7

Sources: Derived by the authors from Texas Population Estimates and Projections
Program 2001; Bureau of Labor Statistics 2002.

differences are particularly large when one examines the net
worth and assets of households. In 2000, for example, the
average (mean) net worth of households in the United States
was $126,618 for Anglos, $34,259 for Blacks, and $43,746 for
Hispanics (Davern and Fisher 2001). As a result, demographic
change involving diverse populations can have substantial
impact on the level of assets in a population.

In this section we examine the implications of population
change on Texans' assets. For this purpose, data on average
dollars of net worth and assets by age and race/ethnicity of
householder were obtained from the U.S. Bureau of the Census
Survey of Income and Program Participation for 1995 (Davern
and Fisher 2001) inflated to be in 2000 dollars and multiplied
by households by age and race/ethnicity. Because data on net
worth were available by age and by race/ethnicity separately
but not by age and race/ethnicity jointly, the effects of these

two variables are examined separately in the analysis. In addition, because separate data were not available on persons from the Other racial/ethnic group, Anglo values were assumed to apply to Other households.

The net worth of Texas households is projected to increase from $709.9 billion to $1.4 trillion from 2000 to 2040 based on the race/ethnicity effects of population growth under the 1.0 scenario, an increase of 103.4 percent (see Table 5.8). Net worth would increase at a slower rate than the increase in the number of households, which is projected to be 162.1 percent. The assets of the average household would thus decrease, from about $96,000 in 2000 to roughly $74,500 in 2040, a decrease of 22.4 percent. The values would also show substantial changes relative to the proportion of net worth and assets resulting from Anglo versus non-Anglo households. Although net worth and assets will remain disproportionately Anglo, with Anglo households accounting for only 29 percent of households but 49.2 percent of net worth in 2040 (see Table 5.9), the proportion of all net worth accounted for by Anglos would decline by 31.8 percent from 2000 to 2040. By contrast, Hispanics, who are projected to account for 52.8 percent of all households in 2040, would account for only 31 percent of net worth, but that percentage would represent an increase of 20 percent from 2000 to 2040.

The data in Table 5.10 show the effects of changes in the age distribution on net worth and assets. Because older householders have larger assets, the effect of the aging of the population is to substantially increase the level of assets. The resulting percentage increases in net worth and all asset categories are greater than the 162.1 percent increase in the number of households. The proportion of net worth and assets accounted for by the older population would also increase (see Table 5.11), with the total percentage of net worth accounted for by the population fifty-five years of age or older increasing from 49.6 percent in 2000 to 59.9 percent in 2040. This effect of the aging of the population is evident for interest-earning

Table 5.8

Race/Ethnicity Effects on Projections of Net Worth and Assets for
Households in Texas in 2000 and 2040 Using the Population Projection
That Assumes 1990–2000 Rates of Net Migration (1.0 Scenario)

Categories of Assets	2000	2040	Percent Difference
Net worth	$ 709,896,741,518	$ 1,444,188,603,304	103.4
Interest-earning assets	416,444,678,728	694,962,422,140	66.9
Regular checking accounts	9,244,116,349	22,283,154,883	141.1
Stocks and mutual funds	299,940,052,315	741,082,606,568	147.1
Equity in business or profession	381,371,946,690	842,735,848,416	121.0
Equity in motor vehicles	71,669,400,586	167,421,386,886	133.6
Equity in own home	534,802,097,857	1,289,022,675,470	141.0
Rental property equity	652,387,202,487	1,499,319,943,638	129.8
Other real estate equity	469,675,888,497	1,108,933,471,751	136.1
U.S. Saving Bonds	28,313,691,464	58,822,167,660	107.8
IRA or KEOGH accounts	263,269,325,874	652,626,452,944	147.9
Other assets	371,673,948,422	577,668,570,957	55.4

Sources: Derived by the authors from Texas Population Estimates and Projections Program
2001; Davern and Fisher 2001.

Table 5.9

Projected Proportion of Net Worth and Assets of Householders in Texas by
Race/Ethnicity in 2000 and 2040 Using the Population Projection That Assumes
1990–2000 Rates of Net Migration (1.0 Scenario)

Race/ Ethnicity	Net worth	Interest-earning assets	Regular checking accounts	Stocks and mutual fund shares	Equity in business or profession	Equity in motor vehicles	Equity in own home	Rental property equity	Other real estate equity	U.S. Savings Bonds	IRA or KEOGH accounts
2000											
Anglo	81.0	92.1	68.2	71.2	76.4	69.7	69.6	74.2	58.5	77.0	71.1
Black	4.1	0.8	9.1	3.9	4.8	9.3	7.4	4.9	22.0	7.7	3.8
Hispanic	11.0	2.6	19.4	21.5	15.1	17.6	19.6	17.3	16.7	11.6	21.7
Other	3.9	4.5	3.3	3.4	3.7	3.4	3.4	3.6	2.8	3.7	3.4
Total	100.0	100.0	100.0	100.0	100.0	100.0	100.0	100.0	100.0	100.0	100.0
2040											
Anglo	49.2	68.2	35.0	35.6	42.7	36.9	35.7	39.9	30.6	45.7	35.4
Black	4.1	1.0	7.8	3.3	4.5	8.2	6.3	4.4	19.3	7.7	3.2
Hispanic	31.0	9.1	46.1	49.8	39.2	43.1	46.6	43.0	40.3	32.0	50.1
Other	15.7	21.7	11.1	11.3	13.6	11.8	11.4	12.7	9.8	14.6	11.3
Total	100.0	100.0	100.0	100.0	100.0	100.0	100.0	100.0	100.0	100.0	100.0

Sources: Derived by the authors from Texas Population Estimates and Projections Program 2001; Davern
and Fisher 2001.

Table 5.10

Age Effects on Projections of Net Worth and Assets for Households in Texas in
2000 and 2040 Using the Population Projection That Assumes 1990–2000 Rates
of Net Migration (1.0 Scenario)

Categories of Assets	2000	2040	Percent Difference
Net worth	$ 824,089,496,224	$ 2,408,070,044,814	192.2
Interest-earning assets	498,981,723,740	1,467,689,335,728	194.1
Regular checking accounts	9,982,625,443	27,600,896,244	176.5
Stocks and mutual funds	301,581,086,876	875,405,769,599	190.3
Equity in business or profession	447,626,496,948	1,183,257,865,061	164.3
Equity in motor vehicles	79,012,319,385	209,168,096,100	164.7
Equity in own home	528,019,623,448	1,493,421,135,285	182.8
Rental property equity	617,595,519,367	1,742,579,793,986	182.2
Other real estate equity	478,931,445,892	1,256,164,778,275	162.3
U.S. Saving Bonds	33,215,100,269	99,370,800,082	199.2
IRA or KEOGH accounts	256,937,781,073	749,279,240,700	191.6
Other assets	477,013,213,831	1,339,570,325,232	180.8

Sources: Derived by the authors from Texas Population Estimates and Projections Program
2001; Davern and Fisher 2001.

Table 5.11

Projected Proportion of Net Worth and Assets in Texas by Age of Householder in 2000
and 2040 Using the Population Projection That Assumes 1990–2000 Rates of Net
Migration (1.0 Scenario)

Age Group	Net worth	Interest-earning assets	Regular checking accounts	Stocks and mutual fund shares	Equity in business or profession	Equity in motor vehicles	Equity in own home	Rental property equity	Other real estate equity	U.S. Savings Bonds	IRA or KEOGH accounts	Other assets
2000												
15-34	7.2	15.8	17.0	9.2	19.9	21.4	12.3	14.5	27.0	7.8	9.3	13.5
35-44	17.6	11.3	20.7	19.7	26.5	23.6	20.4	18.0	20.4	18.5	16.6	21.5
45-54	25.6	21.0	24.0	21.2	23.2	23.7	23.8	23.6	22.7	18.1	25.1	22.7
55-64	21.0	19.0	12.5	22.5	11.2	15.3	17.9	21.8	14.5	17.5	18.9	16.8
65+	28.6	32.9	25.8	27.4	19.2	16.0	25.6	22.1	15.4	38.1	30.1	25.5
Total	100.0	100.0	100.0	100.0	100.0	100.0	100.0	100.0	100.0	100.0	100.0	100.0
2040												
15-34	5.1	11.2	12.9	6.6	15.8	16.9	9.1	10.7	21.6	5.5	6.7	10.1
35-44	12.7	8.2	15.8	14.4	21.3	18.9	15.3	13.6	16.4	13.1	12.0	16.2
45-54	22.3	18.2	22.1	18.5	22.2	22.7	21.4	21.2	22.0	15.4	21.9	20.5
55-64	24.2	21.6	15.2	26.0	14.2	19.4	21.2	25.9	18.6	19.5	21.7	20.1
65+	35.7	40.8	34.0	34.5	26.5	22.1	33.0	28.6	21.4	46.5	37.7	33.1
Total	100.0	100.0	100.0	100.0	100.0	100.0	100.0	100.0	100.0	100.0	100.0	100.0

Sources: Derived by the authors from Texas Population Estimates and Projections Program 2001; Davern
and Fisher 2001.

assets, stocks and mutual funds, and U.S. Savings Bonds, for
which the proportions owned by households with a householder
fifty-five years of age or older are greater than 60 percent, and

least obvious relative to equity in businesses, equity in motor vehicles, and equity in other real estate, for which the proportion owned by those fifty-five years of age or older is roughly 40 percent. However, the percentage of all assets owned by older householders will increase over time. Overall, these data suggest that net worth and assets will generally increase with an aging population and that households with older householders will come to play an increasingly large role in asset ownership in the coming decades.

In Table 5.12 we examine the effects of age and race/ethnicity on net worth and assets by assuming that 2000 distributions for race/ethnicity (in Panel A) and age (in Panel B) apply in 2040. The extent to which change in the population's racial/ethnic composition would decrease net worth and assets and the population's aging would increase net worth and assets is evident. Under existing relationships with race/ethnicity, net worth is reduced by 26.5 percent and all asset categories by at least 7.8 percent relative to what would occur if the race/ethnicity of householders in 2040 were the same as in 2000. On the other hand, the aging of the population increases net worth by 11.4 percent and positively increases equity in all asset categories.

The data on consumer expenditures, net worth, and assets suggest that in the absence of change in the socioeconomic differentials between age and race/ethnicity groups, the projected population changes will markedly impact consumer markets and investments resulting in decreased per-household expenditures and investments. Although change in socioeconomic differentials could change the overall effects on the total volume of future expenditures and investments, expenditures and assets will increasingly involve older and non-Anglo households under any alternative.

Table 5.13 shows total consumer expenditures in 2040 by race/ethnicity for alternative simulations, like those discussed in Chapter 4. The first two columns present information for the baseline projection scenario in which 2000 differentials are

Table 5.12

Race/Ethnicity and Age of Householder Effects on Projected Net Worth
and Assets in Texas in 2040 by Category Assuming 2000 Distribution and
Using the Population Projection That Assumes 1990–2000 Rates of
Net Migration (1.0 Scenario)

	Panel A: Race/Ethnicity of Householder Effects		
Categories of Assets	Assuming 2000 Distribution in 2040	Assuming 1990–2000 Net Migration in 2040	Percent Difference
Net worth	$ 1,964,136,197,568	$ 1,444,188,603,304	-26.5
Interest-earning assets	1,185,077,261,707	694,962,422,140	-41.4
Regular checking accounts	24,685,669,400	22,283,154,883	-9.7
Stocks and mutual funds	812,650,712,861	741,082,606,568	-8.8
Equity in business or profession	1,043,447,475,392	842,735,848,416	-19.2
Equity in motor vehicles	191,975,005,903	167,421,386,886	-12.8
Equity in own home	1,436,382,249,445	1,289,022,675,470	-10.3
Rental property equity	1,777,052,556,302	1,499,319,943,638	-15.6
Other real estate equity	1,202,342,306,782	1,108,933,471,751	-7.8
U.S. Saving Bonds	77,246,732,029	58,822,167,660	-23.9
IRA or KEOGH accounts	713,215,489,070	652,626,452,944	-8.5
Other assets	1,066,229,371,207	577,668,570,957	-45.8

	Panel B: Age of Householder Effects		
Categories of Assets	Assuming 2000 Distribution in 2040	Assuming 1990–2000 Net Migration in 2040	Percent Difference
Net worth	$ 2,161,693,227,502	$ 2,408,070,044,814	11.4
Interest-earning assets	1,308,581,443,078	1,467,689,335,728	12.2
Regular checking accounts	26,173,753,757	27,600,896,244	5.5
Stocks and mutual funds	791,013,176,266	875,405,769,599	10.7
Equity in business or profession	1,173,396,439,476	1,183,257,865,061	0.8
Equity in motor vehicles	207,115,773,249	209,168,096,100	1.0
Equity in own home	1,384,715,739,926	1,493,421,135,285	7.9
Rental property equity	1,619,529,987,935	1,742,579,793,986	7.6
Other real estate equity	1,255,196,925,034	1,256,164,778,275	0.1
U.S. Saving Bonds	87,128,726,816	99,370,800,082	14.1
IRA or KEOGH accounts	673,932,682,945	749,279,240,700	11.2
Other assets	1,250,875,279,147	1,339,570,325,232	7.1

Sources: Derived by the authors from Texas Population Estimates and Projections Program
2001; Davern and Fisher 2001.

assumed to continue throughout the projection period. In the
second two columns we assume that the same closure in
expenditures that occurred in income from 1990 to 2000
continues for each decade from 2000 to 2040. In the final two

Table 5.13

Projected Total Annual Aggregate Consumer Expenditures
(in Billions of 2000 Dollars) and Mean Household Expenditures
(in 2000 Dollars) in Texas in 2040 by Race/Ethnicity Assuming 2000
Income Differentials, 1990–2000 Rates of Closure between Anglo-
Black and Anglo-Hispanic Household Incomes, and Anglo Income
Levels Obtained by All Race/Ethnicity Groups and Using the
Population Projection That Assumes 1990–2000 Rates of Net
Migration (1.0 Scenario)

Race/ Ethnicity	Assuming 2000 Income Differentials		Assuming 1990–2000 Closure in Differentials		Assuming Anglo Incomes for All Groups	
	Aggregate	Mean	Aggregate	Mean	Aggregate	Mean
Anglo	$ 209.2	$ 37,293	$ 209.2	$ 37,293	$ 209.2	$ 37,293
Black	46.8	26,802	54.7	31,304	63.2	36,187
Hispanic	339.2	33,155	354.3	34,631	402.7	39,357
Other	61.1	34,147	61.1	34,147	65.6	36,675
Total	656.3	33,872	679.3	35,057	740.7	38,226

Sources: Derived by the authors from Texas Population Estimates and
Projections Program 2001; Bureau of Labor Statistics 2002.

columns, we examine the implications if all groups came to
have the expenditure levels of Anglos in 2000.

Expenditure levels would increase substantially if
expenditure patterns were to follow income changes (see Table
5.13 and Figure 5.2). Under the 1.0 projection scenario, the
increase is to $679.3 billion in 2040 under the 1990–2000
closure scenario compared to $656.3 billion in 2040 assuming
2000 income differentials, an increase of nearly $23 billion,
and to $740.7 billion assuming Anglo income for all groups, an
increase of more than $84 billion per year. As a result, average
per-household expenditures would change from $37,096 in
2000 to $33,872 in 2040 under the scenario assuming 2000
rates, to $35,057 assuming 1990–2000 rates of closure, and to
$38,226 assuming 2000 Anglo expenditures for all
race/ethnicity groups. In sum, these changes in socioeconomic
differentials among racial/ethnic groups in the state's
population would increase the total expenditures into the Texas
economy.

Figure 5.2

Mean Per-Household Consumer Expenditures in Texas in 2000 and
Projections for 2040* Assuming 2000 Rates in 2040, 1990–2000 Rates
of Closure between Anglo-Black and Anglo-Hispanic Expenditures, and
Anglo Expenditures for All Race/Ethnicity Groups

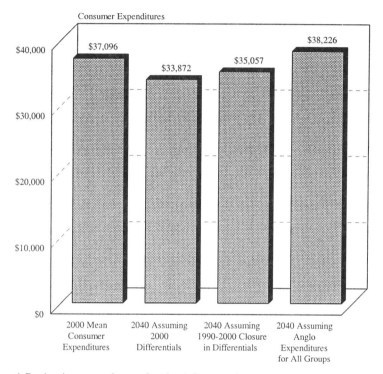

* Projections are shown for the 1.0 scenario

IMPLICATIONS FOR SPECIFIC
PRIVATE-SECTOR MARKETS

The general implications for consumer expenditures and asset
ownership shown above are indicative of general changes likely
to affect overall markets for a variety of goods and services.
Because the effects of population change vary in different
sectors of the economy, the examination of selected sectors can
be quite informative. In this section we examine the
implications for two major sectors of the economy: housing
and health care.

Effects on Housing Demand by Tenure

Population change may substantially affect the demand for
housing and thus the markets for real estate. Table 5.14
indicates some of the differences in housing characteristics
among age and race/ethnicity groups evident in data from the
2000 Census. Median housing values vary from one
racial/ethnic group to another, with values for Blacks being
only 65.9 percent of those for Anglos and 54.9 percent of those
for Asians, and Hispanic-owned units having median values
that are only 59.5 percent of the value for Anglo and 49.5
percent of the value for Asian-owned units. Differences are less
for rents, with median rents for Blacks being 85.2 percent of
the median for Anglos and 86.4 percent of the median for
Asians, and median rents for Hispanics being 79.2 percent and
80.4 percent of Anglo and Asian median rents, respectively.
Ownership rates are also widely different, with Anglo
ownership rates exceeding those for Blacks by 24.3 percent,
those for Hispanics by 14.7 percent, and those for Asians by
18.1 percent. Finally, age differences are also apparent, with
ownership rates peaking in older ages and renters' rates peaking
at younger ages. Demographic factors affect the number of

Table 5.14

Median Owner-Occupied Housing Values, Median Monthly Rents, Ownership
Rates, and Renter Rates in Texas by Race/Ethnicity, and Tenure by Age, 2000

Housing	Race/Ethnicity				
Characteristic	Anglo	Black	Hispanic	Asian	Total
Median Housing Values	$ 94,700	$ 62,400	$ 56,300	$ 113,700	$ 82,500
Median Gross Rents	636	542	504	627	574
Tenure					
Percent Owner	70.8	46.5	56.1	52.7	63.8
Percent Renter	29.2	53.5	43.9	47.3	36.2

Housing	Age Groups				
Characteristic	15–59	60–64	65–74	75+	Total
Tenure					
Percent Owner	58.5	81.3	83.3	78.1	63.8
Percent Renter	41.5	18.7	16.7	21.9	36.2

Source: U.S. Census Bureau 2002a.

households in different types of housing units and the values and rents associated with such units.

The data in Tables 5.15–5.19, in which the projected number of households by tenure are presented, show some of these differences. Under the 1.0 scenario, the total number of owner-occupied units would increase from 4,716,959 in 2000 to 12,404,843 in 2040 and the total number of renter units from 2,676,395 in 2000 to 6,971,954 in 2040, resulting in increases of 163 percent for owner-occupied housing and 160.5 percent for renter housing. Growth in both owner and renter market segments are projected to largely parallel growth in the number of households, which increases by 162.1 percent. The fact that growth in rental housing is slower than that for owner housing reflects the aging of the population and the higher proportions of owners among older age groups (see Table 5.14)

Growth in both owner and renter markets will increasingly reflect the racial/ethnic diversity of the state's population base (see Tables 5.15-5.18). For example, the 2000 to 2040 increase in the number of Anglo owners is only 28.9 percent, but that for Blacks is 136.8 percent, that for Hispanics 521.1 percent, and that for householders from the Other racial/ethnic group is 867.5 percent. Similarly, the renter components of these groups increase by 10.6 percent, 81.6 percent, 408.6 percent, and 544.4 percent, respectively. As a result, only 33.4 percent of owners would be Anglo, 7.4 percent Black, 50.3 percent Hispanic, and 8.9 percent members of the Other racial/ethnic group by 2040. Among renters, the non-Anglo percentages are even higher, with the percentage of Anglos being only 21.1 percent, while 11.9 percent of renters would be Black, 57.3 percent Hispanic, and 9.7 percent members of the Other racial/ethnic group. Of the net change in the number of owner households from 2000 to 2040 (see Table 5.18), Anglo households would account for only 12.1 percent. As for the net change in renter units during the same period, Anglo households would account for only 3.4 percent. Both owner and rental housing markets will increasingly involve non-Anglos.

The effects of the projected aging of the population are also apparent (see Table 5.19). The percentage of all households

Table 5.15

Number of Households in Texas by Race/Ethnicity and Housing Tenure
in 2000 and Projections to 2040 Using the Population Projection That
Assumes 1990–2000 Rates of Net Migration (1.0 Scenario)

Year	Anglo	Black	Hispanic	Other	Total
		Total			
2000	4,540,078	843,712	1,789,623	219,941	7,393,354
2010	4,950,419	1,068,979	2,956,070	414,118	9,389,586
2020	5,327,431	1,324,961	4,676,499	717,860	12,046,751
2030	5,571,513	1,557,897	7,051,958	1,166,697	15,348,065
2040	5,610,322	1,746,730	10,231,880	1,787,865	19,376,797
		Owner			
2000	3,209,443	388,743	1,004,091	114,682	4,716,959
2010	3,562,473	508,827	1,683,602	236,909	5,991,811
2020	3,892,076	653,916	2,735,480	428,350	7,709,822
2030	4,107,312	800,023	4,227,907	713,393	9,848,635
2040	4,137,975	920,475	6,236,864	1,109,529	12,404,843
		Renter			
2000	1,330,635	454,969	785,532	105,259	2,676,395
2010	1,387,946	560,152	1,272,468	177,209	3,397,775
2020	1,435,355	671,045	1,941,019	289,510	4,336,929
2030	1,464,201	757,874	2,824,051	453,304	5,499,430
2040	1,472,347	826,255	3,995,016	678,336	6,971,954

Sources: Derived by the authors from Texas Population Estimates and Projections
Program 2001; U.S. Census Bureau 2002a.

Table 5.16

Percent Change in Projected Number of Households in Texas
by Race/Ethnicity and Housing Tenure Using the Population
Projection That Assumes 1990–2000 Rates of Net Migration
(1.0 Scenario), 2000–40

Time Period	Anglo	Black	Hispanic	Other	Total
		Total			
2000–10	9.0	26.7	65.2	88.3	27.0
2010–20	7.6	23.9	58.2	73.3	28.3
2020–30	4.6	17.6	50.8	62.5	27.4
2030–40	0.7	12.1	45.1	53.2	26.2
2000–40	23.6	107.0	471.7	712.9	162.1
		Owner			
2000–10	11.0	30.9	67.7	106.6	27.0
2010–20	9.3	28.5	62.5	80.8	28.7
2020–30	5.5	22.3	54.6	66.5	27.7
2030–40	0.7	15.1	47.5	55.5	26.0
2000–40	28.9	136.8	521.1	867.5	163.0
		Renter			
2000–10	4.3	23.1	62.0	68.4	27.0
2010–20	3.4	19.8	52.5	63.4	27.6
2020–30	2.0	12.9	45.5	56.6	26.8
2030–40	0.6	9.0	41.5	49.6	26.8
2000–40	10.6	81.6	408.6	544.4	160.5

Sources: Derived by the authors from Texas Population Estimates and Projections
Program 2001; U.S. Census Bureau 2002a.

Table 5.17

Percent of Households in Texas by Race/Ethnicity of Householder
and Housing Tenure in 2000 and Projections to 2040 Using the
Population Projection That Assumes 1990–2000 Rates of Net
Migration (1.0 Scenario)

Year	Anglo	Black	Hispanic	Other
Total				
2000	61.4	11.4	24.2	3.0
2010	52.7	11.4	31.5	4.4
2020	44.2	11.0	38.8	6.0
2030	36.3	10.2	45.9	7.6
2040	29.0	9.0	52.8	9.2
Owner				
2000	68.1	8.2	21.3	2.4
2010	59.4	8.5	28.1	4.0
2020	50.4	8.5	35.5	5.6
2030	41.8	8.1	42.9	7.2
2040	33.4	7.4	50.3	8.9
Renter				
2000	49.7	17.0	29.4	3.9
2010	40.8	16.5	37.5	5.2
2020	33.0	15.5	44.8	6.7
2030	26.6	13.8	51.4	8.2
2040	21.1	11.9	57.3	9.7

Sources: Derived by the authors from Texas Population Estimates and Projections
Program 2001; U.S. Census Bureau 2002a.

Table 5.18

Number and Percent of Net Change in Texas Households by
Race/Ethnicity and Housing Tenure Using the Population Projection That
Assumes 1990–2000 Rates of Net Migration (1.0 Scenario), 2000–40

Race/Ethnicity	Number	Percent
Total		
Anglo	1,070,244	9.0
Black	903,018	7.5
Hispanic	8,442,257	70.4
Other	1,567,924	13.1
Total	11,983,443	100.0
Owner		
Anglo	928,532	12.1
Black	531,732	6.9
Hispanic	5,232,773	68.1
Other	994,847	12.9
Total	7,687,884	100.0
Renter		
Anglo	141,712	3.4
Black	371,286	8.6
Hispanic	3,209,484	74.7
Other	573,077	13.3
Total	4,295,559	100.0

Sources: Derived by the authors from Texas Population Estimates and Projections
Program 2001; U.S. Census Bureau 2002a.

Table 5.19

Percent of Texas Households by Age and Race/Ethnicity of Householder and
Housing Tenure in 2000 and Projections for 2040 Using the Population Projection
That Assumes 1990–2000 Rates of Net Migration (1.0 Scenario)

Age Group	Anglo 2000	Anglo 2040	Black 2000	Black 2040	Hispanic 2000	Hispanic 2040	Other 2000	Other 2040	Total 2000	Total 2040
Total										
15–24	5.5	4.1	7.4	4.7	8.9	5.3	7.4	3.2	6.6	4.7
25–34	16.3	12.7	21.8	15.2	26.0	19.1	26.2	11.6	19.6	16.2
35–44	22.2	14.6	25.7	17.8	26.3	22.5	27.6	16.7	23.8	19.2
45–54	20.6	16.4	19.8	20.4	18.0	20.8	21.9	18.2	19.8	19.3
55–64	14.0	15.9	11.2	16.8	9.7	15.7	10.3	17.7	12.6	16.1
65–74	11.3	15.8	8.3	14.1	6.8	10.3	4.6	18.4	9.6	12.9
75–84	7.8	15.3	4.4	9.0	3.5	5.2	1.7	11.1	6.2	9.0
85+	2.3	5.2	1.4	2.0	0.8	1.1	0.3	3.1	1.8	2.6
Owner										
15–24	1.3	0.9	1.2	0.6	3.0	1.7	1.8	0.7	1.7	1.3
25–34	11.1	8.4	11.1	6.5	19.1	12.8	16.6	6.5	12.9	10.3
35–44	22.6	14.2	24.7	14.9	27.9	22.0	30.5	15.5	24.1	18.3
45–54	22.9	17.6	24.4	22.1	22.0	23.4	28.4	19.9	23.0	21.0
55–64	16.8	18.1	16.3	21.2	13.0	19.4	14.2	20.6	15.8	19.3
65–74	13.8	18.6	12.9	19.2	9.4	13.0	6.0	21.2	12.7	16.0
75–84	9.2	17.2	7.1	12.7	4.5	6.4	2.1	12.2	7.8	10.9
85+	2.3	5.0	2.3	2.8	1.1	1.3	0.4	3.4	2.0	2.9
Renter										
15–24	15.6	12.8	12.7	9.3	16.5	10.9	13.4	7.3	15.3	10.8
25–34	28.7	25.0	31.0	24.9	34.9	28.9	36.8	19.9	31.2	26.7
35–44	21.5	15.8	26.5	20.9	24.1	23.2	24.4	18.7	23.3	20.9
45–54	14.7	13.2	15.8	18.6	12.9	16.8	14.8	15.5	14.3	16.1
55–64	7.6	9.6	6.9	11.9	5.5	10.0	6.1	12.9	6.8	10.4
65–74	5.0	7.7	4.3	8.4	3.6	6.0	3.0	13.9	4.4	7.5
75–84	4.6	10.1	2.1	4.9	2.0	3.4	1.2	9.1	3.3	5.5
85+	2.3	5.8	0.7	1.1	0.5	0.8	0.3	2.7	1.4	2.1

Sources: Derived by the authors from Texas Population Estimates and Projections Program
2001; U.S. Census Bureau 2002a.

with a householder sixty-five years of age or older would
increase from 17.6 percent in 2000 to 24.5 percent by 2040 for
all householders, from 22.5 to 29.8 percent for owner
householders, and from 9.1 percent in 2000 to 15.1 percent in
2040 for renter householders.

Overall, the basic projections of households by tenure
suggest slightly faster increases in owner rather than rental
housing, but with renter householders remaining younger than
owner householders. Because of the projected aging and
racial/ethnic diversification of householders, the percentage of

both owner and renter households involving older and non-Anglo householders will substantially increase. By 2040, 29.8 percent of owners and 15.1 percent of renters will be sixty-five years of age or older (compared to 22.5 and 9.1 percent in 2000) and roughly two-thirds of homeowners and nearly 79 percent of renters will be non-Anglo (compared to roughly 32 and 50 percent, respectively, in 2000).

Effects on Housing Expenditures

The effects of population and household change on housing expenditures are examined in this section. Annual expenditures for housing by age, race/ethnicity, and tenure of householder as reported in the *2000 Consumer Expenditure Survey* (Bureau of Labor Statistics 2002) were multiplied by the projections of households by age, race/ethnicity, and tenure. Because the values are dollar values from the 2000 survey, the projections are in 2000 constant dollars.

The data in Table 5.20 show substantial increases in total expenditures for both owner and renter housing. Owner expenditures would increase from $33.1 billion in 2000 to $79 billion in 2040 and renter expenditures from $15.8 billion in 2000 to $41 billion in 2040, representing increases of 138.7 percent for owner expenditures and 160.2 percent for renter expenditures. Such data suggest that there will be substantial increases in the amount of money spent on real estate products and related services in the coming decades.

These expenditures, like household growth as a whole, will come increasingly from non-Anglo households and older households. By 2040, 67.2 percent of owner expenditures and 78.7 percent of renter expenditures would come from non-Anglo households, with Hispanics responsible for 51.5 percent of owner and 58.4 percent of renter expenditures (see Table 5.21). Also by 2040, 35.9 percent of owner expenditures and 21.6 percent of renter expenditures will come from households with a householder who is fifty-five years of age or older (see Table 5.22). These data show that the amount of money spent on housing will reflect the aging and racial/ethnic diversification of the population.

Table 5.20

Aggregate Annual Expenditures for Housing in Texas by Race/Ethnicity and Housing Tenure in 2000 and Projections to 2040 Using the Population Projection That Assumes 1990–2000 Rates of Net Migration (1.0 Scenario)

Year	Anglo	Black	Hispanic	Other	Total
			Total		
2000	$ 30,899,141,048	$ 4,527,454,222	$ 11,674,055,046	$ 1,765,610,468	$ 48,866,260,784
2010	32,884,943,501	5,640,338,693	19,390,811,337	3,187,531,920	61,103,625,451
2020	34,187,450,530	6,830,075,433	30,581,823,538	5,288,623,425	76,887,972,926
2030	34,778,528,532	7,837,931,995	45,300,526,994	8,172,424,205	96,089,411,726
2040	34,688,437,042	8,653,849,466	64,615,873,425	12,069,782,638	120,027,942,571
			Owner		
2000	$ 22,965,134,432	$ 2,187,249,167	$ 6,880,234,714	$ 1,064,116,688	$ 33,096,735,001
2010	24,625,716,897	2,795,197,014	11,608,543,481	2,012,260,131	41,041,717,523
2020	25,662,579,363	3,440,781,915	18,717,492,742	3,409,745,955	51,230,599,975
2030	26,125,372,698	4,059,927,662	28,212,190,505	5,319,885,455	63,717,376,320
2040	25,952,680,000	4,574,046,496	40,646,046,781	7,820,789,558	78,993,562,835
			Renter		
2000	$ 7,934,006,616	$ 2,340,205,055	$ 4,793,820,332	$ 701,493,780	$ 15,769,525,783
2010	8,259,226,604	2,845,141,679	7,782,267,856	1,175,271,789	20,061,907,928
2020	8,524,871,167	3,389,293,518	11,864,330,796	1,878,877,470	25,657,372,951
2030	8,653,155,834	3,778,004,333	17,088,336,489	2,852,538,750	32,372,035,406
2040	8,735,757,042	4,079,802,970	23,969,826,644	4,248,993,080	41,034,379,736

Sources: Derived by the authors from Texas Population Estimates and Projections Program 2001; U.S. Census Bureau, Census 2000 Summary File 3, [machine-readable data files], 2002a.

The effects of the aging and diversification of the populations on expenditures are demonstrated in Table 5.23. In this table, the first column in the top panel shows the expenditures that would occur if the racial/ethnic composition of the population in 2000 existed in 2040 but the number of households was the total projected in 2040. The second column shows the projected expenditures as presented in the preceding tables in which the 1990–2000 pattern of racial/ethnic change is assumed to occur. In the bottom panel, the first column shows the effects of assuming that the 2000 age distribution exists in 2040 but the number of households is as projected in 2040, and the second column shows the effects of the baseline age assumptions contained in the baseline projections for 2040. The changes in racial/ethnic composition are projected to reduce owner expenditures by more than $7 billion annually and increase renter expenditures by $910.7 million annually, with a net loss across both tenure types of roughly $6.1 billion annually. The aging of the population shows losses for both owner and renter households and a total loss of $9.7 billion

Table 5.21

Percent of Annual Expenditures for Housing in Texas by
Race/Ethnicity and Housing Tenure in 2000 and Projections
to 2040 Using the Population Projection That Assumes
1990–2000 Rates of Net Migration (1.0 Scenario)

Year	Anglo	Black	Hispanic	Other
Total				
2000	63.2	9.3	23.9	3.6
2010	53.9	9.2	31.7	5.2
2020	44.4	8.9	39.8	6.9
2030	36.2	8.2	47.1	8.5
2040	28.9	7.2	53.8	10.1
Owner				
2000	69.4	6.6	20.8	3.2
2010	60.0	6.8	28.3	4.9
2020	50.1	6.7	36.5	6.7
2030	41.0	6.4	44.3	8.3
2040	32.8	5.8	51.5	9.9
Renter				
2000	50.4	14.8	30.4	4.4
2010	41.1	14.2	38.8	5.9
2020	33.3	13.2	46.2	7.3
2030	26.7	11.7	52.8	8.8
2040	21.3	9.9	58.4	10.4

Sources: Derived by the authors from Texas Population Estimates and
Projections Program 2001; U.S. Census Bureau 2002a.

overall because of the lower expenditures of older persons
(whether owner or renter) and the large growth in older
population groups. In sum, in the absence of changes in
differentials, projected demographic growth, while leading to
extensive absolute increases in expenditures, will be less than
would occur if the same population increase were to occur and
2000 demographic characteristics prevailed throughout the
projection period.

The expenditure data, coupled with data on households by
tenure, suggest that population changes projected to occur in
Texas will substantially alter the nature of the state's housing
markets. Not only is it likely that real estate markets will grow
substantially, but also that older and more racially/ethnically
diverse segments will come to play increasingly important
roles. Marketing to older and more diverse groups with
products created to address their needs will obviously become
of increased importance to the real estate industry.

Table 5.22

Proportion of Annual Expenditures for Housing in Texas by Age
of Householder and Housing Tenure in 2000 and Projections to 2040
Using the Population Projection That Assumes 1990–2000 Rates of Net
Migration (1.0 Scenario)

	Age of Householder						
Year	15–24	25–34	35–44	45–54	55–64	65–74	75+
Total							
2000	4.4	22.2	29.2	22.3	11.5	6.3	4.1
2010	4.3	21.7	25.3	23.4	15.0	6.4	3.9
2020	3.8	21.5	25.5	20.6	16.3	8.3	4.0
2030	3.7	19.7	26.0	21.0	15.3	9.1	5.2
2040	3.5	19.5	24.5	21.5	16.4	8.6	6.0
Owner							
2000	1.1	16.4	31.2	25.7	13.9	7.5	4.2
2010	1.1	15.9	26.4	26.8	18.1	7.8	3.9
2020	1.0	15.7	26.2	23.3	19.7	10.0	4.1
2030	0.9	14.4	26.5	23.6	18.5	10.8	5.3
2040	0.8	14.4	24.8	24.1	19.8	10.1	6.0
Renter							
2000	11.2	34.3	25.2	15.1	6.7	3.5	4.0
2010	10.8	33.5	23.1	16.5	8.7	3.6	3.8
2020	9.5	32.9	24.1	15.2	9.5	4.9	3.9
2030	9.2	30.0	25.0	15.9	9.2	5.6	5.1
2040	8.6	29.5	23.8	16.5	9.8	5.7	6.1

Sources: Derived by the authors from Texas Population Estimates and Projections
Program 2001; U.S. Census Bureau 2002a.

Table 5.23

Annual Expenditures for Housing in Texas by Tenure in 2040
Assuming Projected Patterns by Race/Ethnicity and Age of Householder and
Assuming 2000 Distribution and Using the Population Projection That
Assumes 1990–2000 Rates of Net Migration (1.0 Scenario)

Housing Tenure	Assuming 2000 Distribution in 2040	Assuming 1990–2000 Net Migration in 2040	Numerical Difference	Percent Difference
Race/Ethnicity of Householder				
Owner	$ 86,002,893,862	$ 78,993,562,835	$ -7,009,331,027	-8.2
Renter	40,123,679,836	41,034,379,736	910,699,900	2.3
Total	126,126,573,698	120,027,942,571	-6,098,631,127	-4.8
Age of Householder				
Owner	$ 87,819,664,906	$ 78,993,562,835	$ -8,826,102,071	-10.1
Renter	41,929,844,581	41,034,397,736	-895,446,845	-2.1
Total	129,749,509,487	120,027,942,571	-9,721,566,916	-7.5

Sources: Derived by the authors from Texas Population Estimates and Projections
Program 2001; U.S. Census Bureau 2002a.

Effects on the Incidence of Diseases/Disorders and Disabilities

Health care needs are projected to change substantially during the coming years and demographic factors are expected to play a major role in such changes (Pol and Thomas 1992; Kintner et al. 1994). To examine the implications for health care in Texas, we utilized data from the *2000 National Health Interview Survey* (National Center for Health Statistics 2002a) that allow us to obtain estimates of the percentage of persons in various age, sex, and race/ethnicity groups who have certain diseases/disorders. Such rates were then applied to the population projections by age, sex, and race/ethnicity to obtain projections of the number of incidences of diseases/disorders by type of disease/disorder and the age and race/ethnicity of the persons experiencing the incidence of the disease/disorder. Although these data are national in scope, we believe that the incidences within age, sex, and race/ethnicity groups are sufficiently similar across the nation to merit their application to the same age, sex, and race/ethnicity groups in Texas. In addition to this analysis, we examine the implications of population change in the state for the number of persons with disabilities, health professionals, physician office visits, hospital stays, and nursing home residents using a variety of state-based rates and ratios.

Table 5.24 provides the number of incidences of diseases/disorders projected to occur in Texas. Since an individual may have multiple occurrences of more than one disease/disorder per year, the number of incidences exceeds the number of persons in the population. The incidences of diseases/disorders are projected to increase rapidly in Texas as a result of the growth and aging of the population. The projected 161.4 percent increase in the number of diseases/disorders from 2000 to 2040 exceeds the 142.6 percent increase in the total population as a result of aging, and this aging effect is evident across racial/ethnic groups. Anglos, whose population increases by only 10.4 percent from 2000 to

Table 5.24

Projections of Incidences of Diseases/Disorders and Percent Change in
Incidences of Diseases/Disorders in Texas by Race/Ethnicity Using the
Population Projection That Assumes 1990–2000 Rates of Net Migration
(1.0 Scenario), 2000–40

Year	Anglo	Black	Hispanic	Other	Total
	Number of Incidences				
2000	30,537,363	5,556,360	12,113,489	1,337,956	49,545,168
2010	33,431,265	7,039,340	19,445,990	2,564,319	62,480,914
2020	35,922,188	8,668,908	30,458,779	4,630,554	79,680,429
2030	37,739,292	10,150,936	46,188,995	7,819,412	101,898,635
2040	38,131,230	11,428,001	67,601,403	12,334,621	129,495,255
	Percent Change in Incidences				
2000–10	9.5	26.7	60.5	91.7	26.1
2010–20	7.5	23.1	56.6	80.6	27.5
2020–30	5.1	17.1	51.6	68.9	27.9
2030–40	1.0	12.6	46.4	57.7	27.1
2000–40	24.9	105.7	458.1	821.9	161.4

Sources: Derived by the authors from Texas Population Estimates and Projections
Program 2001; National Center for Health Statistics 2002a.

2040 under the 1.0 scenario, show a 24.9 percent increase in
the number of occurrences; Blacks, whose population increases
by 65 percent, show an increase of 105.7 percent in incidences;
Hispanics, with a population increase of 348.7 percent, show a
458.1 percent increase in the number of incidences; and the
Other population, which increases by 546.8 percent, shows an
821.9 percent increase in the number of incidences.

Across all diseases/disorders, the percentage of incidences
involving Anglos declines and the percentages involving
Hispanics and persons from the Other racial/ethnic group
increase (Table 5.25). For example, the percentage of all adults
with high blood pressure disorders who are Anglo decreases
from 63 percent in 2000 to 30.9 percent in 2040 and the
percentage with pregnancy-related disorders declines from 39
to 15.4 percent. On the other hand, the percentage involving
Hispanics increases from 19.1 percent in 2000 to 44.3 percent
in 2040 for high blood pressure and from 41.4 percent to 69.1
percent for pregnancy-related disorders. Similar trends are
evident for nearly all diseases/disorders.

Table 5.25

Projected Percent of the Prevalence of Selected Diseases/Disorders in Texas by
Race/Ethnicity and Type of Disease/Disorder for Adults (18 Years of Age and
Older) in 2000 and 2040 Using the Population Projection That Assumes 1990–2000
Rates of Net Migration (1.0 Scenario)

Disease/Disorder	Anglo 2000	Anglo 2040	Black 2000	Black 2040	Hispanic 2000	Hispanic 2040	Other 2000	Other 2040
High Blood Pressure	63.0	30.9	15.1	12.2	19.1	44.3	2.8	12.6
Coronary Heart Disease	73.5	40.5	8.7	8.2	15.7	40.5	2.1	10.8
Angina Pectoris	70.2	36.3	7.9	6.7	19.6	43.9	2.3	13.1
Heart Attack	71.8	39.1	10.0	9.0	16.3	41.0	1.9	10.9
Other Heart Condition/Disease	72.3	41.7	10.4	10.0	15.1	39.2	2.2	9.1
Stroke	64.6	32.1	13.6	11.6	18.7	41.4	3.1	14.9
Emphysema	80.6	50.7	7.3	8.2	10.3	30.4	1.8	10.7
Asthma	62.1	28.9	11.7	9.4	23.3	52.3	2.9	9.4
Asthma Attack Past Year	62.6	27.2	11.1	8.8	23.7	52.5	2.6	11.5
Ulcer	71.0	38.5	10.4	9.7	16.4	42.2	2.2	9.6
Ulcer Past Year	57.7	25.1	13.9	11.6	25.9	55.0	2.5	8.3
Cancer	82.4	52.9	5.6	6.5	10.3	29.8	1.7	10.8
Diabetes	52.5	21.5	15.5	11.4	29.1	57.5	2.9	9.6
Hayfever Past Year	67.3	31.8	9.9	8.2	19.2	46.7	3.6	13.3
Sinusitis Past Year	68.6	36.5	12.1	11.0	17.1	45.1	2.2	7.4
Chronic Bronchitis Past Year	69.7	36.8	10.5	9.6	18.1	46.5	1.7	7.1
Weak/Failing Kidneys Past Year	53.9	22.2	13.7	10.2	29.1	54.3	3.3	13.3
Liver Condition Past Year	57.5	22.3	11.6	8.5	26.8	55.9	4.1	13.3
Pregnancy related	39.0	15.4	15.9	9.5	41.4	69.1	3.7	6.0
Ever Worn Hearing Aid	75.1	44.5	5.9	4.8	16.8	33.8	2.2	16.9
Vision Impairment	60.8	28.5	12.2	9.4	24.4	52.1	2.6	10.0
Blindness	46.2	19.2	14.4	7.1	37.6	66.8	1.8	6.9
Lost All Teeth	67.7	35.2	11.4	10.2	18.5	41.5	2.4	13.1
Sad Past Month	49.9	19.5	12.7	8.2	34.1	63.1	3.3	9.2
Nervous Past Month	60.3	26.2	9.0	7.0	28.1	59.7	2.6	7.1
Restless Past Month	60.7	27.7	10.8	8.4	25.9	56.4	2.6	7.5
Hopeless Past Month	48.9	17.6	10.4	6.6	37.1	66.4	3.6	9.4
Everything an Effort Past Month	57.2	25.6	13.7	10.0	25.6	55.1	3.5	9.3
Worthlessness Past Month	53.0	20.5	10.5	7.2	32.7	61.1	3.8	11.2
Total	63.1	29.9	10.9	8.9	23.3	51.4	2.7	9.8

Sources: Derived by the authors from Texas Population Estimates and Projections Program
2001; National Center for Health Statistics 2002a.

Such trends are particularly obvious if we examine the
incidences of disabilities in the population (see Table 5.26).
The total number of incidences involving disabilities will
increase by 202.2 percent from 2000 to 2040, and the increases,
as for total diseases and disorders, will be faster for non-Anglo
than for Anglo populations. The increase from 2000 to 2040
would be 52.8 percent for Anglos, 146.5 percent for Blacks,
538.9 percent for Hispanics, and 1,277.6 percent for persons
from the Other racial/ethnic group. These increases are faster

Table 5.26

Projections of the Prevalence of Conditions Associated with Disabilities and
Percent Change in Prevalence of Conditions Associated with Disabilities in Texas
by Race/Ethnicity from 2000 to 2040 Using the Population Projection That
Assumes 1990–2000 Rates of Net Migration (1.0 Scenario)

Year	Anglo	Black	Hispanic	Other	Total
	Number of Incidences				
2000	2,240,626	486,601	801,140	85,730	3,614,097
2010	2,525,027	625,836	1,283,148	181,153	4,615,164
2020	2,854,845	799,421	2,069,464	372,396	6,096,126
2030	3,239,208	1,009,514	3,329,050	688,951	8,266,723
2040	3,422,904	1,199,594	5,118,692	1,181,022	10,922,212
	Percent Change in Incidences				
2000–10	12.7	28.6	60.2	111.3	27.7
2010–20	13.1	27.7	61.3	105.6	32.1
2020–30	13.5	26.3	60.9	85.0	35.6
2030–40	5.7	18.8	53.8	71.4	32.1
2000–40	52.8	146.5	538.9	1,277.6	202.2

Sources: Derived by the authors from Texas Population Estimates and Projections Program
2001; National Center for Health Statistics 2002a.

than the 24.9 percent increase for all diseases/disorders for
Anglos, and similarly than the 105.7 percent increase for
Blacks, 458.1 percent increase for Hispanics, and 821.9 percent
increase for Others because the aging of the population
substantially increases the growth in the number of persons
with disabilities.

The number and prevalence of persons with disabilities
would shift toward non-Anglos. By 2040, 31.3 percent of all
conditions involving a disability would involve an Anglo
compared to 62 percent in 2000, while the percentages would
decrease from 13.5 percent in 2000 to 11 percent in 2040 for
Blacks, increase from 22.2 percent to 46.9 percent for
Hispanics, and increase from 2.4 percent to 10.8 percent in
2040 for Others (see Figure 5.3).

Incidences of diseases/disorders, both in general and
relative to those related to disabilities, will increase
substantially in the coming years and will come to involve
larger numbers and proportions of non-Anglos, particularly
Hispanics. Patients will come to reflect increasing racial/ethnic
diversity.

Figure 5.3

Projected Percent of Persons with Disabilities in Texas Who
Are from Each Racial/Ethnic Group, 2000 and 2040*

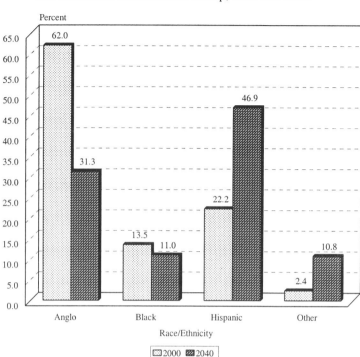

* Projections are shown for the 1.0 scenario

Effects on Health Care Personnel and Costs

The effects of the demographic changes have obvious
implications for health care personnel and health care
operations and costs. In this section we use standard
population-based rates from the Texas Department of Health
and the National Center for Health Statistics to delineate such
effects. As with the data on taxes, it should be noted that the
projections provided here are simply exemplary and not
intended to substitute for the more elaborate data on such
issues prepared by the state's health agency.

The data in Table 5.27 show the implications of population
change for health care personnel assuming the 1.0 population

Table 5.27

Health Care Personnel in Texas by Race/Ethnicity and by Type in 2000
and Projections for 2040 Using the Population Projection That Assumes
1990–2000 Rates of Net Migration (1.0 Scenario)

Health Personnel	Race/Ethnicity				
	Anglo	Black	Hispanic	Other	Total
2000 Actual					
Physicians	23,805	574	2,482	4,905	31,766
Dentists	6,601	148	297	371	7,417
Optometrists	1,697	48	159	273	2,177
Pharmacists	12,940	1,680	1,344	236	16,200
Registered Nurses	103,016	8,788	9,160	10,244	131,208
Veterinarians	4,450	15	31	16	4,512
Podiatrists	708	73	49	60	890
Total	153,217	11,326	13,522	16,105	194,170
Projected to Reflect Population's Race/Ethnicity Distribution					
2000					
Physicians	16,032	1,146	11,412	1,941	30,531
Dentists	4,433	290	1,364	146	6,233
Optometrists	1,150	100	729	108	2,087
Pharmacists	8,706	3,343	6,171	96	18,316
Registered Nurses	69,338	17,492	42,070	4,057	132,957
Veterinarians	2,995	33	146	7	3,181
Podiatrists	480	142	219	24	865
Total	103,134	22,546	62,111	6,379	194,170
2040					
Physicians	17,692	1,893	51,186	12,577	83,348
Dentists	4,905	480	6,107	952	12,444
Optometrists	1,250	161	3,285	697	5,393
Pharmacists	9,618	5,514	27,699	605	43,436
Registered Nurses	76,550	28,865	188,745	26,264	320,424
Veterinarians	3,307	45	635	45	4,032
Podiatrists	534	244	1,008	147	1,933
Total	113,856	37,202	278,665	41,287	471,010

Sources: Derived by the authors from Texas Population Estimates and Projections
Program 2001; Texas Department of Health 2002; U.S. Department of Health and
Human Services 2000c.

projection scenario and applying the population-to-health-
professionals ratios that existed in 2000. The first two panels of
this table show the 2000 data. The top panel shows the actual
number of personnel by race/ethnicity as reported by the Texas
Department of Health. The second panel shows the distribution
as if the number of health professionals by race/ethnicity
reflected the composition of the population by race/ethnicity in
2000. Values assuming that health personnel reflect the

race/ethnicity distribution of the population are then shown for 2040 in the table's third panel. The presentation of data in this manner is not intended to suggest that persons from one racial/ethnic group cannot provide services to persons from another racial/ethnic group. It simply describes the current and potential changes in the future characteristics of health care professionals in Texas if such professionals reflected the population.

Substantial growth in the number of health care professionals will be necessary if Texas is to have adequate health care personnel. The state would need to add 276,840 health professionals by 2040, representing a 142.6 percent increase (which is equal to that for the general population). The data in Table 5.27 suggest that the challenges may be particularly acute relative to the training and recruitment of Black and Hispanic professionals. For example, the number of Hispanic physicians in 2000 was 2,482, only 21.8 percent of the 11,412 that would reflect the proportion of Hispanics in the total population in 2000. By 2040, the proportionate figure would rise to 51,186, representing a nearly twentyfold increase from the current number of Hispanic physicians. Increases exceeding 229.8 percent would be required in the number of Black physicians. Such data make it clear that extensive increases in the number and diversity of health care personnel are likely to occur in the coming years.

Tables 5.28, 5.29, and 5.30 show projected numbers of physician contacts and associated costs, days of hospital care and associated costs, and nursing home residents and costs. The number of physician visits was computed by multiplying the average number of physician visits per population unit for persons of a given age by the number of persons of that age projected for each time period. Costs were obtained by multiplying the number of visits by the average costs per visit for persons of that age. A similar methodology was used to determine the number of hospital days of care and costs: multiplying the average days of care per population unit for

Table 5.28

Physician Contacts and Costs (in 2000 Dollars) in Texas by Age of
Patient and Projections for 2040 Using the Population Projection
That Assumes 1990–2000 Rates of Net Migration (1.0 Scenario)

Age of Patient	Number of Contacts	Total Costs (in thousands)
2000		
<18	11,068,534	$ 1,536,202
18–44	18,018,157	2,500,745
45–54	7,955,812	1,104,199
55–64	6,464,474	897,204
65–74	5,952,126	826,098
75+	6,317,815	876,846
Total	55,776,918	7,741,294
2040		
<18	20,319,756	$ 2,820,181
18–44	39,664,811	5,505,078
45–54	20,696,918	2,872,530
55–64	22,540,343	3,128,368
65–74	22,134,347	3,072,025
75+	25,327,337	3,515,179
Total	150,683,512	20,913,361

Sources: Derived from Texas Population Estimates and Projections Program
2001; National Center for Health Statistics 2001; Cohen et al. 2000.

Table 5.29

Days of Hospital Care and Associated Costs (in 2000 Dollars) in
Texas by Age of Patient in 2000 and Projections for 2040 Using the
Population Projection That Assumes 1990–2000 Rates of Net
Migration (1.0 Scenario)

Age of Patient	Days of Care	Total Costs (in thousands)
2000		
<18	1,091,994	$ 230,894
18–44	2,751,707	993,942
45–54	1,177,623	605,353
55–64	1,270,721	1,151,621
65–74	1,803,150	3,243,392
75+	2,801,768	9,621,665
Total	10,896,963	15,846,867
2040		
<18	2,004,738	$ 423,877
18–44	6,116,316	2,209,268
45–54	3,096,606	1,591,811
55–64	4,464,463	4,046,013
65–74	6,715,870	12,080,036
75+	11,263,916	38,681,860
Total	33,661,909	59,032,865

Sources: Derived from Texas Population Estimates and Projections Program,
2001. National Center for Health Statistics, 2001.

Table 5.30

Number of Nursing Home Residents and Total Monthly Costs
(in 2000 Dollars) in Texas by Age of Resident in 2000 and
Projections for 2040 Using the Population Projection That
Assumes 1990–2000 Rates of Net Migration (1.0 Scenario)

Age of Resident	Number of Residents	Total Costs
2000		
0–64	12,394	$ 34,748,450
65–74	12,041	33,758,760
75–84	24,674	69,177,287
85+	32,228	90,356,063
Total	81,337	228,040,560
2040		
0–64	28,109	$ 78,807,821
65–74	44,928	125,962,438
75–84	101,743	285,251,865
85+	134,491	377,065,828
Total	309,271	867,087,952

Sources: Derived by the authors from Texas Population Estimates
and Projections Program 2001. National Center for Health Statistics
2002b; Texas Health and Human Services Commission 2002.

persons of a given age by the projections of the number of
persons of each age. Average costs per day of care by age of
patient were then used to project total costs. For nursing
homes, the percentage of persons in each age group residing in
nursing homes was multiplied by the population in each age
group, after which the average monthly cost was multiplied by
the number of persons projected to be in nursing homes. As
with our other projections, we do not take into account many
other factors likely to have an impact on actual costs. Rather,
we have attempted to show how population change will affect
health care operations and costs in general in the years ahead.

The data in these tables show very substantial increases in
health care costs and demonstrate the effects of the state's aging
population on health care costs. Under the 1.0 scenario, costs
for physician visits would exceed $20.9 billion per year (in
2000 constant dollars) and hospital care costs $59 billion per
year by 2040. Nursing home costs would be more than $867
million per month by 2040 (more than $10.4 billion per year).
Because the elderly population increases more rapidly than the

total population, increases in health-related factors exceed the
142.6 percent increase in the population from 2000 to 2040
projected under the 1.0 scenario. The number of physician
contacts and related costs would increase by 170.2 percent, the
number of days of hospital care would increase by 208.9
percent, and the number of nursing home residents and related
costs by 280.2 percent (see Figure 5.4). For the population
seventy-five years of age or older, the increases would be 300.9
percent for physician contacts, 302 percent for days of hospital
care, and 315.2 percent for nursing home residents and
associated costs.

Figure 5.4

Percent Change in Selected Health Care Factors in Texas, 2000 to 2040*

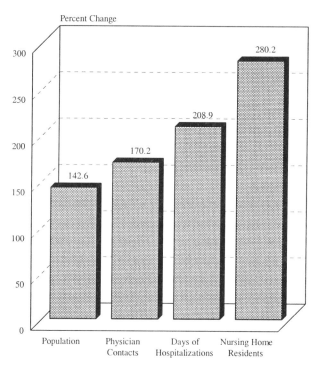

* Projections are shown for the 1.0 scenario

Overall, the data on health care point to rapid growth in the markets for health care products in the coming years, particularly those tied to older populations and to conditions affecting disabilities and nursing home and other forms of long-term care. At the same time, the data show that the population's racial/ethnic diversification will lead to patient populations with different socioeconomic and other characteristics and to the need for substantial training and recruitment of non-Anglo health care professionals. These changes represent both challenges and opportunities for the state's public and private health care sectors in the coming decades.

SUMMARY

In this chapter we have examined the implications of population-related socioeconomic change for factors likely to impact private-sector markets for goods and services. The data suggest that:

1. The Texas economy has shown substantial expansion in the past two decades, particularly in the 1990s. Gross state product, employment, and retail sales grew faster than the population, and the increase in the export of products indicates that numerous factors in addition to population growth have led to the expansion of Texas' economy.

2. The socioeconomic conditions projected for the state will affect consumer expenditures and net worth and asset levels, factors of central importance to Texas businesses. Assuming 2000 socioeconomic differentials under the 1.0 scenario, projections indicate that consumer expenditures, net worth, and assets will fail to keep pace with the growth in households, suggesting that the per-household dollar value of markets and the dollars available for investment will decline. A marked shift toward non-Anglo households would occur such that, by 2040, 68.1 percent of all consumer expenditures and roughly

50.8 percent of net worth would involve non-Anglos (compared to 33.6 percent of expenditures and 19 percent of net worth in 2000). Similarly, nearly 60 percent of all assets would be in households with a householder fifty-five years of age or older by 2040. Household change would also impact consumer expenditures, with increasing proportions of all expenditures involving households other than married-couple households.

3. If the socioeconomic trends of the 1990s (which witnessed increases in Black and Hispanic income relative to Anglo income) were to continue from 2000 to 2040, or if all racial/ethnic groups were to follow the expenditure patterns of Anglos, the effects on consumer expenditures would be substantial. Assuming 1990–2000 levels of closure in expenditures that reflect those in income, the total additional expenditures generated would be nearly $23 billion per year. If Anglo expenditure patterns occurred in all racial/ethnic groups, that increase would exceed $84 billion per year. Average per-household expenditures would decline from $37,096 in 2000 to $33,872 in 2040 under the scenario assuming 2000 rates, to $35,057 under the scenario assuming 1990–2000 rates of closure, and rise to $38,226 under the scenario assuming 2000 Anglo expenditures for all racial/ethnic groups.

4. Housing demand will increase substantially in the coming years with contradictory trends resulting from population change. The aging of the population leads to growth in owner households because of the higher rates of ownership among older householders, but the rapid growth of non-Anglo populations with higher rates of renters leads to faster growth in renter households. As a result, both owner and renter housing will grow rapidly in Texas in the coming years—and at nearly equal rates. For both owner and renter housing, the growth in those units with non-Anglo householders increases such that by 2040 only 33.4 percent of owners and 21.1 percent

of renters would be Anglo, 7.4 percent of owners and 11.9 percent of renters Black, 50.3 percent of owners and 57.3 percent of renters Hispanic, and 8.9 percent of owners and 9.7 percent of renters from the Other racial/ethnic group. Similarly, householders will get older such that by 2040 (again under the 1.0 scenario) 29.8 percent of owners and 15.1 percent of renters would involve a household with a householder who is 65 years of age or older. Expenditures for housing will also reflect such patterns.

5. Health care needs and markets will grow substantially due to the aging of the population. Whether examined from the standpoint of a diverse array of diseases/disorders and disabilities or the growth in days of hospital care, nursing home residents, or other factors, the growth in the demand for health care will exceed population growth. Although the total population increases by 142.6 percent from 2000 to 2040, the number of incidences of diseases/disorders increases by 161.4 percent, physician contacts by 170.2 percent, days of hospital care by 208.9 percent, and nursing home residents by 280.2 percent. Coupled with this growth will be an increasing diversity in the patient population such that by 2040 only 29.9 percent of adult incidences of diseases/disorders would involve Anglos. Similarly, if health care personnel are to reflect the racial/ethnic characteristics of their patients, increases in non-Anglo health care personnel will be required, with a nearly twentyfold increase needed in the number of Hispanic physicians and a more than 200 percent increase in the number of Black physicians.

The coming decades will witness substantial expansion in the state's markets for goods and services, with such expansion increasingly involving older and more racially/ethnically diverse market segments and market segments that involve an increasing diversity of household types. These markets will reflect Texas' population in terms of its age, race/ethnicity, and household characteristics. Per-household expenditures will fail to keep pace with the rate of growth of households if the population's socioeconomic characteristics do not change. Moreover, in the absence of socioeconomic change, such markets are likely to involve higher demands for goods and services required to meet the basic needs of less affluent households. If the socioeconomic differentials among Texas households decrease as a result of relative increases in non-Anglo incomes, the state will experience rapidly expanding markets and potential increases in per-household expenditures for nearly all goods and services. Under any set of socioeconomic conditions, an understanding of Texas' demographics is essential to understanding the future of Texas businesses.

CHAPTER 6

The Labor Force and Labor Force Related Programs

In this chapter we examine the implications of population change for the labor force and for state programs aimed at assisting Texas residents in obtaining labor force training, including those receiving such training as a result of welfare reform legislation (see Chapter 8 for a discussion of the human service implications of these reforms). After reviewing recent changes in the labor force, we provide projections of the labor force and examine the implications of the projected changes for several characteristics of the labor force.

HISTORICAL TRENDS IN THE LABOR FORCE

Texas' labor force has increased rapidly in recent decades with its growth exceeding the rate of growth in the nation's labor force (see Table 6.1). The state's labor force increased from 6,574,676 in 1980 to 9,830,559 in 2000, an increase of 49.5 percent compared to a national increase of 31.8 percent. The rate of growth in the labor force has slowed over the past decade, both in percentage terms and relative to population growth as a result of the disproportionate aging of the population out of the ages usually associated with entrance into the labor force. In the United States, the 9.8 percent increase in the population in the 1980s and the 13.2 percent increase in the 1990s was accompanied by 18.2 percent and 11.5 percent increases in the labor force. Meanwhile, Texas' labor force increased by 25 percent in the 1980s and 19.6 percent in the 1990s, whereas the state's population increased by 19.4 percent

Table 6.1

Civilian Labor Force in the United States and Texas, 1980–2000

Civilian Labor Force	1980	1990	2000	Percent Change		
				1980–90	1990–2000	1980–2000
United States	104,449,817	123,478,450	137,668,798	18.2	11.5	31.8
Texas	6,574,676	8,219,028	9,830,559	25.0	19.6	49.5

Sources: U.S. Census Bureau 2002a, 1991c, and 1983.

in the 1980s and 22.8 percent in the 1990s. Despite the recent patterns of slower growth, the 1980–2000 increase in the labor force resulted in 3,255,883 new members being added to Texas' labor force and 33,218,981 to the U.S. labor force.

The data in Table 6.2 provide a comparison of the occupational and industrial characteristics of the labor forces in Texas and in the United States in 2000. Because changes in categories between 1990 and 2000 make longitudinal comparisons impossible, data for earlier periods are not shown. The data in this table indicate that Texas' labor force was quite similar to that of the nation in 2000. Only its somewhat smaller level of employment in manufacturing and larger percentage employed in construction industries, and related differences in construction- and production-related occupations, show distributional differences greater than 1 percent. Clearly, the characteristics of Texas' labor force increasingly reflect those of the national labor force.

Overall, such data suggest that Texas' labor force has increased substantially in the past several decades. However, like the nation's, it is showing slower rates of growth relative to the population because the baby-boom generation has passed beyond those ages associated with initial labor force entrance and is followed by a relatively smaller cohort. The historical levels of growth in Texas' labor force make it clear, however, that these changes are important for understanding the state's future.

Table 6.2

Percent of Employed Persons 16 Years of Age or Older in the United States
and Texas in 2000 by Occupation and Industry of Employment

	Percent		Percent Difference
	United States	Texas	
Occupation			
Employed civilian population 16 years and older	129,721,512	9,234,372	—
Management, professional, and related	33.6	33.3	-0.3
Service	14.9	14.7	-0.2
Sales and office	26.7	27.2	0.5
Farming, fishing, and forestry	0.7	0.7	0.0
Construction, extraction, and maintenance	9.5	10.9	1.4
Production, transportation, and material moving	14.6	13.2	-1.4
Industry			
Employed civilian population 16 years and older	129,721,512	9,234,372	—
Agriculture, forestry, fishing and			
hunting, and mining	1.9	2.7	0.8
Construction	6.8	8.0	1.2
Manufacturing	14.1	11.9	-2.2
Wholesale trade	3.5	3.9	0.4
Retail trade	11.8	12.0	0.2
Transportation and warehousing, and utilities	5.2	5.8	0.6
Information	3.1	3.1	0.0
Finance, insurance, real estate, and rental and leasing	6.8	6.8	0.0
Professional, scientific, management,			
administrative, and waste management services	9.3	9.5	0.2
Educational, health and social services	20.0	19.3	-0.7
Arts, entertainment, recreation, accommodation			
and food services	7.8	7.3	-0.5
Other services (except public administration)	4.9	5.2	0.3
Public administration	4.8	4.5	-0.3

Source: U.S. Census Bureau 2002a.

PROJECTIONS OF THE CIVILIAN LABOR FORCE AND RELATED FACTORS

Obtaining the projections of the civilian labor force (shown in Tables 6.3–6.7) required the use of relatively elaborate procedures because appropriate data were not yet available from the 2000 Census at the time this volume was completed. Additionally, industry and related classification systems were substantially revised during the 1990s as federal agencies (including the U.S. Census Bureau and Bureau of Labor Statistics) converted from the Standard Industrial Code (SIC) system to the North American Industrial Classification System (NAICS), making historical comparisons nearly impossible.

The labor force projections were completed by applying age-, sex-, and race/ethnicity-specific labor force participation rates to age-, sex-, and race/ethnicity-specific projected population values. Because data were not available on the labor force by age, sex, and race/ethnicity, it was necessary to develop such data as a basis for computing labor force participation rates. To simulate labor force values by age, sex, and race/ethnicity for 2000, 2000 Census data were employed on the total labor force by age and on the total labor force by sex and race/ethnicity. The number of persons in the labor force by age, sex, and race/ethnicity was then estimated using 1990 labor force participation rates to obtain initial age-, sex-, and race/ethnicity-specific values that were then raked to adjust the values to reflect the 2000 Census data that were available on the total labor force by age and on the labor force by sex and race/ethnicity. These values were then examined for reasonableness relative to 1990 and other 2000 data and used as the numerators for the computation of age-, sex-, and race/ethnicity-specific labor force participation rates. These rates were obtained by dividing the labor force values by the population in 2000. These age-, sex-, and race/ethnicity-specific rates were assumed to remain constant across the projected period and applied to the projections of the population to obtain projections of the labor force by age, sex, and race/ethnicity. Because of the assumption of constancy in rates, sex ratios by age and race/ethnicity for the labor force remain constant and sex differences in employment patterns are therefore not discussed.

Data on the educational attainment of the labor force and on the occupational structure of the labor force by demographic characteristic were not available in the 2000 Census. These were simulated using Current Population Survey (CPS) data for Texas averaged for the years 1999 to 2001 to obtain the baseline rates that were applied to the labor force projections. They are, therefore, affected by differences between census and CPS data for these years (see Tables 6.8 and 6.9).

The projections of wages and salary income were obtained by using 2000 Census data. Age-, sex-, race/ethnicity-, and salary-and-wage-level-specific rates for 2000 were developed and applied to the labor force projections to obtain projections of the wage and income levels of future members of the labor force (see Table 6.10).

The projections of the levels of involvement in specific labor force training programs and the costs of such programs were computed using data on the number of participants in 2000 in each of the categories of programs obtained from the Texas Workforce Commission (2002a) and costs from the Texas Legislative Budget Board (2001). The number of participants was then divided by 2000 population values to obtain age-, sex-, and race/ethnicity-specific participation rates, and these rates were applied to projections of the population to obtain projections of the number of participants in each program across the projection period, assuming that the rates of participation remain constant (see Table 6.11).

Because several elements of the 2000 base data required estimation, occupational classification categories were different (and largely not comparable) for the labor force in 2000 from those used in 1990 and labor force training programs had been restructured in the latter part of the 1990s due to welfare reform and other factors, insufficient comparable data were available for 1990 from which to derive rates for alternative simulations. As a result, no alternative projection simulations are provided for the labor force.

As in other chapters, the projections provided here are intended to be simply exemplary and are not appropriate for short-term planning purposes. Near-term projections and more detailed data on Texas' labor force in general should be obtained from the Texas Workforce Commission.

PROJECTIONS OF THE LABOR FORCE

The total labor force increases from 9.8 million in 2000 to nearly 15.7 million in 2040 under the 0.5 scenario and to nearly 23.3 million under the 1.0 scenario, representing increases of 59.6 percent under the 0.5 scenario and 136.7 percent under the 1.0 scenario (see Tables 6.3 and 6.4). These increases are

Table 6.3

Civilian Labor Force in Texas by Race/Ethnicity in 2000 and
Projections to 2040 Assuming Alternative Projection Scenarios

Year	Anglo	Black	Hispanic	Other	Total

Year	Anglo	Black	Hispanic	Other	Total
Assuming Rates of Net Migration Equal to One-Half of 1990–2000 (0.5 Scenario)					
2000	5,741,765	1,053,552	2,700,075	335,167	9,830,559
2010	5,923,856	1,257,844	3,803,488	464,118	11,449,306
2020	5,774,312	1,389,297	5,047,718	583,281	12,794,608
2030	5,584,578	1,454,344	6,433,953	696,647	14,169,522
2040	5,441,430	1,508,040	7,927,467	811,942	15,688,879
Assuming Rates of Net Migration Equal to 1990–2000 (1.0 Scenario)					
2000	5,741,765	1,053,552	2,700,075	335,167	9,830,559
2010	6,038,211	1,319,679	4,392,161	581,844	12,331,895
2020	5,997,764	1,532,682	6,691,490	911,887	15,133,823
2030	5,907,902	1,687,921	9,764,451	1,344,888	18,705,162
2040	5,853,781	1,842,923	13,661,252	1,912,166	23,270,122

Sources: Derived by the authors from Texas Population Estimates and Projections
Program 2001; U.S. Census Bureau 2002a.

Table 6.4

Percent Change in Projected Civilian Labor Force in Texas by
Race/Ethnicity Assuming Alternative Projection Scenarios, 2000–40

Year	Anglo	Black	Hispanic	Other	Total
Assuming Rates of Net Migration Equal to One-Half of 1990–2000 (0.5 Scenario)					
2000–10	3.2	19.4	40.9	38.5	16.5
2010–20	-2.5	10.5	32.7	25.7	11.8
2020–30	-3.3	4.7	27.5	19.4	10.7
2030–40	-2.6	3.7	23.2	16.5	10.7
2000–40	-5.2	43.1	193.6	142.2	59.6
Assuming Rates of Net Migration Equal to 1990–2000 (1.0 Scenario)					
2000–10	5.2	25.3	62.7	73.6	25.4
2010–20	-0.7	16.1	52.4	56.7	22.7
2020–30	-1.5	10.1	45.9	47.5	23.6
2030–40	-0.9	9.2	39.9	42.2	24.4
2000–40	2.0	74.9	406.0	470.5	136.7

Sources: Derived by the authors from Texas Population Estimates and Projections
Program 2001; U.S. Census Bureau 2002a.

slower rates of growth than the 67.9 and 142.6 percent
increases projected for the total population, reflecting the
continuing influence of the aging of the population.

Nevertheless, the labor force will have characteristics
reflective of the population. The non-Anglo labor force grows
more rapidly than the Anglo labor force. For example, whereas
the number of Anglos declines by 5.2 percent from 2000 to

2040 under the 0.5 scenario and increases by only 2 percent under the 1.0 scenario, the increases for the Black population are 43.1 percent and 74.9 percent, the increases for the Hispanic population are 193.6 and 406 percent, and the increases for the Other population are 142.2 and 470.5 percent under the 0.5 and 1.0 scenarios, respectively. As a result, whereas the percentage of the labor force composed of Anglos was 58.4 percent in 2000, with Blacks accounting for 10.7 percent, Hispanics for 27.5 percent, and persons from the Other racial/ethnic group for 3.4 percent, by 2040 under the 0.5 scenario, 34.7 percent of the labor force would be composed of Anglos, 9.6 percent of Blacks, 50.5 percent of Hispanics, and 5.2 percent of persons from the Other racial/ethnic group. Under the 1.0 scenario, the 2040 percentages are 25.2 percent, 7.9 percent, 58.7 percent, and 8.2 percent for Anglos, Blacks, Hispanics, and persons from the Other racial/ethnic group, respectively (see Table 6.5). Under the 0.5 scenario, the net change in the labor force from 2000 to 2040 is entirely attributable to the non-Anglo labor force (because the number of Anglos in the labor force decreases by 5.1 percent), with 89.2 percent attributable to the Hispanic labor force alone. Under the 1.0 scenario, 99.2 percent of the net change from 2000 to 2040 is attributable to non-Anglos, with Hispanics accounting for 81.6 percent (see Table 6.6). The change in the labor force reflects the change in Texas' population, which is growing substantially and diversifying rapidly.

Table 6.7 also shows that the labor force will age as the population ages. Although 32.7 percent of the labor force was forty-five years of age or older in 2000, 41.2 percent of the labor force will be forty-five years or older by 2040 under the 0.5 scenario and 40.6 percent under the 1.0 scenario (in which there is faster growth in younger non-Anglo populations). Similarly, the workforce less than thirty-five years of age decreases from 40.7 percent in 2000 to 35.8 percent in 2040 under the 0.5 scenario and to 35.5 percent in 2040 under the 1.0

Table 6.5

Percent of Civilian Labor Force in Texas by Race/Ethnicity in 2000
and Projections to 2040 Assuming Alternative Projection Scenarios

Year	Anglo	Black	Hispanic	Other
2000	58.4	10.7	27.5	3.4
Assuming Rates of Net Migration Equal to				
One-Half of 1990–2000 (0.5 Scenario)				
2010	51.7	11.0	33.2	4.1
2020	45.0	10.9	39.5	4.6
2030	39.4	10.3	45.4	4.9
2040	34.7	9.6	50.5	5.2
Assuming Rates of Net Migration Equal to 1990–2000 (1.0 Scenario)				
2010	49.0	10.7	35.6	4.7
2020	39.7	10.1	44.2	6.0
2030	31.6	9.0	52.2	7.2
2040	25.2	7.9	58.7	8.2

Sources: Derived by the authors from Texas Population Estimates and
Projections Program 2001; U.S. Census Bureau 2002a.

Table 6.6

Number and Percent of Net Change in the Civilian Labor Force
in Texas Due To Each Race/Ethnicity Group, Assuming Alternative
Projection Scenarios, 2000–40

Race/Ethnicity	Number	Percent
Assuming Rates of Net Migration Equal to		
One-Half of 1990–2000 (0.5 Scenario)		
Anglo	-300,335	-5.1
Black	454,488	7.8
Hispanic	5,227,392	89.2
Other	476,775	8.1
Total	5,858,320	100.0
Assuming Rates of Net Migration Equal to 1990–2000 (1.0 Scenario)		
Anglo	112,016	0.8
Black	789,371	5.9
Hispanic	10,961,177	81.6
Other	1,576,999	11.7
Total	13,439,563	100.0

Sources: Derived by the authors from Texas Population Estimates and
Projections Program 2001; U.S. Census Bureau 2002a.

scenario. The aging of the population clearly results in an aging
of the labor force.

The projections point to a labor force that is likely to grow
substantially, although less rapidly than the population due to

Table 6.7

Percent of the Civilian Labor Force in Texas by Age and
Race/Ethnicity in 2000 and Projections for 2040 Assuming
Alternative Projection Scenarios

Age Group	Percent Labor Force				
	Anglo	Black	Hispanic	Other	Total
2000					
16–19	5.1	6.3	8.1	4.9	6.1
20–24	9.0	11.8	14.8	9.8	10.9
25–34	21.9	25.6	26.7	25.0	23.7
35–44	26.9	26.7	25.4	32.9	26.6
45–54	22.4	18.7	16.5	20.3	20.4
55–59	6.8	5.5	4.5	3.8	5.9
60–64	4.0	2.9	2.4	1.9	3.3
65+	3.9	2.5	1.6	1.4	3.1
Assuming Rates of Net Migration Equal to One-Half of 1990–2000 (0.5 Scenario)					
2040					
16–19	4.3	4.3	5.7	3.5	5.0
20–24	8.8	9.6	10.8	6.7	9.7
25–34	20.9	20.9	21.7	16.5	21.1
35–44	21.3	21.7	23.7	28.5	23.0
45–54	21.7	22.7	20.8	22.6	21.3
55–59	8.9	9.9	8.4	7.2	8.7
60–64	5.8	5.4	5.1	5.5	5.4
65+	8.3	5.5	3.8	9.5	5.8
Assuming Rates of Net Migration Equal to 1990–2000 (1.0 Scenario)					
2040					
16–19	4.3	4.3	5.2	3.2	4.7
20–24	8.6	9.9	10.3	6.3	9.5
25–34	20.8	21.0	22.3	15.8	21.3
35–44	21.4	21.9	24.6	28.4	23.9
45–54	21.8	22.7	21.8	24.3	22.1
55–59	8.9	9.6	8.3	7.5	8.5
60–64	5.8	5.2	4.6	5.8	5.0
65+	8.4	5.4	2.9	8.7	5.0

Sources: Derived by the authors from Texas Population Estimates and Projections
Program 2001; Bureau of Labor Statistics and U.S. Census Bureau 2002.

the population's aging. The labor force will become
increasingly non-Anglo such that it changes from roughly 58
percent Anglo in 2000 to between 65.3 percent (under the 0.5
scenario) and 74.8 percent (under the 1.0 scenario) non-Anglo
by 2040. The labor force also ages, with more than 40 percent
of all workers being forty-five years of age or older by 2040
under both scenarios.

IMPLICATIONS OF POPULATION CHANGE FOR THE FUTURE CHARACTERISTICS OF THE LABOR FORCE

In this section we examine the implications of change in the labor force for a variety of socioeconomic factors. Table 6.8 and Figure 6.1 show data on the projected changes in the labor force's educational level, Table 6.9 and Figure 6.2 projected changes in its occupational distribution, and Table 6.10 and Figure 6.3 projected changes in salary and wages in the coming decades. All projections assume that 2000 age and race/ethnicity patterns for education, occupation, and salaries and wages prevail throughout the entire projection period. Due to space limitations only data for the 1.0 scenario are shown.

Implications for the Educational Level of the Workforce

Hispanics will account for a larger percentage of the total number of people at all educational levels than they did in 2000. When compared to the total labor force, however, Anglos and persons from the Other racial/ethnic group form larger proportions in the categories with the highest levels of education, whereas the opposite is generally true for Hispanics. For example, under the 1.0 scenario, Hispanics would account for 58.7 percent of the labor force in 2040 but make up 58.7 percent or more of the labor force only in the categories of less than a ninth grade education and nine to twelve years of education (but no high school diploma). Anglo percentages exceed their percentage of the labor force (25.2 percent) under the 1.0 scenario only for education levels higher than high school, while the percentage is higher only in the bachelor's and graduate and professional degree categories of educational attainment for persons in the Other racial/ethnic group. The data in Table 6.8 suggest continuing differentials in educational attainment among racial/ethnic groups in Texas.

Figure 6.1 shows data on educational attainment for the total labor force. However, an examination of the total percentages by educational level shows that, in the absence of change in the educational characteristics of Blacks and Hispanics—populations that are projected to grow more rapidly

Table 6.8

Civilian Labor Force in Texas by Level of Educational Attainment and Race/Ethnicity in 2000 and Projections for 2040 Using the Population Projection That Assumes 1990–2000 Rates of Net Migration (1.0 Scenario) (Percentaged within Level of Educational Attainment)

Level of Attainment	Anglo		Black		Hispanic		Other		Total
	Number	%	Number	%	Number	%	Number	%	Number
2000									
Less than 9th grade	64,146	9.5	19,976	3.0	542,133	80.9	43,982	6.6	670,237
9th to 12th grade, no diploma	480,025	40.7	116,227	9.9	546,132	46.4	35,419	3.0	1,177,803
High school graduate	1,601,107	56.0	373,673	13.1	796,273	27.9	84,449	3.0	2,855,502
Some college	1,336,364	62.3	308,940	14.4	451,937	21.1	47,384	2.2	2,144,625
Associate degree	461,422	67.8	71,848	10.5	129,772	19.0	18,321	2.7	681,363
Bachelors degree	1,414,037	79.2	114,476	6.4	185,394	10.4	70,653	4.0	1,784,560
Graduate/professional	384,664	74.4	48,412	9.4	48,434	9.4	34,959	6.8	516,469
Total labor force	5,741,765	58.4	1,053,552	10.7	2,700,075	27.5	335,167	3.4	9,830,559
2040									
Less than 9th grade	93,104	2.5	49,827	1.4	3,240,568	89.4	242,998	6.7	3,626,497
9th to 12th grade, no diploma	478,499	14.3	192,737	5.7	2,483,330	74.0	202,303	6.0	3,356,869
High school graduate	1,626,899	24.3	657,836	9.9	3,868,828	58.0	521,098	7.8	6,674,661
Some college	1,349,303	31.7	532,691	12.5	2,153,615	50.5	225,870	5.3	4,261,479
Associate degree	460,233	35.2	120,565	9.2	637,312	48.6	92,291	7.0	1,310,401
Bachelors degree	1,441,381	47.9	189,573	6.3	971,824	32.3	405,469	13.5	3,008,247
Graduate/professional	404,362	39.2	99,694	9.7	305,775	29.6	222,137	21.5	1,031,968
Total labor force	5,853,781	25.2	1,842,923	7.9	13,661,252	58.7	1,912,166	8.2	23,270,122

Sources: Derived by the authors from Texas Population Estimates and Projections Program 2001; Bureau of Labor Statistics and U.S. Census Bureau 2002.

than the Anglo population—the state's labor force will be less well educated in the future than it was in 2000. For example, 5.3 percent of the labor force had a graduate degree and 18.2 percent a bachelor's degree in 2000, but 4.4 would have a graduate degree and 12.9 percent a bachelor's degree in 2040 under the 1.0 scenario. On the other hand, although only 18.8 percent had less than a high school education in 2000, that number would increase to 30.1 percent in 2040 under the 1.0 scenario. It is clear that demographic change, in the absence of socioeconomic change, will lead to a less well-educated labor force in Texas.

Implications for Occupational Skill Levels

Table 6.9 shows data similar in form to those in Table 6.8 but for occupational characteristics of the labor force. The data in Table 6.9 show that the percentage of non-Anglos increases over time. What is also obvious, however, is that in the absence

Figure 6.1

Percent of Civilian Labor Force in Texas by Educational
Attainment in 2000 and Projections for 2040*

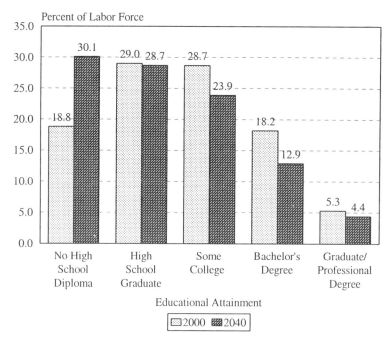

* Projections are shown for the 1.0 scenario

of changes in the occupational distribution of the non-Anglo
labor force, Anglos would continue to occupy a
disproportionate share of executive and professional positions
while non-Anglos would continue to account for a
disproportionate share of people in nontechnical and
nonmanagerial occupations. For example, under the 1.0
scenario, although Anglos would make up only 25.2 percent of
the labor force by 2040, they would still account for 39.4
percent of those in executive positions and 42.2 percent of
those in professional positions. Hispanics, who would make up
58.7 percent of the labor force would account for only 40
percent of those in executive positions and 39 percent of those
in professional positions. On the other hand, Anglos would

Table 6.9

Civilian Labor Force by Occupation and Race/Ethnicity in 2000 and Projections
for 2040 Using the Population Projection That Assumes 1990–2000 Rates of Net
Migration (1.0 Scenario) (Percentaged within Occupation)

Occupation	Anglo		Black		Hispanic		Other		Total
	Number	%	Number	%	Number	%	Number	%	Number
2000									
Executive, administrative, and managerial	971,174	74.5	102,536	7.9	188,972	14.5	40,467	3.1	1,303,149
Professional specialty	1,076,671	75.4	103,966	7.3	189,265	13.3	56,983	4.0	1,426,885
Technicians and related support	233,928	67.4	26,892	7.7	68,259	19.7	18,058	5.2	347,137
Sales	748,950	67.0	80,392	7.2	256,351	23.0	30,952	2.8	1,116,645
Administrative support	794,101	58.2	188,818	13.9	347,712	25.5	32,416	2.4	1,363,047
Protective service	145,983	65.5	45,195	20.2	29,929	13.4	2,090	0.9	223,197
Other services	292,729	35.2	165,638	19.9	334,162	40.2	38,709	4.7	831,238
Precision production	580,636	52.1	57,697	5.2	444,917	39.9	31,056	2.8	1,114,306
Machine operators and assemblers	158,877	35.7	48,385	10.9	203,461	45.7	34,378	7.7	445,101
Transportation and material moving	196,397	49.9	71,266	18.1	117,557	29.8	8,767	2.2	393,987
Handlers and equipment cleaners	136,106	36.0	34,959	9.3	186,727	49.4	20,067	5.3	377,859
Farming, forestry and fishing	171,646	58.8	17,592	6.0	98,914	33.9	3,669	1.3	291,821
Unemployed	234,567	39.4	110,216	18.5	233,849	39.2	17,555	2.9	596,187
Total labor force	5,741,765	58.4	1,053,552	10.7	2,700,075	27.5	335,167	3.4	9,830,559
2040									
Executive, administrative, and managerial	990,549	39.4	191,811	7.6	1,004,100	40.0	325,726	13.0	2,512,186
Professional specialty	1,063,200	42.2	179,159	7.1	981,398	39.0	293,345	11.7	2,517,102
Technicians and related support	220,697	32.3	45,801	6.7	332,434	48.7	84,198	12.3	683,130
Sales	779,523	33.5	138,061	5.9	1,200,456	51.6	208,616	9.0	2,326,656
Administrative	805,998	27.3	297,334	10.1	1,660,681	56.2	188,552	6.4	2,952,565
Protective service	165,206	39.7	77,271	18.5	142,057	34.1	32,299	7.7	416,833
Other services	300,492	12.3	327,548	13.3	1,651,826	67.3	173,988	7.1	2,453,854
Precision production	583,594	18.2	107,105	3.3	2,366,635	73.3	169,269	5.2	3,226,603
Machine operators and assemblers	154,316	10.2	90,793	5.9	1,102,847	72.2	178,909	11.7	1,526,865
Transportation and material moving	214,079	20.6	124,876	12.1	657,027	63.5	38,895	3.8	1,034,877
Handlers and equipment cleaners	131,689	10.9	55,093	4.5	928,067	76.4	99,984	8.2	1,214,833
Farming, forestry and fishing	211,961	25.4	36,170	4.3	566,337	67.8	20,855	2.5	835,323
Unemployed	232,477	14.8	171,901	11.0	1,067,387	68.0	97,530	6.2	1,569,295
Total labor force	5,853,781	25.2	1,842,923	7.9	13,661,252	58.7	1,912,166	8.2	23,270,122

Sources: Derived by the authors from Texas Population Estimates and Projections Program 2001; Bureau of Labor Statistics and U.S. Census Bureau 2002.

account for only 10.2 percent of machine operators, 10.9
percent of handlers and equipment cleaners, and 14.8 percent
of the unemployed, but Hispanics would account for 72.2
percent of machine operators, 76.4 percent of handlers, and 68
percent of the unemployed. Blacks will account for similarly

Figure 6.2

Percent of Civilian Labor Force in Texas by Occupation
in 2000 and Projections for 2040*

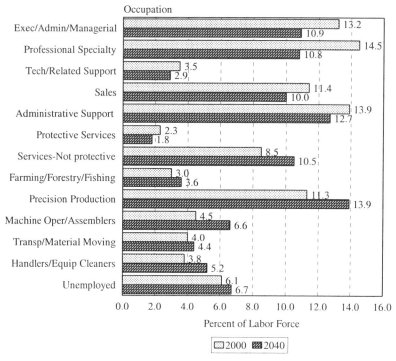

* Projections are shown for the 1.0 Scenario

disproportionate shares of the unemployed and will continue to be underrepresented in the executive, professional, and technical occupations. Labor force members from the Other racial/ethnic group will be disproportionately concentrated in executive, professional, and technical occupations at levels similar (proportionate to their share of the population) to Anglos.

The data in Figure 6.2 again show that, in the absence of change in the occupational structure of the Black and Hispanic populations, their growth will lead to declines in the percentages of the labor force in executive, professional, and technical occupations, to increases in the percentages in less technical jobs, and to an increase in the percentage of the labor force that is unemployed. Under the 1.0 scenario, the percentages of the labor force in executive and professional positions will decline about 2 to 4 percent by 2040 compared to the percentages in these categories in 2000, while the percentages in the operator, handler, and similar positions increase. Current demographic patterns, if accompanied by current occupational differentials among race/ethnicity groups, will lead to a labor force that is generally less skilled in the future than it is today.

Implications for Earnings

Table 6.10 presents data on earnings in the labor force that are similar to those for education and occupation. Because earnings (that is, salary and wages) are not reported for all positions and the source for these data is different (the 2000 Census) from the source for the two preceding items examined (the CPS), the values for the total labor force presented in this table are slightly different from those in the preceding tables. Anglos and persons from the Other racial/ethnic group are proportionately overrepresented at upper salary and wage levels and underrepresented at lower salary and wage levels in 2000 and are projected to continue to be so in the future under the 1.0 scenario (see Table 6.10). For example, Anglos, who would account for 25.8 percent of the labor force with earnings in 2040, would form a percentage of the labor force larger than 25.8 percent for only those salary and wage levels of $25,000 or more. Similarly, labor force members in the Other racial/ethnic group would account for 8.6 percent of the labor force in 2040 and would account for a percentage larger than 8.6 percent for only those salary and wage categories of $35,000 or more. On the other hand, the patterns for Blacks and Hispanics are quite different. For Blacks, the proportion of the total labor force in 2040 would be 7.7 percent, but they would account for more than 7.7 percent in four of the six categories below $50,000 and be underrepresented at all higher salary and

Table 6.10

Wage and Salary of Civilian Labor Force in Texas in 2000 by Race/Ethnicity and
Projections for 2040 Using the Population Projection That Assumes 1990–2000
Rates of Net Migration (1.0 Scenario) (Percentaged within Income Group)

Wage and Salary Incomes	Anglo		Black		Hispanic		Other		Total
	Number	%	Number	%	Number	%	Number	%	Number
2000									
$ < 5,000	463,095	54.7	102,915	12.2	253,297	29.9	27,502	3.2	846,809
5,000-9,999	328,033	48.9	74,329	11.1	246,033	36.7	22,232	3.3	670,627
10,000-14,999	353,512	43.8	90,401	11.2	336,770	41.7	26,824	3.3	807,507
15,000-24,999	679,598	49.6	167,627	12.2	476,527	34.7	47,882	3.5	1,371,634
25,000-34,999	672,193	61.4	127,481	11.6	261,239	23.8	34,805	3.2	1,095,718
35,000-49,999	684,438	70.2	92,109	9.4	165,553	17.0	33,089	3.4	975,189
50,000-74,999	523,784	77.2	46,356	6.8	78,038	11.5	30,868	4.5	679,046
75,000-99,999	191,235	82.2	10,951	4.7	19,834	8.5	10,761	4.6	232,781
100,000 or more	235,002	85.6	8,751	3.2	20,019	7.3	10,725	3.9	274,497
Labor Force	4,130,890	59.4	720,920	10.4	1,857,310	26.7	244,688	3.5	6,953,808
2040									
$ < 5,000	470,179	22.6	179,527	8.7	1,269,979	61.2	155,675	7.5	2,075,360
5,000-9,999	332,930	18.2	129,466	7.1	1,239,177	67.8	125,728	6.9	1,827,301
10,000-14,999	359,063	15.1	157,313	6.6	1,710,399	71.9	152,799	6.4	2,379,574
15,000-24,999	691,753	18.7	292,652	7.9	2,441,013	66.0	273,853	7.4	3,699,271
25,000-34,999	686,144	27.9	223,315	9.1	1,343,187	54.8	200,337	8.2	2,452,983
35,000-49,999	701,221	36.8	162,069	8.5	853,780	44.7	190,880	10.0	1,907,950
50,000-74,999	540,037	44.8	82,131	6.8	404,602	33.5	179,700	14.9	1,206,470
75,000-99,999	197,753	51.5	19,467	5.1	103,051	26.9	63,356	16.5	383,627
100,000 or more	243,528	57.1	15,578	3.7	104,313	24.4	63,268	14.8	426,687
Labor Force	4,222,608	25.8	1,261,518	7.7	9,469,501	57.9	1,405,596	8.6	16,359,223

Sources: Derived by the authors from Texas Population Estimates and Projections Program 2001; Bureau of Labor Statistics and U.S. Census Bureau 2002.

wage levels. Hispanics, who are expected to be 57.9 percent of the labor force with earnings in 2040, would account for that percentage or more only in those categories less than $25,000. Overall, then, the data in Table 6.10 suggest that under the 1.0 scenario there will be a continuation of lower earnings among two of the three non-Anglo groups, with the pattern of lower earnings being particularly evident among Hispanics.

Figure 6.3 shows earnings for the total labor force using the 1.0 scenario. Projected demographic change will markedly impact the earnings structure of employees if the salary and wage differentials among racial/ethnic groups remain as they were in 2000. For example, the median wage and salary level of all workers with earnings was $23,398 in 2000 but would be $20,129 (in 2000 constant dollars) in 2040. Similarly, whereas 17 percent of the labor force was earning $50,000 or more in 2000, only 12.3 percent would have earnings at that level in

Figure 6.3

Percent of Civilian Labor Force in Texas by Earnings
in 2000 and Projections for 2040*

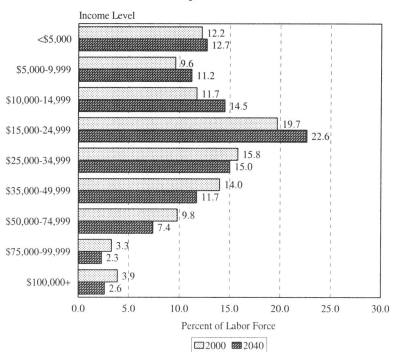

* Projections are shown for the 1.0 scenario

2040; 33.5 percent had earnings below $15,000 per year in
2000, but that number would increase to 38.4 percent in 2040.
Unless there are changes in earnings differentials, the relative
earnings of the labor force in 2040 under the 1.0 scenario
would be less (in 2000 constant dollars) than they were in
2000.

Implications for Workforce Training Programs
The data in Table 6.11 and Figure 6.4 show the implications of
the projected labor force for those enrolled in workforce
training programs in Texas. As noted above, these projections
indicate the percentage of the labor force that would be in
specific programs given the 2000 rates of participation in these

programs as projected from Texas Workforce Commission data. Data are again shown for only the 1.0 scenario.

The total number of participants in all labor force training programs would increase from 273,411 in 2000 to 739,959 in 2040 (see Table 6.11, Panel A), a numerical increase of 466,548, and a percentage increase of 170.6 percent (see Table 6.11, Panel B). Enrollment in these programs, which are intended to serve those with the highest level of need for training, is projected to grow more rapidly than the population, which increases by 142.6 percent from 2000 to 2040 under the 1.0 scenario, and faster than the 136.7 percent rate of growth projected in the labor force under the 1.0 scenario.

Total enrollment in these programs involves larger proportions of participants who are non-Anglo than in the labor force as a whole. For example, whereas 21.7 percent of all participants were Anglo in 2000, 29 percent were Black, 47.9 percent were Hispanic, and 1.4 percent were from the Other racial/ethnic group (see Table 6.11, Panel C), 58.4 percent of the labor force as a whole was Anglo, 10.7 percent Black, 27.5 percent Hispanic, and 3.4 percent from the Other racial/ethnic group. The higher proportions of non-Anglos in these programs than in the labor force continue into the future. The 2040 percentages would be 7.6 percent, 15.1 percent, 74.6 percent, and 2.7 percent for Anglo, Black, Hispanic, and Other participants, respectively. By comparison, the workforce in 2040 is 25.2 percent Anglo, 7.9 percent Black, 58.7 percent Hispanic, and 8.2 percent members of the Other racial/ethnic group.

Percent changes in enrollment for specific programs are shown for the 1.0 scenario in Figure 6.4. The data show rapid growth in virtually all programs. The most rapid growth will occur in Title III and IV programs (related to veterans and defense closures) and the Workforce Investment Act (WIA) dislocated worker program, while the slowest growth will be in the WIA Youth program and programs resulting from welfare reform legislation. The number of participants in the Title III

Table 6.11

Participants in Workforce Training Programs in Texas, Percent Change in
Projected Participants and Percent of Participants by Race/Ethnicity, Using the
Population Projection That Assumes 1990–2000 Rates of Net Migration
(1.0 Scenario), 2000–40

Year	Anglo	Black	Hispanic	Other	Total
Panel A: Participants in Workforce Training Programs					
2000	59,504	79,292	130,872	3,743	273,411
2010	60,793	94,363	201,249	6,341	362,746
2020	59,082	102,139	289,254	9,874	460,349
2030	57,777	107,128	406,966	14,324	586,195
2040	56,369	111,558	551,963	20,069	739,959
Panel B: Percent Change in Projected Participants in Workforce Training Programs					
2000-2010	2.2	19.0	53.8	69.4	32.7
2010-2020	-2.8	8.2	43.7	55.7	26.9
2020-2030	-2.2	4.9	40.7	45.1	27.3
2030-2040	-2.4	4.1	35.6	40.1	26.2
2000-2040	-5.3	40.7	321.8	436.2	170.6
Panel C: Percent of Participants in Workforce Training Programs by Race/Ethnicity					
2000	21.7	29.0	47.9	1.4	100.0
2010	16.8	26.0	55.5	1.7	100.0
2020	12.9	22.2	62.8	2.1	100.0
2030	9.9	18.3	69.4	2.4	100.0
2040	7.6	15.1	74.6	2.7	100.0

Sources: Derived by the authors from Texas Population Estimates and Projections Program
2001; Texas Workforce Commission 2002a.

and IV programs will increase by 350.7 and the number in the
dislocated worker program by 202.6 percent from 2000 to
2040. The percentage increase for the same period for the WIA
Youth program is projected to be 134.2 percent and that for the
welfare-related programs 162.5 percent. In all programs,
however, absolute growth in the number of participants is
extensive, and these programs have, and are projected to
continue to have, largely non-Anglo participants. More than 86
percent of all of the participants in each of these programs in
2040 are projected to be non-Anglo and at least 50 percent in
all programs are projected to be Hispanic, with Hispanics
accounting for approximately 70 percent or more of all
participants in five of the six program areas.

Table 6.12 shows the fiscal implications of growth in these
specialized programs. State expenditures for all of these
programs would increase from $97.1 million in 2000 to $276.8

Figure 6.4

Percent Change in Workforce Training Programs and
in the Total Labor Force in Texas, 2000 to 2040*

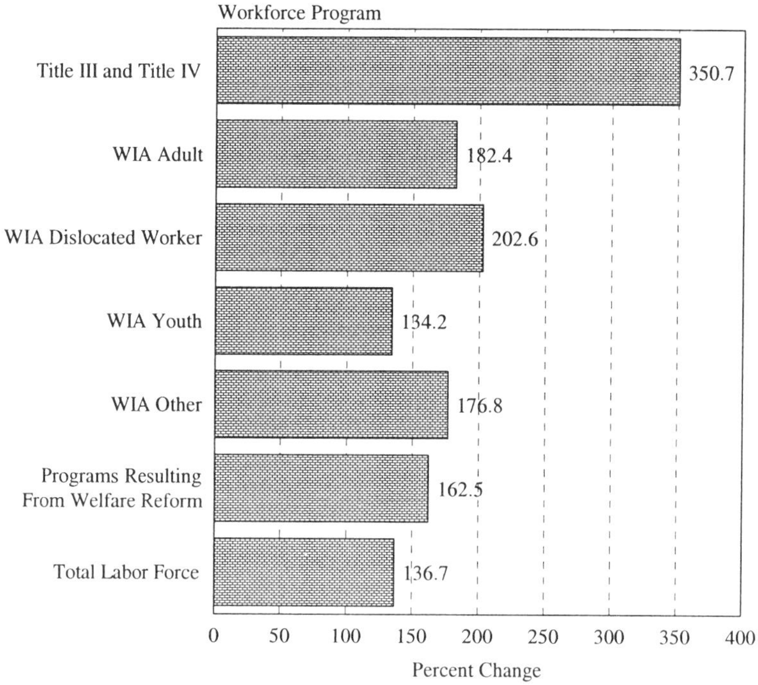

Workforce Program

* Projections are shown for the 1.0 scenario

million under the 1.0 scenario. The increase in expenditures from 2000 to 2040 would be approximately $179.8 million. The changing characteristics of Texas' population are likely to have substantial implications for the costs for workforce training programs.

The data on workforce programs indicate that such programs will grow rapidly in the coming years as a result of the higher levels of involvement of the fastest growing segments of Texas' labor force in these programs. The extensive growth of non-Anglo, particularly Hispanic, labor force members will lead such programs to have higher percentages of growth than either the population or the labor force. The increase in the number of participants in these programs will bring comparable increases in costs. Such

Table 6.12

Total State Expenditures and State Expenditures for Selected Workforce Training Programs
in Texas (in thousands of 2000 Dollars) and Projections to 2040 Using the Population
Projection That Assumes 1990–2000 Rates of Net Migration (1.0 Scenario)

Year	All Programs	Title III and IV	WIA Adult	WIA Dislocated Worker	WIA Youth	WIA Other	All Welfare
2000	97,089.9	4,212.3	20,488.4	29,977.4	7,666.9	792.5	33,952.4
2010	130,110.3	6,456.8	27,487.7	40,377.2	9,826.9	1,059.1	44,902.5
2020	167,826.0	9,442.6	35,510.2	53,171.3	11,663.5	1,356.6	56,681.7
2030	216,503.1	13,651.0	45,364.5	69,801.9	14,914.4	1,739.3	71,031.9
2040	276,839.4	18,985.1	57,869.2	90,719.8	17,957.0	2,193.9	89,114.6

Sources: Derived by the authors from Texas Population Estimates and Projections Program 2001; Texas Workforce Commission 2001a and 2002b; and Texas Workforce Commission Letter 09-01 2001b.

programs will play an increasing role in addressing the training needs of Texas' workforce in the coming years.

SUMMARY

In this chapter we have examined the implications of population change for the state's labor force. Projections were provided and the implications of the projected changes in the labor force traced across several dimensions. Because of a lack of sufficient 2000 Census data on Texas' labor force at the time this publication was prepared and because categories for several labor force characteristics were being used for the first time, it was impossible to provide historical comparisons for several of these characteristics. The results of the analysis indicate that:

1. The state's labor force has increased rapidly in recent decades, with its growth exceeding the rate of growth in the nation's labor force. Texas' labor force increased from 6,574,676 in 1980 to 9,830,559 in 2000, an increase of 49.5 percent, compared to an increase of 31.8 percent for the nation. The rate of growth in the labor force has slowed over the past decade, both in percentage terms and relative to population growth, as a result of the aging of the population out of the initial labor force entrance years of age. The state's labor force increased by 25 percent in the 1980s but only 19.6 percent in the 1990s, whereas its population increased by 19.4 percent in

the 1980s and 22.8 percent in the 1990s. Despite the recent patterns of slower growth, 3,255,883 persons were added to Texas' labor force between 1980 and 2000. These patterns are similar to those in the nation as a whole and Texas' labor force is similar to that in the nation in terms of the percentages of the labor force employed in different occupations and industries.

2. The labor force is projected to increase from 9.8 million in 2000 to nearly 15.7 million in 2040 under the 0.5 scenario and to nearly 23.3 million under the 1.0 scenario, representing percentage increases of 59.6 percent under the 0.5 scenario and 136.7 percent increase under the 1.0 scenario. These are slower growth rates than the 67.9 and 142.6 percent increases projected for the total population, reflecting the continuing influence of the aging of the population.

3. The non-Anglo labor force grows more rapidly than the Anglo labor force. For example, under the 1.0 scenario, the number of Anglos increases by only 2 percent, but the increases are 74.9 percent for the Black population, 406 percent for the Hispanic population, and 470.5 percent for the Other population. As a result, whereas 58.4 percent of the labor force was Anglo in 2000, with Blacks accounting for 10.7 percent, Hispanics for 27.5 percent, and persons from the Other racial/ethnic group for 3.4 percent, by 2040 Anglos will compose 25.2 percent, while 7.9 percent will be Black, 58.7 percent Hispanic, and 8.2 percent persons from the Other racial/ethnic group.

4. The labor force will age as the population ages. Although 32.7 percent of the labor force was forty-five years of age or older in 2000, by 2040 the percentage forty-five years of age or older would be 40.6 percent under the 1.0 scenario. The percentage of the workforce less than thirty-five years of age decreases from 40.7 percent in 2000 to 35.5 percent in 2040.

5. Projections of the educational characteristics of the labor force show that Hispanics will form a larger percentage of the

total number of labor force members at all educational levels than they did in 2000. Anglos and persons from the Other racial/ethnic group form larger proportions of the labor force in the categories with the highest levels of education than in the total labor force, but the opposite is true for Hispanics and Blacks. As a result, unless racial/ethnic differentials in educational attainment change, Texas' labor force in the future will be less well educated than it was in 2000. Whereas 5.3 percent of the labor force had a graduate degree and 18.2 percent a bachelor's degree in 2000, in 2040 4.4 percent would have a graduate degree and 12.9 percent a bachelor's degree under the 1.0 scenario. In addition, while only 18.8 percent had less than a high school education in 2000, by 2040 30.1 percent would have only that level of education.

6. Projections of the occupational characteristics of the labor force show that the percentage of non-Anglos increases over time under both scenarios. In the absence of changes in the occupational distribution of the labor force, Anglos would continue to occupy a disproportionate share of executive and professional positions while non-Anglos would continue to occupy a disproportionate share of the nontechnical and nonmanagerial occupations. Current demographic patterns, if accompanied by current occupational differentials among racial/ethnic groups, will lead to a labor force that is generally less skilled in the future than it is today.

7. Projections of earnings show that Anglos and persons from the Other racial/ethnic group are proportionately overrepresented at upper wage and salary levels and underrepresented at lower wage levels in 2000 and are projected to continue to be so in the future, while the opposite is true for Blacks and Hispanics. Unless changes occur in occupational patterns among racial/ethnic groups, projected demographic change will reduce the average level of salary and wages. The median wage level of all workers with earnings was $23,398 in 2000 but would be only $20,129 in 2040 (in 2000 constant dollars) under the 1.0 scenario.

8. Projections of the number of persons in workforce training programs indicate that the total number of participants in all programs would increase from 273,411 in 2000 to 739,959 in 2040 under the 1.0 scenario, a numerical increase of 466,548, and a percentage increase of 170.6 percent. Growth in the enrollment in these programs exceeds the increase in the population (which is expected to be 142.6 percent from 2000 to 2040 under the 1.0 scenario), and the 136.7 percent rate of growth projected in the labor force from 2000 to 2040 under the 1.0 scenario, because these programs involve larger proportions of participants who are non-Anglo than the labor force as a whole. Anglos accounted for 21.7 percent of participants in these programs in 2000, 29 percent were Black, 47.9 percent were Hispanic, and 1.4 percent from the Other racial/ethnic group. At the same time, 58.4 percent of the labor force as a whole were Anglo, 10.7 percent Black, 27.5 percent Hispanic, and 3.4 percent from the Other racial/ethnic group. Under the 1.0 scenario by 2040, 7.6 percent, 15.1 percent, 74.6 percent, and 2.7 percent of all participants would be Anglo, Black, Hispanic, and Other participants, respectively. State expenditures for these programs would increase from $97.1 million in 2000 to $276.8 million under the 1.0 scenario, a 2000 to 2040 increase of nearly $179.8 million.

The labor force will grow rapidly in the future, although more slowly than the population, and become increasingly diverse and older. If differentials in the socioeconomic characteristics of the labor force do not change, the state's future labor force will be less well educated, less skilled, earn lower salaries and wages, and thus be in greater need of labor force training (with substantial associated costs). The state's demographics have substantial implications for the future of Texas' labor force, and through the labor force, its economic competitiveness.

CHAPTER 7

Public Elementary, Secondary, and Higher Education

Population change affects both educational demands and costs. In this chapter we examine the implications of population patterns in Texas on the demand for, and costs of, public elementary and secondary education and selected aspects of higher education. Because data on enrollment by age, sex, and race/ethnicity were not available from the 2000 Census at the time this volume was completed, it was not possible to project total enrollment changes for the state that would include both public- and private-sector forms of educational involvement as reported in the Census. The emphasis in this chapter is thus on the effects of population change on public education enrollment and costs.

      This chapter follows the pattern in previous chapters in that we first provide a brief history of recent patterns of change in education in Texas and then present projections of the number of persons enrolled in public elementary and secondary schools and public community colleges and public universities. We examine the implications of such enrollment changes for enrollment in selected specialized elementary and secondary programs, for public education costs, for the number of college students with unmet financial needs, and for the level of financial assistance needed from all sources and from the state. As with other projections in this volume, the projections provided here are intended to be exemplary of only the population-related changes in educational enrollment and costs. They should not be confused with the official projections provided by the Texas Education Agency or the Texas Higher Education Coordinating Board, which are more inclusive and take into account a number of additional considerations not examined here. The projections from these agencies are more appropriate for short-term planning purposes.

HISTORICAL PATTERNS OF EDUCATIONAL INVOLVEMENT, ATTAINMENT, AND COSTS

The 1980s and 1990s witnessed dramatic changes in education in Texas. Elementary and secondary education experienced substantial changes resulting from increased testing and increased accountability at all levels. The Hopwood decision (*Hopwood v Texas,* 21 F.3d 603 [5th Cir. 1994]), the development of the TEXAS Grant Program (Acts 1999, 76th Leg., ch. 1590, §§ 1, eff. June 19, 1999), and the creation of the Closing the Gaps Program (Texas Higher Education Coordinating Board 2001c) were a few of the changes that impacted higher education. These and other policy changes and conditions have markedly affected education in the state. Population-related change is clearly only one of many factors impacting education in Texas.

Enrollment in education has increased rapidly in the past two decades (see Tables 7.1 and 7.2). The number of persons enrolled in elementary and secondary schools increased by 45.3 percent from 1980 to 2000, only slightly less than the 46.5 percent population growth rate. Growth was faster in the 1990s than in the 1980s, and a comparison of Tables 7.1 and 7.2 suggests that, while much of the growth in both decades was in public education, private and other forms of education have become larger parts of total elementary and secondary enrollment in the state over the last decade. Nearly 3.3 million of the 3.6 million persons (90.2 percent) enrolled in elementary and secondary education were in public schools in 1990 and 4 million of the 4.7 million persons enrolled in elementary and secondary education in 2000 (84.3 percent) were accounted for by public education. Care must be taken in interpreting such

Table 7.1

Enrollment and Percent Change in Enrollment for Texas Residents Enrolled
in Elementary and Secondary Schools and Colleges in Texas, 1980–2000[a]

School Level	1980	1990	2000	1980–1990	1990–2000	1980–2000
				Percent Change		
Elementary and Secondary[b]	3,264,840	3,606,848	4,745,370	10.5	31.6	45.3
College	732,217	1,199,047	1,202,890	63.8	0.3	64.3
Total	3,997,057	4,805,895	5,948,260	20.2	23.8	48.8

Sources: U.S. Census Bureau, 2002a; 1991c, 1983.

[a] Data shown are self-reported enrollment as presented in the decennial censuses for the census years
indicated. The enrollment so reported includes enrollment in any type of institution or form of school
(private, public, home school, etc.) and any level of involvement (post-graduate, part-time, etc.).

[b] Includes persons in preprimary education and related programs.

Table 7.2

Enrollment in Texas Public Elementary and Secondary Schools, Selected Education
Programs, and Public Community Colleges and Universities by Race/Ethnicity, and
Percent Change in Enrollment, 1980–2000

Time Period	Anglo Number	%	Black Number	%	Hispanic Number	%	Other Number	%	Total Number
Total Public Colleges and Public Universities									
1980	435,157	75.8	52,555	9.2	77,071	13.4	8,957	1.6	573,740
1990	535,942	69.7	69,436	9.0	136,650	17.8	26,808	3.5	768,836
2000	484,891	58.1	90,921	10.9	212,427	25.4	46,914	5.6	835,153
% Change 1980–1990	23.2		32.1		77.3		199.3		34.0
% Change 1990–2000	-9.5		30.9		55.5		75.0		8.6
Total Elementary and Secondary									
1980	1,634,355	56.3	434,667	15.0	796,614	27.5	34,431	1.2	2,900,067
1990	1,632,005	50.2	471,191	14.5	1,081,368	33.2	69,767	2.1	3,254,331
2000	1,727,491	43.1	576,715	14.4	1,582,323	39.6	114,129	2.9	4,000,658
% Change 1980–1990	-0.1		8.4		35.7		102.6		12.2
% Change 1990–2000	5.9		22.4		46.3		63.6		22.9
Bilingual/ESL									
1990	3,479	1.3	940	0.3	254,940	93.8	12,582	4.6	271,941
2000	6,430	1.3	2,418	0.5	464,075	93.6	22,592	4.6	495,515
% Change 1990–2000	84.8		157.2		82.0		79.6		82.2
Gifted and Talented									
1990	147,713	71.2	14,193	6.9	36,366	17.6	8,857	4.3	207,129
2000	198,487	59.2	33,400	10.0	86,612	25.9	16,402	4.9	334,901
% Change 1990–2000	34.4		135.3		138.2		85.2		61.7
Special Education									
1990	168,155	50.9	58,362	17.7	100,574	30.5	2,832	0.9	329,923
2000	220,564	45.2	86,451	17.7	176,161	36.1	4,898	1.0	488,074
% Change 1990–2000	31.2		48.1		75.2		73.0		47.9
Career and Technology Education									
1990	206,947	50.2	69,756	16.9	129,769	31.4	6,311	1.5	412,783
2000	345,791	46.7	111,481	15.0	263,875	35.6	19,670	2.7	740,817
% Change 1990–2000	67.1		59.8		103.3		211.7		79.5

Sources: Texas Education Agency 2001; Texas Higher Education Coordinating Board 2001a.

data, however, because census data are self-reported for a somewhat different time period than the data on public enrollment, which are actual agency enrollment data. Available data are insufficient to allow us to examine the implications of private education for the state's future education needs.

The bottom panels of Table 7.2 show that there have been increases in enrollment in specialized elementary and secondary educational programs as well. In the 1990s, growth in all of these programs was faster than growth in enrollment generally and faster than the 22.8 percent rate of population increase. The data on costs in Table 7.3 show that costs in each of these specialized program areas also increased faster than the population. As is also obvious, however, many of these costs were driven by growth in the specific populations needing such services. For example, although costs for bilingual and English as a Second Language (ESL) education increased by 66.7 percent from 1990 to 2000, the per-student cost declined by 11.1 percent. Overall, expenditures on elementary and secondary education increased from $17.5 to $23.1 billion (31.6 percent) in 2000 constant dollar terms from 1990 to 2000, and per-student expenditures increased by 7 percent.

These data show rapid growth in higher education enrollment in the 1980s, but much slower growth in the 1990s. The 1980s were impacted by the last of the baby boomers entering into higher education, while the 1990s were impacted by the much smaller "baby bust" generation. Total higher education enrollment increased by 63.8 percent in the 1980s but by just 0.3 percent in the 1990s, while public higher education enrollment increased by 34 percent in the 1980s and 8.6 percent in the 1990s. Because higher education enrollment as self-reported in the census can include any involvement in any postsecondary course or curriculum, it is difficult to directly compare public to total enrollment data, but relative patterns of change across the two decades are similar in census and agency data.

Table 7.3

General Revenue Expenditures (in 2000 Dollars) for Texas Public Elementary
and Secondary Schools, Selected Education Programs, and Public Colleges and
Universities, and Percent Change in Expenditures, 1990 and 2000

| Program | Expenditures | | | | Percent Change 1990–2000 | |
| | 1990 | | 2000 | | | |
	Total	Per Student	Total	Per Student	Total	Per Student
Total Elementary and Secondary	$ 17,548,698,571	$ 5,392	$ 23,092,358,439	$ 5,772	31.6	7.0
Bilingual/ESL	354,346,821	1,303	590,748,041	1,159	66.7	-11.1
Gifted and Talented	135,356,821	653	245,961,232	717	81.7	9.8
Special Education	1,047,145,311	3,174	1,739,689,310	3,599	66.1	13.4
Career and Technology Education	408,431,566	989	566,681,113	738	38.7	-25.4
Total Public Colleges and Public Universities	2,207,969,578	3,032	2,611,362,728	3,297	18.3	8.7

Sources: Texas Education Agency 2002a and 2002b; Texas Higher Education Coordinating Board 2002c.

The data in Table 7.3 indicate that general revenue expenditures on public higher education increased by 18.3 percent and that per-student expenditures increased by 8.7 percent between 1990 and 2000. These values include only general revenue costs for higher education programs and do not include any tuition or fee increases instituted by colleges or universities, local tax funds (for community colleges), research funds, endowment funds, or other funds generated by college or university activities. Total expenditures from all sources are significantly higher than those shown here.

As for income, educational attainment and enrollment in the 1990s showed patterns of progress, but continued disparity existed among the state's racial/ethnic groups (see Table 7.4). In comparison to 12.8 percent of Anglos and 19.3 percent of Asians, 24.2 percent of Blacks and 50.7 percent of Hispanics 25 years of age or older had less than a high school level of education. Thirty percent of Anglos and 47.8 percent of Asians had a bachelor's degree or higher but only 15.4 percent of

Table 7.4

Percent of Population 25 Years of Age or Older in Texas
by Educational Attainment Level and Race/Ethnicity, 2000

Educational	Percent				
Attainment Level	Anglo	Black	Hispanic	Asian	Total
Less than 9th grade	3.5	6.5	31.5	9.0	11.5
9th to 12th grade, no diploma	9.3	17.7	19.2	10.3	12.9
High school graduate					
(includes equivalency)	25.7	29.9	22.0	14.3	24.8
Some college, no degree	25.6	24.8	14.9	12.7	22.4
Associate degree	5.9	5.7	3.4	5.9	5.2
Bachelor's degree	20.3	10.7	6.1	27.3	15.6
Graduate or professional degree	9.7	4.7	2.9	20.5	7.6

Source: U.S. Census Bureau 2002a.

Blacks and 9 percent of Hispanics held such degrees. There was progress in the 1990s, however (see Table 7.5). The percentage increase in the proportion of high school graduates was 14.5 percent from 1990 to 2000 for Blacks and 10.5 percent for Hispanics compared to a 7 percent increase for Anglos and a 2 percent increase for Asians. Similarly, the percentage increase in the proportion of college graduates from 1990 to 2000 was 15.7 percent for Asians and 19 percent for Anglos but 27.5 percent for Blacks and 21.9 percent for Hispanics. The total percentages of persons with high school diplomas increased by 9.6 percent for Blacks from 1990 to 2000, by 5.7 percent for Anglos, by 4.7 percent for Hispanics, and by 1.6 percent for Asians. The percentage of persons twenty-five years of age or older who are college graduates increased from 1990 to 2000 by 6.5 percent for Asians, 4.8 percent for Anglos, 3.3 percent for Blacks, and by 1.6 percent for Hispanics. These differentials reflect not only educational achievement but also population change because inmigrating persons may either enhance or reduce the educational levels that a group would otherwise have shown. Nevertheless, these data suggest that the 1990s witnessed improvements in educational attainment, while 2000 data point to the need for

Table 7.5

Percent of Population 25 Years of Age or Older in Texas Who Are High
School Graduates and Higher or College Graduates and Higher by
Race/Ethnicity, and Percent Change, 1990–2000

Educational Attainment Level	Anglo	Black	Hispanic	Asian	Total
1990					
Percent High School Graduates and Higher	81.5	66.2	44.6	79.1	72.1
Percent College Graduates and Higher	25.2	12.0	7.3	41.3	20.3
2000					
Percent High School Graduates and Higher	87.2	75.8	49.3	80.7	75.7
Percent College Graduates and Higher	30.0	15.3	8.9	47.8	23.2
Percent Change in Percent, 1990–2000					
High School Graduate or Higher	7.0	14.5	10.5	2.0	5.0
College Graduate or Higher	19.0	27.5	21.9	15.7	14.3

Sources: U.S. Census Bureau 2002a and 1991c.

additional improvements if gaps in attainment are to be
decreased.

Table 7.6 provides another measure of change in
educational involvement in Texas. This table shows the
percentage of persons in major college-attending ages (eighteen
to thirty-five years of age) enrolled in public community
colleges and universities in both 1990 and 2000. These data
again provide both positive and negative indications relative to
educational progress in the state in the 1990s. Enrollment in
community colleges increased for all racial/ethnic groups and,
as a result, the total enrollment rate increased. Increases were
generally larger for non-Anglos than Anglos. For public
universities, however, the rates of enrollment for Hispanics
declined from 1990 to 2000, while those for other groups,
particularly Blacks, increased. Because of the large size of the
Hispanic population among college-age persons, these changes

Table 7.6

Public Community College and University Enrollment Rates (Per 100
Persons Ages 18 –35) in Texas by Race/Ethnicity, 1990 and 2000

Year	Anglo	Black	Hispanic	Other	Total
Community College					
1990	6.3	4.1	4.4	5.6	5.5
2000	6.5	5.2	4.8	6.8	5.7
Public University					
1990	7.4	4.0	3.5	10.0	6.0
2000	7.5	4.7	3.3	10.3	5.7

Sources: Derived by the authors from U.S. Census Bureau 2002a; Texas Higher
Education Coordinating Board 2001a.

led to a decrease in the total enrollment rate in public
universities between 1990 and 2000.

Texas educational programs have shown significant
increases in the past two decades, increasing both the number
of persons involved in education and the expenditures for
education. The data on achievement, however, are very mixed
relative to educational attainment while showing substantial
continuing educational differentials. The historical data on
education suggest that future population change may be of
particular importance for understanding the future of education
in Texas and that public interest in, and concern about,
education is likely to continue to be based on its recognized
importance in achieving adequate socioeconomic resources. As
shown in Figure 7.1, income levels vary substantially by level
of education. In the United States in 2000, the average income
of a household in which the householder was without a high
school degree was only $28,974 compared to $45,368 for a
household in which the householder was a high school graduate
and $84,029 for a householder with a bachelor's degree. Such
differences when experienced over a lifetime have implications
for the quality of life of the individuals involved and for the
private and public sector economies to which they contribute.
Education is likely to continue to be an area of concern for both
public policy makers and private-sector decision makers.

Figure 7.1

Average Annual Household Income in the United States
by Educational Attainment in 2000*

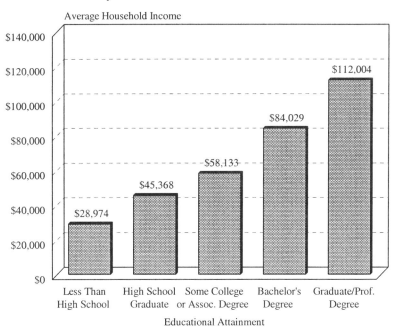

* From March 2001 Current Population Survey, U.S. Bureau of the Census

PROJECTIONS OF ENROLLMENT, COSTS, NEED, AND FINANCIAL ASSISTANCE

The projections in this chapter were completed using a variety of data sources and methods. Enrollment projections by educational level were made by developing age-, sex-, and race/ethnicity-specific rates of participation in public schools at each level from data provided by the Texas Education Agency (2001) and the Texas Higher Education Coordinating Board (2001a). These projections are of Texas residents enrolled in public elementary and secondary schools, public community colleges, and public universities in the state. Public college enrollments exclude persons enrolled in the health-related institutions (whose enrollment patterns are different from those for public colleges and universities), out-of-state students, international students, and, of course, students enrolled in private colleges and universities. In the set of projections used here, 2000 age, sex, and race/ethnicity rates of enrollment are assumed to prevail throughout the projection period. These rates were applied to the population projections to obtain projections of those enrolled across the projection period.

The cost projections use 2000 per-student costs as computed from expenditure data provided by the Texas Education Agency (2002a, 2002b) and the Texas Higher Education Coordinating Board (2002c) and assume these per-student costs continue over the projection period. All cost data are, therefore, in 2000 constant dollars. Projections for the number of students in specialized elementary and secondary programs were made by computing age-, sex-, and race/ethnicity-specific rates of participation in such programs for all students, then multiplying these rates by the total number of students projected.

The projections of the number of students with unmet financial needs and financial assistance involved the use of three databases and corresponding assumptions. Data on the income distributions of students by race/ethnicity in Texas public community colleges and universities were obtained from the comptroller's disparity study (Texas Comptroller of Public Accounts 1998, Murdock et al. 1998) and updated appropriately. Data on financial need and assistance were obtained from the Texas Higher Education Coordinating Board's Financial Aid Database (2002b) on programs available to students at various income levels, the contributions of federal and state sources to each program, and the average costs for attending public community colleges and universities. Data on family contributions to total costs were determined using federal guidelines (U.S. Department of Education 2000).

Given these data sources, the income distributions were applied to the projections of the number of students to obtain income distributions for students. These race/ethnicity-specific income distributions were assumed to apply to the racial/ethnic groups across the projection period. For each income level, the amount of expected household contribution to college costs was determined for each household income category using federal guidelines. This step was taken to eliminate students without unmet need. The number of students with any level of unmet need was therefore determined for each income level in 2000 and this proportion assumed for subsequent years in the projections for each income category. Since each income level can be used to determine the amount of unmet need, we were able to project the number of students with different amounts of (dollars of) unmet need. Financial assistance was determined by analyzing expected assistance from federal and state sources for each aid program available to persons qualifying at each income level. Because of the assumption of constant income distributions for each race/ethnicity group over time and the fact that the number of persons with unmet financial need and financial assistance (including state assistance levels) are determined by income levels, it is population change that drives the projections of all other factors. Similarly, because of the assumption that the aid programs available by income level are fixed over time and the state's assistance levels within programs are fixed, the state's proportion of assistance remains at a relatively fixed level over time, except for the period from 2000 to 2010 during which we assume that the $300 million TEXAS Grant Program becomes fully utilized. The projections provided here will not reflect any changes in income distribution by race/ethnicity, financial assistance programs available, and federal/state proportions of assistance.

PROJECTIONS OF PUBLIC SCHOOL ENROLLMENT

Projections of the number of persons enrolled in each level of education are shown in Tables 7.7–7.10. Due to space limitations projections are shown only for the 1.0 scenario. Total enrollment at all levels of education would increase from roughly 4.8 million residents in public educational institutions

Table 7.7

Total Public Education (All Levels), Public Elementary and Secondary
School, Public Community College, Public University, and Total Public
College and University Enrollment in Texas by Race/Ethnicity in 2000
and Projections to 2040 Using the Population Projection That Assumes
1990–2000 Rates of Net Migration (1.0 Scenario)

Year	Anglo	Black	Hispanic	Other	Total
Total Public Education (All Levels)					
2000	2,186,097	661,995	1,785,676	160,507	4,794,275
2010	2,114,040	683,790	2,328,788	228,599	5,355,217
2020	2,069,649	698,248	3,199,022	315,913	6,282,832
2030	1,973,400	724,415	4,246,985	422,932	7,367,732
2040	1,832,427	711,819	5,456,943	578,411	8,579,600
Public Elementary and Secondary Schools					
2000	1,727,733	576,977	1,582,538	114,979	4,002,227
2010	1,632,174	579,433	2,026,823	161,258	4,399,688
2020	1,608,472	586,270	2,786,400	217,725	5,198,867
2030	1,516,195	606,549	3,670,164	283,491	6,076,399
2040	1,395,371	588,439	4,679,891	390,090	7,053,791
Public Community Colleges					
2000	230,497	46,742	124,057	19,782	421,078
2010	239,162	56,778	184,574	29,805	510,319
2020	231,187	61,807	252,369	43,818	589,181
2030	228,522	65,548	353,220	62,823	710,113
2040	218,426	68,598	475,574	86,269	848,867
Public Universities					
2000	227,867	38,276	79,081	25,746	370,970
2010	242,704	47,579	117,391	37,536	445,210
2020	229,990	50,171	160,253	54,370	494,784
2030	228,683	52,318	223,601	76,618	581,220
2040	218,630	54,782	301,478	102,052	676,942
Total Public Colleges and Universities					
2000	458,364	85,018	203,138	45,528	792,048
2010	481,866	104,357	301,965	67,341	955,529
2020	461,177	111,978	412,622	98,188	1,083,965
2030	457,205	117,866	576,821	139,441	1,291,333
2040	437,056	123,380	777,052	188,321	1,525,809

Sources: Derived by the authors from Texas Population Estimates and Projections
Program 2001; Texas Education Agency 2001; Texas Higher Education
Coordinating Board 2001a.

in 2000 to nearly 8.6 million under the 1.0 scenario. This
represents an increase of 79 percent. This increase is smaller
than the percent increase projected to occur in the total
population and suggests that the aging of the population leads
educational enrollment to slow in the coming years.
Nevertheless, growth as in the 1.0 scenario could result in

Table 7.8

Percent Change in Projected Total Public Education (All Levels),
Public Elementary and Secondary School, Public Community
College, Public University, and Total Public College and University
Enrollment in Texas Using the Population Projection That Assumes
1990–2000 Rates of Net Migration (1.0 Scenario), 2000–40

Time Period	Anglo	Black	Hispanic	Other	Total
Total Public Education (All Levels)					
2000–10	-3.3	3.3	30.4	42.4	11.7
2010–20	-2.1	2.1	37.4	38.2	17.3
2020–30	-4.7	3.7	32.8	33.9	17.3
2030–40	-7.1	-1.7	28.5	36.8	16.4
2000–40	-16.2	7.5	205.6	260.4	79.0
Public Elementary and Secondary Schools					
2000–10	-5.5	0.4	28.1	40.2	9.9
2010–20	-1.5	1.2	37.5	35.0	18.2
2020–30	-5.7	3.5	31.7	30.2	16.9
2030–40	-8.0	-3.0	27.5	37.6	16.1
2000–40	-19.2	2.0	195.7	239.3	76.2
Public Community Colleges					
2000–10	3.8	21.5	48.8	50.7	21.2
2010–20	-3.3	8.9	36.7	47.0	15.5
2020–30	-1.2	6.1	40.0	43.4	20.5
2030–40	-4.4	4.7	34.6	37.3	19.5
2000–40	-5.2	46.8	283.4	336.1	101.6
Public Universities					
2000–10	6.5	24.3	48.4	45.8	20.0
2010–20	-5.2	5.4	36.5	44.8	11.1
2020–30	-0.6	4.3	39.5	40.9	17.5
2030–40	-4.4	4.7	34.8	33.2	16.5
2000–40	-4.1	43.1	281.2	296.4	82.5
Total Public Colleges and Universities					
2000–10	5.1	22.7	48.7	47.9	20.6
2010–20	-4.3	7.3	36.6	45.8	13.4
2020–30	-0.9	5.3	39.8	42.0	19.1
2030–40	-4.4	4.7	34.7	35.1	18.2
2000–40	-4.6	45.1	282.5	313.6	92.6

Sources: Derived from Texas Population Estimates and Projections Program 2001; Texas Education Agency 2001; Texas Higher Education Coordinating Board 2001a.

nearly 3.8 million additional students being added to Texas' educational system over the next forty years.

Non-Anglo population growth will account for a majority of the projected increase. For example, under the 1.0 scenario, Anglo enrollment declines by 16.2 percent but Black enrollment increases by 7.5 percent, Hispanic enrollment increases by 205.6 percent, and enrollment in the Other

Table 7.9

Percent of Total Public Education (All Levels), Public
Elementary and Secondary School, Public Community College,
Public University, and Total Public College and University
Enrollment in Texas by Race/Ethnicity in 2000 and Projections
to 2040 Using the Population Projection That Assumes
1990–2000 Rates of Net Migration (1.0 Scenario)

Year	Anglo	Black	Hispanic	Other
Total Public Education (All Levels)				
2000	45.7	13.8	37.2	3.3
2010	39.4	12.8	43.5	4.3
2020	33.0	11.1	50.9	5.0
2030	26.9	9.8	57.6	5.7
2040	21.4	8.3	63.6	6.7
Public Elementary and Secondary Schools				
2000	43.2	14.4	39.5	2.9
2010	37.0	13.2	46.1	3.7
2020	30.9	11.3	53.6	4.2
2030	24.9	10.0	60.4	4.7
2040	19.9	8.3	66.3	5.5
Public Community Colleges				
2000	54.7	11.1	29.5	4.7
2010	46.9	11.1	36.2	5.8
2020	39.3	10.5	42.8	7.4
2030	32.3	9.2	49.7	8.8
2040	25.7	8.1	56.0	10.2
Public Universities				
2000	61.5	10.3	21.3	6.9
2010	54.5	10.7	26.4	8.4
2020	46.5	10.1	32.4	11.0
2030	39.3	9.0	38.5	13.2
2040	32.3	8.1	44.5	15.1
Total Public Colleges and Universities				
2000	58.0	10.7	25.6	5.7
2010	50.5	10.9	31.6	7.0
2020	42.5	10.3	38.1	9.1
2030	35.4	9.1	44.7	10.8
2040	28.7	8.1	50.9	12.3

Sources: Derived by the authors from Texas Population Estimates and
Projections Program 2001; Texas Education Agency 2001; Texas
Higher Education Coordinating Board 2001a.

category increases by 260.4 percent. Overall, because Anglo
enrollment declines, all of the net increase will be due to non-
Anglo populations. By 2040, under the 1.0 scenario, only 21.4
percent of the persons enrolled would be Anglo while 8.3
percent would be Black, 63.6 percent Hispanic, and 6.7 percent

Table 7.10

Number and Percent of Net Change in Projected Total Public
Education (All Levels), Public Elementary and Secondary School,
Public Community College, Public University, and Total Public
College and University Enrollment in Texas Due To Each
Race/Ethnicity Group, Using the Population Projection That
Assumes 1990–2000 Rates of Net Migration (1.0 Scenario), 2000–40

Race/ Ethnicity	Number	Percent
Total Public Education (All Levels)		
Anglo	-353,670	-9.3
Black	49,824	1.3
Hispanic	3,671,267	97.0
Other	417,904	11.0
Total	3,785,325	100.0
Public Elementary and Secondary Schools		
Anglo	-332,362	-10.9
Black	11,462	0.4
Hispanic	3,097,353	101.5
Other	275,111	9.0
Total	3,051,564	100.0
Public Community Colleges		
Anglo	-12,071	-2.8
Black	21,856	5.1
Hispanic	351,517	82.2
Other	66,487	15.5
Total	427,789	100.0
Public Universities		
Anglo	-9,237	-3.0
Black	16,506	5.4
Hispanic	222,397	72.7
Other	76,306	24.9
Total	305,972	100.0
Total Public Colleges and Universities		
Anglo	-21,308	-2.9
Black	38,362	5.2
Hispanic	573,914	78.2
Other	142,793	19.5
Total	733,761	100.0

Sources: Derived by the authors from Texas Population Estimates and
Projections Program 2001; Texas Education Agency 2001; Texas Higher
Education Coordinating Board 2001a.

persons from the Other racial/ethnic group. Non-Anglos will
largely determine the future of educational enrollment in Texas.

Enrollment in elementary and secondary education increase
by more than 3 million to more than 7 million by 2040 under

the 1.0 scenario. Since the total enrollment growth at all levels of education is 3.8 million under the 1.0 scenario, elementary and secondary enrollment will be responsible for the vast majority of enrollment growth in the state (more than 78 percent). The projected change represents a 2000 to 2040 increase in enrollment of 76.2 percent.

The extent to which enrollment increases will result from non-Anglo populations is even more apparent for elementary and secondary education than for total public education because of the younger age structure of the non-Anglo population. By 2040, under the 1.0 scenario, 19.9 percent of those enrolled in public elementary and secondary schools would be Anglo, 8.3 percent Black, 66.3 percent Hispanic, and 5.5 percent persons from the Other racial/ethnic group. Of the total net increase in public elementary and secondary enrollment from 2000 to 2040 under the 1.0 scenario, non-Anglos would account for all of the increase, with Hispanics accounting for the vast majority of the non-Anglo increase.

The data show quite different patterns between public community colleges and universities. The number of residents enrolled in universities was roughly 50,000 less than that in community colleges in 2000 (370,970 in universities and 421,078 in community colleges), and the faster enrollment growth in community colleges leads to a marked expansion in this difference over time. Under the 1.0 scenario community college enrollment would be 848,867 compared to 676,942 for public universities by 2040. Overall, these data suggest that public community colleges and universities will increase their combined resident enrollment from 792,048 in 2000 to 1,525,809 in 2040 under the 1.0 scenario. Total enrollment would increase by 92.6 percent from 2000 to 2040, with community college enrollment increasing by 101.6 percent and university enrollment by 82.5 percent.

Both community college and university enrollment will become more diverse, but the diversity will be greater in community colleges than in universities. Under the 1.0

scenario, 74.3 percent of community college students and 67.7 percent of public university students would be non-Anglo in 2040 and all of the net change in enrollment from 2000 to 2040 would be due to non-Anglo populations.

For all enrollment categories, the data in these tables suggest that enrollment will grow more slowly than the population and that enrollment will increasingly involve non-Anglo populations. Community colleges will increase enrollment more rapidly than public universities because of their higher rates of enrollment for Hispanics and other non-Anglo groups, which are the fastest growing components of the population. Public education at all levels in Texas will be altered significantly by changes in non-Anglo populations.

IMPLICATIONS OF PROJECTED CHANGE IN PUBLIC ENROLLMENT

The implications of the projected changes in enrollment are examined relative to three factors. First, we examine the implications of change in public elementary and secondary education for enrollment in specialized programs. Second, we examine the implications of public elementary and secondary school and college and university enrollment for total educational costs. We then examine the implications of projected change in public higher education for the level of financial need for students attending public colleges and universities and for likely levels of unmet financial need. Due to space limitations, we again present data for only the 1.0 scenario.

Tables 7.11–7.13 and Figure 7.2 show projected changes in enrollment in several specialized public elementary and secondary education programs. These data suggest that the projected population changes would increase enrollment in these programs. Although total enrollment in public elementary and secondary schools increases by 76.2 percent under the 1.0 scenario, enrollment in the Bilingual/ESL, Economically Disadvantaged, Immigrant, Limited English Proficiency, and Title I programs would all increase by larger percentages than

Table 7.11

Enrollment in Selected Public Elementary and Secondary School Programs in
Texas by Race/Ethnicity in 2000 and Projections for 2040 Using the Population
Projection That Assumes 1990–2000 Rates of Net Migration (1.0 Scenario)

Program	Anglo	Black	Hispanic	Other	Total
2000					
Bilingual/ESL	7,336	2,766	464,459	23,714	498,275
Economically Disadvantaged	359,510	369,393	1,190,363	36,734	1,956,000
Gifted and Talented	198,574	33,827	86,807	17,354	336,562
Immigrants	3,587	1,837	61,917	6,463	73,804
Limited English Proficiency (LEP)	8,498	3,214	516,745	27,013	555,470
Special Education	220,853	86,806	176,391	6,170	490,220
Title I	513,926	319,111	1,149,095	30,568	2,012,700
Career and Technology Education	345,957	111,644	264,034	20,314	741,949
2040					
Bilingual/ESL	5,382	2,614	1,342,446	78,683	1,429,125
Economically Disadvantaged	293,846	372,081	3,508,910	126,261	4,301,098
Gifted and Talented	156,840	34,167	249,133	59,549	499,689
Immigrants	3,119	2,039	182,485	21,211	208,854
Limited English Proficiency (LEP)	6,306	3,073	1,500,613	90,338	1,600,330
Special Education	176,432	88,561	521,844	20,487	807,324
Title I	387,810	306,010	3,270,388	99,764	4,063,972
Career and Technology Education	276,169	120,301	795,926	68,407	1,260,803

Sources: Derived by the authors from Texas Population Estimates and Projections
Program 2001; Texas Education Agency 2001.

Table 7.12

Percent Change in Projected Enrollment in Selected Public Elementary
and Secondary School Programs in Texas by Race/Ethnicity, Using the
Population Projection That Assumes 1990–2000 Rates of Net
Migration (1.0 Scenario), 2000–40

Program	Anglo	Black	Hispanic	Other	Total
Bilingual/ESL	-26.6	-5.5	189.0	231.8	186.8
Economically Disadvantaged	-18.3	0.7	194.8	243.7	119.9
Gifted and Talented	-21.0	1.0	187.0	243.1	48.5
Immigrants	-13.0	11.0	194.7	228.2	183.0
Limited English Proficiency (LEP)	-25.8	-4.4	190.4	234.4	188.1
Special Education	-20.1	2.0	195.8	232.0	64.7
Title I	-24.5	-4.1	184.6	226.4	101.9
Career and Technology Education	-20.2	7.8	201.4	236.7	69.9

Sources: Derived by the authors from Texas Population Estimates and
Projections Program 2001; Texas Education Agency 2001.

Table 7.13

Percent of Enrollment in Selected Public Elementary and Secondary School
Programs by Race/Ethnicity in 2000 and Projections for 2040 Using the Population
Projection That Assumes 1990–2000 Rates of Net Migration (1.0 Scenario)

Program	Anglo	Black	Hispanic	Other
2000				
Bilingual/ESL	1.5	0.6	93.1	4.8
Economically Disadvantaged	18.4	18.9	60.8	1.9
Gifted and Talented	59.0	10.1	25.7	5.2
Immigrants	4.9	2.5	83.8	8.8
Limited English Proficiency (LEP)	1.5	0.6	93.0	4.9
Special Education	45.1	17.7	35.9	1.3
Title I	25.5	15.9	57.1	1.5
Career and Technology Education	46.6	15.0	35.7	2.7
2040				
Bilingual/ESL	0.4	0.2	93.9	5.5
Economically Disadvantaged	6.8	8.7	81.6	2.9
Gifted and Talented	31.4	6.8	49.9	11.9
Immigrants	1.5	1.0	87.3	10.2
Limited English Proficiency (LEP)	0.4	0.2	93.8	5.6
Special Education	21.9	11.0	64.6	2.5
Title I	9.5	7.5	80.5	2.5
Career and Technology Education	21.9	9.5	63.2	5.4

Sources: Derived by the authors from Texas Population Estimates and Projections Program
2001; Texas Education Agency 2001.

total enrollment. Those programs are used the most by the elements of Texas' population that are projected to grow the most rapidly: that is, the programs projected to increase most rapidly are those with the largest percentage of Hispanic participants and those projected to grow least rapidly are those with the highest proportion of Anglo participants. For all programs, however, the percentage of non-Anglo participants increases over time. For example, although the percentage of non-Anglos in the Gifted and Talented Program was only 41 percent in 2000, by 2040 the percentage of non-Anglos would be 68.6 percent under the 1.0 scenario (see Table 7.13). In sum, these programs will grow significantly given the projected changes in the population and will, like total enrollment, come to reflect the racial/ethnic composition of the population and of public elementary and secondary enrollment.

Table 7.14 provides data showing the implications of the projected changes in enrollment for public costs for public

Figure 7.2

Percent Change in Enrollment in Selected Elementary and
Secondary School Programs in Texas, 2000 to 2040*

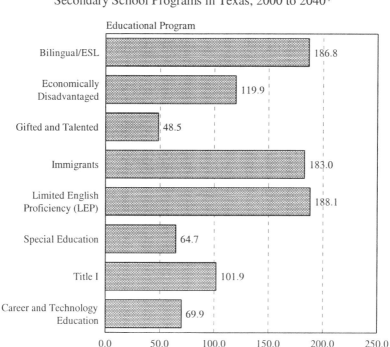

* Projections are shown for the 1.0 scenario

elementary and secondary schools, community colleges, and universities, and several of the above-noted specialized elementary and secondary programs. Because these projections are based on per-student costs, they grow as enrollment grows such that their percentage changes are the same as the percentage changes in enrollments in these programs. The costs of such programs can be expected to show significant increases in the coming years. From 2000 to 2040, under the 1.0 scenario, total elementary and secondary school costs would increase by roughly $17.6 billion and public college and university costs by $2.3 billion. Substantial increases are also

Table 7.14

State Education Expenditures (in 2000 Dollars) for Total Public Elementary
and Secondary Schools, Total Community Colleges, Total Public
Universities, Total Public Colleges and Universities, and Selected
Elementary and Secondary Education Programs in Texas in 2000 and
Projections to 2040 Using the Population Projection That Assumes
1990–2000 Rates of Net Migration (1.0 Scenario)

Year	Total Public Elementary and Secondary	Total Community Colleges	Total Public Universities	Total Public Colleges and Universities
2000	$ 23,101,414,556	$ 825,704,483	$ 1,785,656,676	$ 2,611,361,159
2010	25,395,615,092	1,000,699,837	2,143,009,431	3,143,709,268
2020	30,008,588,165	1,155,342,698	2,381,632,888	3,536,975,586
2030	35,073,825,724	1,392,481,885	2,797,690,846	4,190,172,731
2040	40,715,469,183	1,664,568,766	3,258,446,778	4,923,015,544

Selected Elementary and Secondary Education Programs

Year	Bilingual/ ESL	Gifted and Talented	Special Education	Career and Technology Education
2000	$ 518,028,752	$ 244,720,917	$ 1,650,334,925	$ 537,903,489
2010	653,056,711	251,846,691	1,772,822,351	587,075,017
2020	895,899,940	287,389,765	2,056,313,546	669,941,773
2030	1,162,517,755	323,842,465	2,381,303,821	796,141,011
2040	1,485,781,627	363,333,799	2,717,871,554	914,065,971

Sources: Derived by the authors from Texas Population Estimates and Projections
Program 2001; Texas Education Agency 2002a and 2002b; Texas Higher Education
Coordinating Board 2002c.

shown for each of the programs for which specialized
assistance would be provided.

Tables 7.15–7.17 present the projected number of college
students with financial need unmet by household resources for
the coming years. These data point to a rapid increase in the
number of students requiring financial assistance. For example,
under the 1.0 scenario, the number increases by nearly 660,000
to 1,285,387 in 2040. This represents an increase of 105.4
percent, greater than the 92.6 percent rate of growth in total
enrollment projected under the same scenario (see Table 7.8).
Reflecting the higher proportion of non-Anglos (who tend to
have lower incomes) enrolled, the increases are greater for
public community colleges than for public universities. The
increase from 2000 to 2040 in the number of students requiring

Table 7.15

Number of Students with Financial Need Unmet by Household Resources
Enrolled at Public Colleges and Universities in Texas by Race/Ethnicity in 2000
and Projections to 2040 Using the Population Projection That Assumes
1990–2000 Rates of Net Migration (1.0 Scenario)

Year	Anglo	Black	Hispanic	Other	Total
Public Community Colleges					
2000	146,761	41,091	110,268	15,732	313,852
2010	152,222	49,889	164,064	23,704	389,879
2020	147,171	54,310	224,324	34,848	460,653
2030	145,488	57,594	313,971	49,963	567,016
2040	139,065	60,267	422,717	68,611	690,660
Public Universities					
2000	179,581	36,082	73,575	22,789	312,021
2010	191,252	44,843	109,218	33,218	378,531
2020	181,240	47,285	149,095	48,116	425,736
2030	180,218	49,310	208,034	67,806	505,368
2040	172,297	51,631	280,487	90,312	594,727
Total Public Colleges and Universities					
2000	326,342	77,173	183,843	38,515	625,873
2010	343,474	94,732	273,282	56,922	768,410
2020	328,411	101,595	373,419	82,964	886,389
2030	325,706	106,904	522,005	117,769	1,072,384
2040	311,362	111,898	703,204	158,923	1,285,387

Sources: Derived by the authors from Texas Population Estimates and Projections Program
2001; Murdock et al. 1998; Texas Higher Education Coordinating Board 2001b; U.S.
Department of Education 2000.

at least some assistance is 120.1 percent for community
colleges and 90.6 percent for public universities under the 1.0
scenario.

Because of racial/ethnic differences in income, the
percentage of all those with unmet financial need from non-
Anglo groups is larger than their total percentage of enrollment.
For example, of those enrolled in 2040, 28.7 percent, 8.1
percent, 50.9 percent, and 12.3 percent are projected to be
Anglos, Blacks, Hispanics, and persons from the Other
racial/ethnic group, respectively. Of all persons requiring at
least some assistance in 2040 under the 1.0 scenario, 24.2
percent would be Anglo, 8.7 percent Black, 54.7 percent
Hispanic, and 12.4 percent persons from the Other racial/ethnic
group.

Table 7.16

Percent Change in Projected Number of Students with Financial Need
Unmet by Household Resources Enrolled at Public Colleges and
Universities in Texas Using the Population Projection That Assumes
1990–2000 Rates of Net Migration (1.0 Scenario), 2000–40

Year	Anglo	Black	Hispanic	Other	Total
Public Community Colleges					
2000–10	3.7	21.4	48.8	50.7	24.2
2010–20	-3.3	8.9	36.7	47.0	18.2
2020–30	-1.1	6.0	40.0	43.4	23.1
2030–40	-4.4	4.6	34.6	37.3	21.8
2000–40	-5.2	46.7	283.4	336.1	120.1
Public Universities					
2000–10	6.5	24.3	48.4	45.8	21.3
2010–20	-5.2	5.4	36.5	44.9	12.5
2020–30	-0.6	4.3	39.5	40.9	18.7
2030–40	-4.4	4.7	34.8	33.2	17.7
2000–40	-4.1	43.1	281.2	296.4	90.6
Total Public Colleges and Universities					
2000–10	5.2	22.8	48.6	47.8	22.8
2010–20	-4.4	7.2	36.6	45.8	15.4
2020–30	-0.8	5.2	39.8	42.0	21.0
2030–40	-4.4	4.7	34.7	34.9	19.9
2000–40	-4.6	45.0	282.5	312.6	105.4

Sources: Derived by the authors from Texas Population Estimates and
Projections Program 2001; Murdock et al. 1998; Texas Higher Education
Coordinating Board 2001b; U.S. Department of Education 2000.

Overall then, these data suggest that the number of persons requiring assistance will grow rapidly and will reflect the socioeconomic differences in Texas' population in 2000. The population of students requiring at least some assistance will increase faster than enrollment and will show even larger proportions of non-Anglos than total enrollment.

The data in Tables 7.18 and 7.19 show the projected number of persons by level of financial assistance required after household contributions have been taken into account. The percentage distributions across racial/ethnic groups remain constant over time and across scenarios because of the assumption in these projections that race/ethnicity-specific income distributions for 2000 remain constant across the projection period.

Table 7.17

Percent of Students with Financial Need Unmet
by Household Resources Enrolled at Public Colleges and
Universities by Race/Ethnicity in Texas in 2000 and Projections
to 2040 Using the Population Projection That Assumes 1990–
2000 Rates of Net Migration (1.0 Scenario)

Year	Anglo	Black	Hispanic	Other
Public Community Colleges				
2000	46.8	13.1	35.1	5.0
2010	39.0	12.8	42.1	6.1
2020	31.9	11.8	48.7	7.6
2030	25.6	10.2	55.4	8.8
2040	20.2	8.7	61.2	9.9
Public Universities				
2000	57.5	11.6	23.6	7.3
2010	50.5	11.8	28.9	8.8
2020	42.6	11.1	35.0	11.3
2030	35.6	9.8	41.2	13.4
2040	28.9	8.7	47.2	15.2
Total Public Colleges and Universities				
2000	52.1	12.3	29.4	6.2
2010	44.7	12.3	35.6	7.4
2020	37.0	11.5	42.1	9.4
2030	30.3	10.0	48.7	11.0
2040	24.2	8.7	54.7	12.4

Sources: Derived by the authors from Texas Population Estimates and
Projections Program 2001; Murdock et al. 1998; Texas Higher
Education Coordinating Board 2001b; U.S. Department of Education
2000.

Table 7.18 shows that the levels of need vary across
racial/ethnic groups. For example, of those requiring financial
assistance in community colleges in 2000, 21 percent of
Anglos, 49.1 percent of Blacks, 51.6 percent of Hispanics, and
44.1 percent of persons from the Other racial/ethnic group
required the maximum assistance of $7,500 to $9,999. In
public universities, 62.6 percent of Blacks, 63.5 percent of
Hispanics, and 53.8 percent of persons in the Other
racial/ethnic group required more than $10,000 in assistance
compared to 29.4 percent of Anglos.

The percentage distributions for the total population show
changes over time that reflect the characteristics of the

Table 7.18

Number and Percent of Students with Financial Need Unmet by Household Resources in
Public Colleges and Universities by Need Category within Race/Ethnicity Groups in Texas in
2000 and Projections for 2040 Using the Population Projection That Assumes 1990–2000
Rates of Net Migration (1.0 Scenario)

Need Category	Anglo		Black		Hispanic		Other		Total	
	Number	%	Number	%	Number	%	Number	%	Number	%
2000			**Public Community Colleges**							
$ 7,500–9,999	30,860	21.0	20,158	49.1	56,943	51.6	6,930	44.1	114,891	36.6
6,000–7,499	54,329	37.0	13,374	32.5	33,852	30.7	5,135	32.6	106,690	34.0
4,000–5,999	31,692	21.6	4,261	10.4	11,450	10.4	2,149	13.7	49,552	15.8
<4,000	29,880	20.4	3,298	8.0	8,023	7.3	1,518	9.6	42,719	13.6
Total	146,761	100.0	41,091	100.0	110,268	100.0	15,732	100.0	313,852	100.0
			Public Universities							
$ >10,000	52,761	29.4	22,581	62.6	46,707	63.5	12,252	53.8	134,301	43.0
7,500–9,999	33,725	18.8	5,360	14.9	10,372	14.1	3,599	15.8	53,056	17.0
6,000–7,499	14,973	8.3	1,948	5.4	3,872	5.2	1,371	6.0	22,164	7.1
4,000–5,999	30,304	16.9	2,856	7.9	5,936	8.1	2,331	10.2	41,427	13.3
<4,000	47,818	26.6	3,337	9.2	6,688	9.1	3,230	14.2	61,073	19.6
Total	179,581	100.0	36,082	100.0	73,575	100.0	22,783	100.0	312,021	100.0
			Total Public Colleges and Universities							
$ >10,000	52,761	16.2	22,581	29.3	46,707	25.4	12,252	31.8	134,301	21.5
7,500–9,999	64,585	19.8	25,518	33.0	67,315	36.6	10,529	27.3	167,947	26.8
6,000–7,499	69,302	21.2	15,322	19.9	37,724	20.5	6,506	16.9	128,854	20.6
4,000–5,999	61,996	19.0	7,117	9.2	17,386	9.5	4,480	11.7	90,979	14.5
<4,000	77,698	23.8	6,635	8.6	14,711	8.0	4,748	12.3	103,792	16.6
Total	326,342	100.0	77,173	100.0	183,843	100.0	38,515	100.0	625,873	100.0
2040			**Public Community Colleges**							
$ 7,500–9,999	29,235	21.0	29,549	49.0	218,274	51.6	30,270	44.1	307,328	44.5
6,000–7,499	51,493	37.0	19,617	32.6	129,811	30.7	22,365	32.6	223,286	32.3
4,000–5,999	30,020	21.6	6,236	10.3	43,778	10.4	9,339	13.6	89,373	13.0
<4,000	28,317	20.4	4,865	8.1	30,854	7.3	6,637	9.7	70,673	10.2
Total	139,065	100.0	60,267	100.0	422,717	100.0	68,611	100.0	690,660	100.0
			Public Universities							
$ >10,000	50,595	29.4	32,299	62.6	177,991	63.5	48,643	53.9	309,528	52.0
7,500–9,999	32,378	18.8	7,696	14.9	39,609	14.1	14,212	15.7	93,895	15.8
6,000–7,499	14,390	8.3	2,780	5.4	14,791	5.3	5,445	6.0	37,406	6.3
4,000–5,999	29,059	16.9	4,097	7.9	22,540	8.0	9,218	10.2	64,914	10.9
<4,000	45,875	26.6	4,759	9.2	25,556	9.1	12,794	14.2	88,984	15.0
Total	172,297	100.0	51,631	100.0	280,487	100.0	90,312	100.0	594,727	100.0
			Total Public Colleges and Universities							
$ >10,000	50,595	16.2	32,299	28.9	177,991	25.3	48,643	30.6	309,528	24.1
7,500–9,999	61,613	19.8	37,245	33.3	257,883	36.7	44,482	28.0	401,223	31.2
6,000–7,499	65,883	21.2	22,397	20.0	144,602	20.6	27,810	17.5	260,692	20.3
4,000–5,999	59,079	19.0	10,333	9.2	66,318	9.4	18,557	11.7	154,287	12.0
<4,000	74,192	23.8	9,624	8.6	56,410	8.0	19,431	12.2	159,657	12.4
Total	311,362	100.0	111,898	100.0	703,204	100.0	158,923	100.0	1,285,387	100.0

Sources: Derived from Texas Population Estimates and Projections Program 2001; Murdock et al. 1998;
Texas Higher Education Coordinating Board 2001b, 2002a, 2002b; U.S. Department of Education 2000.

projected population. In both community colleges and public
universities, the percentage of those with high levels of need is
projected to increase over time. For example, whereas 36.6

Table 7.19

Percent of Students with Financial Need Unmet by Household
Resources in Public Colleges and Universities by Race/Ethnicity
within Need Category in Texas in 2000 and Projections for 2040
Using the Population Projection That Assumes 1990–2000 Rates of
Net Migration (1.0 Scenario)

Need Category	Anglo	Black	Hispanic	Other	Total
2000	**Public Community Colleges**				
$ 7,500–9,999	26.9	17.6	49.5	6.0	100.0
6,000–7,499	51.0	12.5	31.7	4.8	100.0
4,000–5,999	64.0	8.6	23.1	4.3	100.0
<4,000	69.9	7.7	18.8	3.6	100.0
Total	46.8	13.1	35.1	5.0	100.0
	Public Universities				
$ >10,000	39.3	16.8	34.8	9.1	100.0
7,500–9,999	63.5	10.1	19.6	6.8	100.0
6,000–7,499	67.5	8.8	17.5	6.2	100.0
4,000–5,999	73.2	6.9	14.3	5.6	100.0
<4,000	78.3	5.4	11.0	5.3	100.0
Total	57.5	11.6	23.6	7.3	100.0
	Total Public Colleges and Universities				
$ >10,000	39.3	16.8	34.8	9.1	100.0
7,500–9,999	38.4	15.2	40.1	6.3	100.0
6,000–7,499	53.8	11.9	29.3	5.0	100.0
4,000–5,999	68.2	7.8	19.1	4.9	100.0
<4,000	74.8	6.4	14.2	4.6	100.0
Total	52.1	12.3	29.4	6.2	100.0
2040	**Public Community Colleges**				
$ 7,500–9,999	9.6	9.6	71.0	9.8	100.0
6,000–7,499	23.1	8.8	58.1	10.0	100.0
4,000–5,999	33.6	7.0	49.0	10.4	100.0
<4,000	40.0	6.9	43.7	9.4	100.0
Total	20.2	8.7	61.2	9.9	100.0
	Public Universities				
$ >10,000	16.4	10.4	57.5	15.7	100.0
7,500–9,999	34.5	8.2	42.2	15.1	100.0
6,000–7,499	38.4	7.4	39.6	14.6	100.0
4,000–5,999	44.8	6.3	34.7	14.2	100.0
<4,000	51.5	5.4	28.7	14.4	100.0
Total	28.9	8.7	47.2	15.2	100.0
	Total Public Colleges and Universities				
$ >10,000	16.4	10.4	57.5	15.7	100.0
7,500–9,999	15.3	9.3	64.3	11.1	100.0
6,000–7,499	25.2	8.6	55.5	10.7	100.0
4,000–5,999	38.3	6.7	43.0	12.0	100.0
<4,000	46.5	6.0	35.3	12.2	100.0
Total	24.2	8.7	54.7	12.4	100.0

Sources: Derived by the authors from Texas Population Estimates and
Projections Program 2001; Murdock et al. 1998; Texas Higher Education
Coordinating Board 2001b, 2002a, and 2002b; U.S. Department of Education
2000.

percent of those from community colleges needing assistance in 2000 would require $7,500 to $9,999 in assistance, the percentage at this level of need in 2040 (under the 1.0 scenario and in 2000 constant dollars) would be 44.5 percent. In public universities, the percentage with the highest level of need (more than $10,000) is 43 percent in 2000 but is projected to be 52 percent in 2040 under the 1.0 scenario.

Levels of need will largely vary by race/ethnicity in accordance with the growth in their total populations and their socioeconomic resources (see Table 7.19). For example, whereas 26.9 percent of those with the highest level of need among community college enrollees needing assistance were Anglo in 2000, by 2040 the percentage of participants who are Anglo would decline to only 9.6 under the 1.0 scenario. The proportions for Blacks are 17.6 percent in 2000 but 9.6 percent in 2040, for Hispanics 49.5 percent in 2000 and 71 percent in 2040, and for the Other racial/ethnic group 6 percent in 2000 and 9.8 percent in 2040. Non-Anglos, particularly Hispanics, have higher levels of need and are likely to form increasing proportions of those with need.

The amounts of financial assistance projected to be provided in the future from all nonhousehold sources and by the State of Texas are shown in Table 7.20. Both the level of financial assistance required overall and that for the state are fixed per capita amounts within need levels. The amount of such aid provided is assumed to remain at the 2000 level with the exception that the TEXAS Grant Program appropriation of $300 million enacted in the Texas' legislature's 1999 and 2001 sessions is assumed to be included in the level of state assistance provided by 2010. All dollar values are in 2000 constant dollars.

The absolute level of financial assistance required will increase in the coming years under the 1.0 scenario. The total level of financial assistance, estimated to be $671.9 million in 2000, would grow to nearly $1.2 billion by 2010 and to nearly $2.2 billion by 2040. These represent increases of 219.9

Table 7.20

Total and State Financial Assistance Expenditures (in 2000 Constant
Dollars) for Public Higher Education Students in Texas in 2000 and
Projections for 2010 and 2040 Using the Population Projection That
Assumes 1990–2000 Rates of Net Migration (1.0 Scenario)

Household Income	All Expenditures	State Expenditures
2000		
$ <10,000	$ 220,986,578	$ 47,918,456
10,000–19,999	182,282,208	37,470,863
20,000–29,999	143,411,299	33,714,407
30,000–39,999	64,709,606	18,998,756
40,000–49,999	29,741,063	10,756,151
50,000–59,999	13,573,506	5,899,333
60,000+	17,169,279	10,177,243
Total	671,873,539	164,935,209
Average	848	208
2010		
$ <10,000	$ 314,244,500	$ 102,565,379
10,000-19,999	279,774,850	101,956,862
20,000–29,999	230,691,527	100,271,779
30,000–39,999	130,930,283	78,447,374
40,000–49,999	73,064,445	51,271,670
50,000–59,999	50,177,410	41,105,459
60,000+	115,259,217	105,521,129
Total	1,194,142,232	581,139,652
Average	1,250	608
2040		
$ <10,000	$ 651,719,974	$ 209,932,622
10,000–19,999	558,436,395	200,953,531
20,000–29,999	412,089,258	177,011,358
30,000–39,999	207,055,693	123,143,992
40,000–49,999	105,975,048	74,143,153
50,000–59,999	68,465,264	56,065,213
60,000+	145,504,855	133,234,982
Total	2,149,246,487	974,484,851
Average	1,409	639

Sources: Derived by the authors from Texas Population Estimates and Projections
Program 2001; Murdock et al. 1998; Texas Higher Education Coordinating Board
2001b, 2002a, and 2002b; U.S. Department of Education 2000.

percent from 2000 to 2040. Reflecting the increasing level of
need among students requiring financial assistance, these rates
of increase are larger than the increase in enrollment of 92.6
percent or the total increases in the number of persons requiring
at least some level of assistance of 105.4 percent from 2000 to
2040.

The dollar amount of assistance grows as the total level of assistance grows because of the use of per capita values and shows similar levels of percentage change by income category relative to total assistance under the 1.0 scenario. Whereas state aid was $164.9 million in 2000, it is projected to be $581.1 million by 2010 and $974.5 million in 2040. This represents a 2000 to 2040 percentage increase of 490.8 percent. The large numerical and percentage increases between 2000 and 2010 are a result of the assumption that the $300 million TEXAS Grant Program would be fully utilized by 2010. Percentage increases are smaller for subsequent decades.

A comparison of the 2000 to 2010 data shows how significant the TEXAS Grant Program is in increasing the state's support for financial assistance. In 2000, the state's contribution to the total financial assistance provided is approximately 24.5 percent, but with the TEXAS Grant Program in place, the state's contribution is more than 45 percent for all years after 2010.

The change in the dollar value of assistance provided by the state after 2010 can be seen as what the state would need to contribute to maintain its (approximately 45 percent) share of total financial assistance. A comparison of 2010 to 2040 shows that the state would need to increase its level of expenditures by about $393 million under the 1.0 scenario. The average contribution per enrollee is $600 to $650 for the state and approximately $1,200 to $1,400 from all sources, compared to estimated costs of $8,200 for attending a community college and $11,555 for public universities in Texas in 2000–01 (Texas Higher Education Coordinating Board 2002d). Most students will need to obtain substantial additional resources through loans, work-related income, and other sources. The total level of financial assistance required will increase significantly and the state's expenditures on financial assistance will also have to increase if the financial assistance requirements of Texas students are to be addressed.

SUMMARY

The analysis in this chapter has examined the implications of population change for public education enrollment and costs in the coming decades. Projected elementary and secondary enrollment and public community college and public university enrollment were examined under projections that assume that 2000 rates of enrollment will continue throughout the projection period from 2000 through 2040. Given these projections, the implications of such population-related changes are examined for the costs of educational programs, for the number of students requiring financial assistance in public community colleges and universities, and for the total level of financial need likely to be provided from all sources, including the state. The results of the analysis suggest that:

1. Texas has witnessed enrollment increases at all education levels in the past decade, coupled with increases in expenditures and development of a number of major policy initiatives. Total enrollment in elementary and secondary education (both public and private) increased by 45.3 percent from 1980 to 2000, and 4 million students were enrolled in public institutions in 2000. The number of Texas residents enrolled in Texas public colleges and universities (at both the graduate and undergraduate levels) increased by 8.6 percent from 1990 to 2000 and stood at more than 835,000 in 2000. Public costs for education in 2000 were more than $23 billion for elementary and secondary education, having increased by 31.6 percent in real dollar terms from 1990 to 2000. General revenue costs for educational programs at public colleges and universities were more than $2.6 billion in 2000, having increased by more than 18.3 percent from 1990 to 2000 in 2000 constant dollars. The 1990s decade brought increases in the number of high school and college graduates among all racial/ethnic groups, with the largest percentage being non-Anglo students. Large racial/ethnic differences in enrollment rates and levels of educational attainment continued, however,

suggesting the contradictory nature of change during the decade.

2. Projections assuming 2000 age-, sex-, and race/ethnicity-specific rates of enrollment show increases in the total number of Texas' residents enrolled in public educational institutions at all levels by 2040—from 4.8 million in 2000 to 8.6 million under the 1.0 scenario. This represents an increase of nearly 3.8 million or 79 percent from 2000 to 2040. Enrollment is expected to increase more slowly than the population, which will increase by 142.6 percent.

3. Non-Anglos will account for a majority of the enrollment increase. Under the 1.0 scenario, Anglo enrollment declines by 16.2 percent from 2000 to 2040, while Black enrollment increases by 7.5 percent, Hispanic enrollment by 205.6 percent, and the enrollment of persons in the Other racial/ethnic group by 260.4 percent. By 2040 21.4 percent of all those enrolled in school would be Anglo, 8.3 percent Black, 63.6 percent Hispanic, and 6.7 percent members of the Other racial/ethnic group.

4. The data for public elementary and secondary enrollment show enrollment increasing by nearly 3.1 million to 7.1 million in 2040 under the 1.0 scenario. More than 80 percent of total public enrollment in all schools would be in elementary and secondary schools. By 2040, under the 1.0 scenario, 19.9 percent of those enrolled in public elementary and secondary schools would be Anglo while 8.3 percent would be Black, 66.3 percent Hispanic, and 5.5 percent would be persons from the Other racial/ethnic group.

5. The data on public colleges and universities show different patterns for community colleges and universities because of higher rates of enrollment for Black and Hispanic populations in community colleges than in universities. The

number of residents enrolled in universities was roughly 50,000 less than that in community colleges in 2000 (370,970 in universities and 421,078 in community colleges), but the faster growth of enrollment in community colleges leads to expansion in this difference over time. Under the 1.0 scenario, community college enrollment would be 848,867 in 2040 compared to 676,942 in public universities (with community college enrollments increasing by 101.6 percent and university enrollment by 82.5 percent). Both community college and university enrollment will become more diverse, but the diversity will be greater in community colleges than in universities with 74.3 percent of community college students and 67.7 percent of public university students in 2040 being non-Anglo, compared to 45.3 percent and 38.5 percent in 2000.

6. The implications of such changes relative to enrollment in specialized elementary and secondary programs (Bilingual/ESL, Economically Disadvantaged, Gifted and Talented, Immigrant, Limited English Proficiency, Special Education, Title I, and Career and Technology Education) were examined. Those programs most impacted by non-Anglo enrollment increases, such as Bilingual/ESL, Economically Disadvantaged, Immigrant, Limited English Proficiency, and Title I, would all experience increases exceeding 100 percent in the projected number of students involved in these programs from 2000 to 2040, compared to an overall growth rate 76.2 percent in elementary and secondary school enrollment.

7. The implications of enrollment growth for public education costs at all levels were also examined using the 1.0 scenario. These costs were calculated on a per-student basis and show percentage increases equivalent to increases in enrollment, but the absolute cost increases are substantial. Total elementary and secondary school costs would increase by roughly $17.6 billion and public college and university costs would increase by $2.3 billion.

8. Projections of the number of persons attending college with levels of financial need unmet by household resources were made using the 1.0 scenario. The number of students requiring at least some form of financial assistance to pay college costs will increase faster than total enrollment. For example, enrollment increases by 101.6 percent in public community colleges and by 82.5 percent in public universities between 2000 and 2040, but the number of students with financial need unmet by household resources increases by 120.1 percent for community colleges and by 90.6 percent for public universities. Those in need are also projected to be increasingly non-Anglo. Whereas 28.7 percent of all those enrolled in 2040 would be Anglo, 8.1 percent Black, 50.9 percent Hispanic, and 12.3 percent persons from the Other racial/ethnic group, 24.2 percent of all those with at least some level of unmet need would be Anglo, 8.7 percent Black, 54.7 percent Hispanic, and 12.4 percent persons from the Other racial/ethnic group. Because of the faster growth in non-Anglo enrollment, particularly Hispanic, and the lower socioeconomic resources among non-Anglo populations, the percentage of students with the highest level of need increases. For example, the percentage of community college students with any level of unmet need in the highest level-of-need category ($7,500–$9,999) increases from 36.6 percent in 2000 to 44.5 percent in 2040 and whereas 43 percent of university students were in the highest need category ($10,000 or more) in 2000, 52 percent would be in 2040.

9. The total level of financial assistance to be provided to college students in Texas was also projected using the 1.0 scenario. The total level of financial need would increase from $671.9 million in 2000 to $1.2 billion by 2010 and to nearly $2.2 billion by 2040, a percentage increase of 219.9 percent from 2000 to 2040. This 2000 to 2040 rate of increase is larger than the projected 92.6 percent enrollment increase or the total increase in the number of persons requiring at least some level

of assistance of 105.4 percent. State aid was $164.9 million in 2000, but it is projected to be $581.1 million by 2010 and $974.5 million in 2040. This represents a 2000 to 2040 increase of 490.8 percent. The large increase between 2000 and 2010 is largely the result of assuming that the $300 million TEXAS Grant Program would be fully utilized by 2010. It increases the state's proportion of all assistance that would be required from approximately 24.5 percent in 2000 to more than 45 percent under all scenarios and years after 2010. Despite this increase, given estimated annual attendance costs of $8,200 for community colleges and $11,555 for senior colleges in 2000, the state's level of assistance of $600 to $650, and the approximately $1,200 to $1,400 in financial aid from all sources (in 2000 constant dollars), the amount students must obtain to attend college through loans, work, and other means is substantial. The total level of financial assistance required by students will increase, and the state's expenditures on financial assistance will also likely have to increase if the financial assistance requirements of Texas students are to be addressed.

The number of persons to be educated in Texas public elementary and secondary schools and public community colleges and public universities will increase in the coming years. In the absence of changes in population patterns and/or relative socioeconomic resources, the projected enrollment growth will increase: (1) the number of persons in and the associated costs of specialized educational programs; (2) total public costs for education; (3) the number of students with unmet financial need; (4) and the total level of financial assistance required by students and to be provided by the state. Educational change will represent a significant challenge for Texas in the coming decades.

CHAPTER 8

Human Services

In this chapter we examine the implications of population change for human services in Texas. Specifically, we examine the implications for three major federal-state programs: Food Stamps, Medicaid, and Temporary Assistance for Needy Families (TANF). After reviewing historical patterns of change in these programs we then project the future number of participants in each program and associated costs.

HISTORICAL PATTERNS OF HUMAN SERVICES PROGRAMS

During the past several decades, human services programs experienced unprecedented rates of growth and decline. Caseloads for TANF, Food Stamps, and Medicaid generally expanded rapidly in the late 1980s, peaked in the mid-1990s, and declined thereafter (see Figure 8.1). One result of these patterns is that by 2000 the TANF caseload in Texas was smaller than in 1975. Because of new welfare policies enacted in the mid-1990s, changes that occurred later in the decade are most critical to understanding the recent patterns of human services in Texas.

Between 1995 and 2000, the TANF caseload declined by more than 50 percent in both the United States and Texas. Similarly, Texas' Food Stamp caseload declined by almost 50 percent during the same period, while the national caseload decreased by about 35 percent. The change has not been as dramatic for Medicaid enrollment. The nation's Medicaid caseload actually increased by about 6 percent between 1995 and 2000, but Texas' Medicaid caseload declined almost 15

Figure 8.1

TANF, Food Stamp, and Medicaid Enrollment in Texas, 1980 to 2000

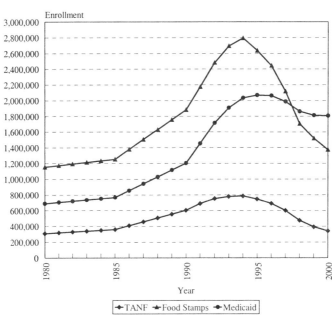

percent, falling from more than 2 million persons in 1995 to nearly 1.7 million in 2000 (see Table 8.1). Overall, Texas reduced its TANF caseload by more than half and experienced greater declines in its Food Stamp and Medicaid programs than in the United States as a whole during the latter half of the 1990s.

The reasons for these declines were twofold. First, both the federal government and the majority of states, including Texas, enacted welfare reform legislation (most notably the Federal Personal Responsibility and Work Opportunity Reconciliation Act of 1996 [U.S. Public Law 104-193, 104th Cong., 2nd sess., August 22, 1996, PRWORA] and the Texas' Achieving Change for Texas and Choices programs) that significantly altered the eligibility rules for human services. Second, the latter part of the 1990s was an unprecedented period of economic expansion. Welfare reform reduced caseloads through its emphasis on moving recipients into full-time

Table 8.1

Number and Percent Change in Enrollment for Aid to Families with Dependent Children
(AFDC)/Temporary Assistance for Needy Families (TANF), Food Stamps, and Medicaid in
the United States and Texas, 1995–2000

Area	1995	1996	1997	1998	1999	2000	Percent Change 1995-2000
Aid to Families with Dependent Children /Temporary Assistance for Needy Families							
United States	13,931,000	12,877,000	11,423,000	9,132,000	7,455,000	5,781,000	-58.5
Texas	748,178	690,021	600,128	474,755	369,938	341,691	-54.3
Food Stamps							
United States	26,619,000	25,542,000	22,858,000	19,788,000	18,183,000	17,155,000	-35.6
Texas	2,637,195	2,467,550	2,117,429	1,705,795	1,457,347	1,372,616	-48.0
Medicaid							
United States	36,281,586	36,117,956	34,872,275	40,649,482	37,958,192	38,535,065	6.2
Texas	2,039,743	2,021,795	1,934,199	1,802,307	1,733,987	1,738,452	-14.8

Sources: U.S. Department of Health and Human Services 2002a, 2000a, and 2000b; U.S. Department of
Agriculture 2002. Texas Department of Human Services 2001 and 2000.

employment and its use of stricter rules for both eligibility and
the receipt of benefits. The expanding economy reduced
caseloads through the creation of jobs that reduced the levels of
poverty for many human services recipients.

In a manner similar to caseload size, human services
expenditures declined or slowed during the late 1990s (see
Table 8.2). The changes in expenditure patterns did not,
however, necessarily parallel those for caseloads. For example,
the national TANF caseload declined almost 59 percent
between 1995 and 2000 while program expenditures actually
rose by almost 1 percent. In Texas, the TANF caseload
declined 54.3 percent and expenditures declined by 3.4 percent.
For the Food Stamp program, the U.S. caseload declined 35.6
percent compared to a 37.4 percent reduction in expenditures.
In Texas, the Food Stamp caseload decreased 48 percent and
expenditures fell 42.8 percent. The U.S. Medicaid program's
caseload increased 6.2 percent and expenditures went up 20.3
percent between 1995 and 2000. Texas, on the other hand, had
a 14.8 percent decline in its Medicaid caseload, but program
expenditures increased by 8.9 percent.

Because costs either decreased less or actually increased
while the number of recipients declined rapidly, costs per

Table 8.2

Federal and Texas' Expenditures for Aid to Families with Dependent Children (AFDC)/Temporary Assistance for Needy Families (TANF), Food Stamps, and Medicaid (in Millions of 2000 Dollars), and Per-Recipient Costs in Texas, 1995–2000

Area	1995	1996	1997	1998	1999	2000	Percent Change 1995-2000
Aid to Families with Dependent Children /Temporary Assistance for Needy Families							
United States	$ 16,978.1	$ 15,766.0	$ 15,997.9	$ 18,265.2	$ 17,344.7	$ 17,136.5	0.9
Texas total	827.6	679.8	841.6	798.1	794.8	799.1	-3.4
Federal costs	524.0	423.5	571.8	532.5	534.9	547.7	4.5
Texas state costs	303.7	256.3	269.8	265.6	259.9	251.4	-17.2
Texas annual costs per recipient	405.85	371.43	449.52	559.52	702.53	735.87	81.3
Food Stamps							
United States	$ 27,891.8	$ 26,745.3	$ 23,122.1	$ 20,202.3	$ 18,991.0	$ 17,461.1	-37.4
Texas total	2,886.8	2,672.1	2,212.5	1,810.7	1,689.9	1,650.5	-42.8
Federal costs	2,712.5	2,510.5	2,062.5	1,658.0	1,499.4	1,432.8	-47.2
Texas state costs	174.3	161.6	150.0	152.7	190.5	217.6	24.9
Texas annual costs per recipient	66.09	65.51	70.83	89.50	130.71	158.56	139.9
Medicaid							
United States	$ 100,459.7	$ 101,211.6	$ 102,187.0	$ 104,869.6	$ 114,583.8	$ 120,898.7	20.3
Texas total	10,375.8	10,405.4	10,334.0	10,956.5	11,897.0	11,295.7	8.9
Federal costs	6,568.9	6,482.5	6,464.9	6,823.7	7,429.7	6,931.1	5.5
Texas state costs	3,806.9	3,922.8	3,869.0	4,132.8	4,467.3	4,364.7	14.7
Texas annual costs per recipient	1,866.36	1,940.27	2,000.34	2,293.06	2,576.33	2,510.67	34.5

Sources: U.S. Census Bureau 2002b and 2000; U.S. Department of Health and Human Services 2002b and 2001.

recipient increased in Texas for all three human services programs from 1995 to 2000. For example, between 1995 and 2000, Texas' costs per recipient rose 81.3 percent for TANF, 139.9 percent for the Food Stamp program, and 34.5 percent for Medicaid. By the year 2000, the state was spending $735.87 for TANF, $158.56 for Food Stamp, and $2,510.67 for each Medicaid recipient. Much of the increase in costs per recipient can be traced to increasing program costs. For example, welfare reform initiated a variety of employment services for TANF recipients, and Medicaid costs were affected by increases in the cost of medical services.

In summary, federal and state policy changes resulted in a decline in human services caseloads in Texas during the latter half of the 1990s. At the same time, total expenditures either increased or declined more slowly than caseloads and Texas' expenditures per recipient increased. As a result, although this was a period of unprecedented caseload decline, human services continued to represent a large component in the state's budget. In 2000, about a third of the state's budget was spent on health and human services programs (see Table 4.4), more than was spent on any functional area other than education. In spite of recent caseload declines, human services remain an important component in the state's system of revenues and expenditures. Because of such patterns, it is clearly important to understand how changes in Texas' population may impact the future demand for human services.

PROJECTING HUMAN SERVICES ENROLLMENTS AND COSTS

The projections of human services enrollments discussed in this chapter were completed using the average of 1999–2001 age-, sex-, and race/ethnicity-specific enrollment rates computed from data provided by the Texas Department of Human Services (TDHS) (2001a). These values were divided by 2000 data from the 2000 Census to produce age-, sex-, and race/ethnicity-specific participation rates. The participation rates so obtained were then applied to the population projections used throughout this volume to obtain projections of future caseload populations assuming that the 2000 participation rates continue throughout the projection period. The projections of the number of participants were then used with per capita cost estimates (Texas Department of Human Services 2001) to project program costs. As with other projections in this volume, the projections presented in this chapter are intended only to explore the implications of long-term trends. They are not as inclusive as those provided by the Texas Health and Human Services Commission (THHSC) for short-term planning purposes.

PROJECTIONS OF FUTURE DEMANDS FOR HUMAN SERVICES PROGRAMS

Projections of human services programs by race/ethnicity and program are shown in Tables 8.3–8.5. Given the participation, programmatic, administrative, and other differences in these programs, we provide projections of the number of participants for each of the three programs separately. Due to space limitations we provide projections for only the 1.0 scenario.

Projections of TANF Recipients
The data in Table 8.3 (Panels A and B) show increases in TANF participation from 405,287 recipients in 2000 to 1,008,932 by 2040, an increase of 148.9 percent. The growth in TANF is thus projected to be about the same as the increase in the population of 142.6 percent.

The population of recipients will reflect general population change in that percentage increases are larger for Hispanics and persons from the Other racial/ethnic group and smaller for Blacks and Anglos. In fact, because of decreased rates of population growth, the number of Anglo recipients declines and the number of Black recipients increases from 2000 to 2040 by 22.3 percent. The number of Hispanics increases by 260 percent and the number of persons from the Other racial/ethnic group increases by 355.8 percent. As a result, by 2040 the percentages of Anglo, Black, Hispanic, and Other recipients are expected to be 5.9, 14, 78.6, and 1.5, respectively. These compare to 16.4 percent of Anglo, 28.5 percent of Black, 54.3 percent of Hispanic, and 0.8 percent of Other racial/ethnic group recipients in 2000 (see Panel C). Hispanics are projected to be an increasing proportion of all recipients and to account for at least 94 percent of all net additions to the number of recipients between 2000 and 2040 (see Panel D).

Projections of Food Stamp Recipients
The number of Food Stamp recipients will increase more rapidly than the number of TANF recipients, going from 1,007,067 recipients in 2000 to 3,229,632 (see Table 8.4 Panel A). This represents an increase from 2000 to 2040 of 220.7 percent, which is significantly larger than the 142.6 percent population increase or the 148.9 percent increase in the number

Table 8.3

Temporary Assistance for Needy Families (TANF) Enrollment in Texas, Percent
Change in Enrollment, Percent of Enrollment by Race/Ethnicity, and Net Change
in Enrollment, Using the Population Projection That Assumes 1990–2000 Rates of
Net Migration (1.0 Scenario), 2000–40

Year/Period	Anglo	Black	Hispanic	Other	Total
Panel A: TANF Enrollment					
2000	66,215	115,626	220,165	3,281	405,287
2010	67,744	125,651	319,685	5,164	518,244
2020	66,264	135,526	448,194	7,473	657,457
2030	62,971	139,129	601,647	10,657	814,404
2040	59,917	141,456	792,604	14,955	1,008,932
Panel B: Percent Change in Projected TANF Enrollment					
2000–10	2.3	8.7	45.2	57.4	27.9
2010–20	-2.2	7.9	40.2	44.7	26.9
2020–30	-5.0	2.7	34.2	42.6	23.9
2030–40	-4.8	1.7	31.7	40.3	23.9
2000–40	-9.5	22.3	260.0	355.8	148.9
Panel C: Percent of TANF Enrollment by Race/Ethnicity					
2000	16.4	28.5	54.3	0.8	100.0
2010	13.1	24.2	61.7	1.0	100.0
2020	10.1	20.6	68.2	1.1	100.0
2030	7.7	17.1	73.9	1.3	100.0
2040	5.9	14.0	78.6	1.5	100.0

Panel D: Number and Percent of Net Change in TANF Enrollment, 2000–40		
	Number	Percent
Anglo	-6,298	-1.0
Black	25,830	4.3
Hispanic	572,439	94.8
Other	11,674	1.9
Total	603,645	100.0

Sources: Derived by the authors from Texas Population Estimates and Projections Program
2001; Texas Department of Human Services 1999–2001a.

of TANF recipients. This change reflects the fact that rates of
participation in the Food Stamp program are higher among
Texas' fastest growing population group, Hispanics, and to a
lesser extent among persons from the Other racial/ethnic group.

As with the data for the TANF program, the Food Stamps
data show that the program's recipients will increasingly be
non-Anglos, particularly Hispanic. The 2000 to 2040 increases
are 8.5 percent for Anglos, 46.4 percent for Blacks, 318.6
percent for Hispanics, and 1,436.8 percent for persons from the
Other racial/ethnic group (see Panel B). By 2040, 6.2 percent of
Anglo, 9.1 percent of Black, 79.2 percent of Hispanic, and 5.5
percent of persons from the Other racial/ethnic group are
expected to be recipients (see Panel C). This compares to 18.3
percent of Anglos, 19.9 percent of Blacks, 60.6 percent of

Table 8.4

Food Stamp Recipients in Texas, Percent Change in Recipients, Percent of Recipients
by Race/Ethnicity, and Net Change in Recipients, Using the Population Projection
That Assumes 1990–2000 Rates of Net Migration (1.0 Scenario), 2000–40

Year/Period	Anglo	Black	Hispanic	Other	Total
Panel A: Food Stamp Recipients					
2000	184,521	199,980	610,921	11,645	1,007,067
2010	200,005	229,812	929,245	24,108	1,383,170
2020	205,572	257,781	1,343,312	50,218	1,856,883
2030	204,578	277,960	1,871,591	99,488	2,453,617
2040	200,270	292,829	2,557,578	178,955	3,229,632
Panel B: Percent Change in Projected Food Stamp Recipients					
2000–10	8.4	14.9	52.1	107.0	37.3
2010–20	2.8	12.2	44.6	108.3	34.2
2020–30	-0.5	7.8	39.3	98.1	32.1
2030–40	-2.1	5.3	36.7	79.9	31.6
2000–40	8.5	46.4	318.6	1,436.8	220.7
Panel C: Percent of Food Stamp Recipients by Race/Ethnicity					
2000	18.3	19.9	60.6	1.2	100.0
2010	14.5	16.6	67.2	1.7	100.0
2020	11.1	13.9	72.3	2.7	100.0
2030	8.3	11.3	76.3	4.1	100.0
2040	6.2	9.1	79.2	5.5	100.0

Panel D: Number and Percent of Net Change in Food Stamp Recipients, 2000–40

	Number	Percent
Anglo	15,749	0.7
Black	92,849	4.2
Hispanic	1,946,657	87.6
Other	167,310	7.5
Total	2,222,565	100.0

Sources: Derived by the authors from Texas Population Estimates and Projections Program
2001; Texas Department of Human Services 1999–2001a.

Hispanics, and 1.2 percent from the Other racial/ethnic group
in 2000 (see Panel C). Of the total net change in the number of
Food Stamp recipients from 2000 to 2040, 99.3 or more
percent would come from non-Anglo populations, including
87.6 percent that would be due to Hispanic recipients (see
Panel D).

Projections of Medicaid Recipients

Medicaid enrollment would be substantially larger than
enrollment in any other human services program and would
show rates of growth greater than TANF but less than Food
Stamps. The total number of Medicaid recipients will increase
(see Table 8.5 Panel A) from 1,886,937 in 2000 to 5,319,029 in
2040 (compared to 2040 TANF enrollment of 1,008,932 and

Food Stamp enrollment of 3,229,632, respectively). This is an increase of 181.9 percent (compared to increases of 148.9 percent for TANF and 220.7 percent for Food Stamps).

As with other human services programs, Medicaid enrollment will reflect the increasing involvement of non-Anglo populations, but the Anglo population will retain a higher level of involvement than for either TANF or Food Stamps. For example, Anglo enrollment is projected to increase by 30.5 percent from 2000 to 2040, Black enrollment by 58.9 percent, Hispanic enrollment by 300.3 percent, and the enrollment of persons from the Other racial/ethnic group by 978.6 percent (see Panel B). However, the number of Anglo recipients is expected to decline from 2000 to 2040 for TANF and increase by only 8.5 percent for Food Stamps. As a result of such patterns, although enrollment in the Medicaid program shows rapid increases in the percentage of Hispanics and persons from the Other racial/ethnic group, the changes are less dramatic than those for TANF and Food Stamps. By 2040 (see Panel C), the Medicaid population would be 12.5 percent Anglo, 12.8 percent Black, 69.6 percent Hispanic, and 5.1 percent persons from the Other racial/ethnic group (these compare to 2040 percentages of 5.9, 14, 78.6, and 1.5 percent for TANF and 6.2, 9.1, 79.2, and 5.5 percent for Food Stamps for the same groups). Although Anglo involvement in the Medicaid program is projected to be roughly twice the percentage that it is in the other human services programs, it is still evident that non-Anglo populations will come to increasingly dominate the number of Medicaid participants, as in the TANF and Food Stamp programs. Between 2000 and 2040 (see Panel D), more than 95 percent of the net additions to the number of Medicaid recipients would be non-Anglo, including an 81.1 percent Hispanic increase.

In sum, the data on projected enrollment in the TANF, Food Stamp, and Medicaid programs show rapid increases in the number of persons enrolled in each of them. Although TANF programs are projected to increase at about the same

Table 8.5

Medicaid Recipients in Texas, Percent Change in Recipients, Percent of Recipients
by Race/Ethnicity, and Net Change in Recipients, Using the Population Projection
That Assumes 1990–2000 Rates of Net Migration (1.0 Scenario), 2000–40

Year/Period	Anglo	Black	Hispanic	Other	Total
Panel A: Medicaid Recipients					
2000	508,077	428,061	925,836	24,963	1,886,937
2010	546,054	485,930	1,333,515	33,572	2,399,071
2020	585,850	553,460	1,907,489	69,686	3,116,485
2030	631,453	623,279	2,676,028	143,793	4,074,553
2040	663,170	680,220	3,706,383	269,256	5,319,029
Panel B: Percent Change in Projected Medicaid Recipients					
2000–10	7.5	13.5	44.0	34.5	27.1
2010–20	7.3	13.9	43.0	107.6	29.9
2020–30	7.8	12.6	40.3	106.3	30.7
2030–40	5.0	9.1	38.5	87.3	30.5
2000–40	30.5	58.9	300.3	978.6	181.9
Panel C: Percent of Medicaid Recipients by Race/Ethnicity					
2000	26.9	22.7	49.1	1.3	100.0
2010	22.8	20.3	55.5	1.4	100.0
2020	18.8	17.8	61.2	2.2	100.0
2030	15.5	15.3	65.7	3.5	100.0
2040	12.5	12.8	69.6	5.1	100.0

Panel D: Number and Percent of Net Change in Medicaid Recipients, 2000–40

	Number	Percent
Anglo	155,093	4.5
Black	252,159	7.3
Hispanic	2,780,547	81.1
Other	244,293	7.1
Total	3,432,092	100.0

Sources: Derived by the authors from Texas Population Estimates and Projections Program
2001; Texas Department of Human Services 1999–2001a.

rate as the total population, Food Stamp and Medicaid enrollments would increase more rapidly than the total population because of the high rates of involvement in these programs of the fastest growing segments of Texas's population. Nevertheless, despite program differences, the absolute levels of growth will be extensive. The 2000 to 2040 increases would be more than six hundred thousand for TANF, more than 2.2 million for Food Stamps, and more than 3.4 million for Medicaid. The enrollment in all of these programs will increasingly involve non-Anglo, particularly Hispanic, participants. As a result, the delivery system is likely to generate additional requirements due to language and other factors. The growth in human services programs is likely to challenge the state if the factors leading to the use of such programs do not change in the coming years.

COST IMPLICATIONS OF CHANGE IN HUMAN SERVICES PROGRAMS

The application of 2000 per-recipient costs to the number of projected recipients shown in Tables 8.3–8.5 provides a projection of total expenditures for these programs per year in 2000 constant dollars (see Table 8.6). Because the costs shown are projected on a per-recipient basis, the percentage changes in costs are identical to those for the percentage increases in the number of recipients. The total and state costs for these

Table 8.6

Total Costs and State Costs (in 2000 Dollars) for TANF, Food Stamps, and Medicaid in Texas by Race/Ethnicity of Recipient in 2000 and Projections to 2040 Using the Population Projection That Assumes 1990–2000 Rates of Net Migration (1.0 Scenario)

Year	Anglo	Black	Hispanic	Other	Total
			Panel A: TANF		
Total Costs					
2000	$ 130,557,157	$ 227,981,602	$ 434,102,792	$ 6,469,199	$ 799,110,750
2010	133,571,910	247,748,052	630,327,941	10,181,940	1,021,829,843
2040	118,139,291	278,911,019	1,562,789,768	29,487,009	1,989,327,087
State Costs					
2000	$ 41,079,908	$ 71,734,584	$ 136,590,773	$ 2,035,538	$ 251,440,803
2010	42,028,503	77,954,113	198,333,165	3,203,755	321,519,536
2040	37,172,618	87,759,564	491,732,987	9,278,110	625,943,279
			Panel B: Food Stamps		
Total Costs					
2000	$ 302,406,929	$ 327,742,303	$ 1,001,223,401	$ 19,084,704	$ 1,650,457,337
2010	327,783,275	376,633,234	1,522,916,775	39,510,008	2,266,843,292
2040	328,217,577	479,910,246	4,191,551,679	293,284,948	5,292,964,450
State Costs					
2000	$ 39,878,897	$ 43,219,915	$ 132,032,971	$ 2,516,731	$ 217,648,514
2010	43,225,318	49,667,242	200,829,532	5,210,250	298,932,342
2040	43,282,590	63,286,551	552,746,792	38,675,967	697,991,900
			Panel C: Medicaid		
Total Costs					
2000	$ 3,041,494,340	$ 2,562,495,662	$ 5,542,319,281	$ 149,435,663	$ 11,295,744,946
2010	3,268,835,531	2,908,916,059	7,982,802,458	200,971,601	14,361,525,649
2040	3,969,925,427	4,071,991,607	22,187,469,449	1,611,843,480	31,841,229,963
State Costs					
2000	$ 1,175,233,413	$ 990,148,324	$ 2,141,552,170	$ 57,741,940	$ 4,364,675,847
2010	1,263,078,049	1,124,005,165	3,084,554,870	77,655,427	5,549,293,511
2040	1,533,979,185	1,573,417,557	8,573,238,195	622,816,321	12,303,451,258

Sources: Derived by the authors from Texas Population Estimates and Projections Program 2001; Texas Department of Human Services 1999–2001a and 1999–2001b; U.S. Census Bureau 2002b and 2000; U.S. Department of Health and Human Services 2002b.

programs will be substantial. Under the 1.0 scenario, these increases in state costs would be roughly $375 million for TANF, $480 million for Food Stamps, and more than $7.9 billion for Medicaid.

Taken together, the data in Tables 8.3–8.6 suggest extensive increases in the number of human services recipients in Texas. This growth in the state's demand for human services will likely require increases in the personnel and facilities needed to deliver these services and in their costs.

SUMMARY

In this chapter we have examined the implications of population change for human services in Texas. These include the implications for TANF, Food Stamps, and Medicaid. The results suggest:

1. During the latter part of the 1990s, human services programs showed dramatic changes as a result of welfare reform legislation and waivers enacted at both the federal and state levels. As a result, between 1995 and 2000, the TANF caseload declined by more than 50 percent for both the United States and Texas, and Texas' Food Stamp caseload declined by almost 50 percent compared to a roughly 35 percent decrease for the nation. The number of Medicaid recipients nationwide increased by about 6 percent between 1995 and 2000, while Texas' Medicaid caseload declined almost 15 percent, falling from some 2 million persons in 1995 to about 1.7 million in 2000. During the latter half of the 1990s, Texas reduced its TANF caseload by more than half and experienced greater declines in its Food Stamp and Medicaid programs than those that occurred in the nation as a whole.

2. Human services expenditures declined or slowed during the latter part of the 1990s but did not necessarily parallel those for caseloads. Although the TANF caseload in the United States declined almost 59 percent between 1995 and 2000, expenditures rose by almost 1 percent. Texas' TANF caseload

declined 54.3 percent in the 1995–2000 period while expenditures declined by 3.4 percent. For the Food Stamp program, the U.S. caseload declined 35.6 percent and expenditures fell 37.4 percent. At the same time, Texas' Food Stamp caseload decreased 48 percent and expenditures declined 42.8 percent. The Medicaid program experienced a nationwide caseload increase of 6.2 percent but a 20.3 percent increase in expenditures between 1995 and 2000. In Texas, which had a 14.8 percent decline in its Medicaid caseload during the same period, program expenditures increased by 8.9 percent. Because costs either decreased less or in some cases increased while the number of recipients declined rapidly, Texas saw costs per recipient increase. Between 1995 and 2000, the state's per-recipient costs rose 81.3 percent for TANF, 139.9 percent for Food Stamps, and 34.5 percent for Medicaid to per-recipient costs of $735.87 for TANF, $158.56 for Food Stamps, and $2,510.67 for Medicaid.

3. The projected number of TANF recipients will increase from 405,287 recipients in 2000 to 1,008,932 by 2040, a percentage increase of 148.9 percent, about the same as the 142.6 percent increase in the population. The number of Anglo recipients will decline and the number of Black recipients will increase by 22.3 percent from 2000 to 2040. The number of Hispanics will increase by 260 percent and the number of persons from the Other racial/ethnic group by 355.8 percent. By 2040 the percentage of recipients who would be Anglo, Black, Hispanic, and Other will be 5.9, 14, 78.6, and 1.5 percent, respectively.

4. The number of Food Stamp recipients will increase more rapidly than the number of TANF recipients, increasing from 1,007,067 recipients in 2000 to 3,229,632 recipients by 2040. This represents an increase of 220.7 percent, an increase that is significantly larger than the 142.6 percent increase in population or the 148.9 percent increase in the number of TANF recipients. Percentage increases from 2000 to 2040 are

projected to be 8.5 for Anglos, 46.4 for Blacks, 318.6 for Hispanics, and 1,436.8 for persons from the Other racial/ethnic group. By 2040, the Food Stamp population would be 6.2 percent Anglo, 9.1 percent Black, 79.2 percent Hispanic, and 5.5 percent persons from the Other racial/ethnic group.

5. Medicaid enrollment would be substantially larger than that in any other human services program. The total number of Medicaid recipients increases from 1,886,937 in 2000 to 5,319,029 in 2040. The increase in the number of Medicaid recipients is 181.9 percent (compared to increases of 148.9 percent for TANF and 220.7 percent for Food Stamps). By 2040, the Medicaid population would be 12.5 percent Anglo, 12.8 percent Black, 69.6 percent Hispanic, and 5.1 percent persons from the Other racial/ethnic group.

6. The application of 2000 per-recipient costs to the number of projected recipients shows that the total and state costs for these programs may be substantial. Under the 1.0 scenario, the increases in state costs from 2000 to 2040 would be roughly $375 million for TANF, $480 million for Food Stamps, and more than $7.9 billion for Medicaid.

Overall, the projections point to a dramatically changing historical environment for human services programs in Texas, with resulting uncertainty for their future. The projections presented here show that nearly 9.6 million persons will be involved in these programs by 2040, compared to about 3.3 million in 2000. The number of new enrollees and the associated costs will substantially impact the resources needed to provide these services to Texans.

CHAPTER 9

Youth Correctional Services and the Prison System

In this chapter we examine the implication of population change for the number of persons in Texas adult prisons and youth correctional facilities. After briefly describing recent trends in the populations in such facilities, we provide projections of the number of Texas residents in the facilities. We then examine the cost implications of the projections.

HISTORICAL TRENDS IN TEXAS CORRECTIONAL POPULATIONS

According to 2000 Census data (U.S. Census Bureau 2001b), Texas ranked second in the nation in the number of people in correctional institutions and first in terms of incarceration rates. Moreover, the numbers of persons involved in the Texas juvenile correction system and in the adult prison system have grown rapidly: more than doubling the population in the juvenile correction system from 1979 to 1999 and quintupling the number in the adult prison system during the same period. Between 1979 and 1999, the population in the state's juvenile correctional facilities increased by 155.1 percent compared to 51.5 percent for the nation and Texas' adult prison population increased by 414.2 percent from 1980 to 2000, compared to a 310.6 percent increase in the nation (see Table 9.1).

Data on the demographic and offense characteristics of juvenile and adult offenders (see Tables 9.2 and 9.3) reveal that while many of the characteristics of offenders remained relatively stable across time, there are some exceptions. The

Table 9.1

Number and Percent Change in Persons in Juvenile Facilities
in Texas, Adults in State Prisons in Texas, and Juveniles and Adults
in Prisons in the United States, 1979–99 and 1980–2000

	Juvenile Offenders					
	Year			Percent Change		
Area	1979	1989	1999	1979–89	1989–99	1979–99
Texas	3,118	4,396	7,954	41.0	80.9	155.1
United States	71,922	93,945	108,931	30.6	16.0	51.5

	Adult Offenders					
	Year			Percent Change		
Area	1980	1990	2000	1980–90	1990–2000	1980–2000
Texas	28,543	49,157	146,761	72.2	198.6	414.2
United States	319,598	743,382	1,312,354	132.6	76.5	310.6

Sources: U.S. Department of Justice 1988, 1989, 1992a, 1992b, 1994, 2001a, 2002.
Texas Department of Criminal Justice 1981, 1991, 2001, and 2002.

percentage of all youth offenders who were Black showed a
decline from 1990 to 2000, while the percentages of those who
were Anglo, Hispanic, and members of the Other racial/ethnic
group increased. Additionally, the age at commitment was
generally older in 2000 than in 1990. For adult offenders, the
aging of prison populations is apparent: there was a 6.6 percent
proportional decrease in offenders under 25 years of age, a 7.1
percent decrease in the proportion of 25- to 29-year-olds, and a
4.8 percent decrease in the percentage of 30- to 34-year-olds.
On the other hand, the proportion of 35- to 39-year-olds
increased by 3.5 percent, the proportion of 40- to 59-year-olds
by 14.3 percent, and the proportion of all prisoners 60 years of
age or older by 0.7 percent. The 1990–2000 data suggest
stability in the proportions of Anglo and Other prisoners and a
decline in the percentage of Black prisoners, matched by a
nearly equal increase in the proportion of Hispanic prisoners.

Table 9.3 shows the characteristics of offenses committed
by adults. These data show an increase in the total percentage
of inmates imprisoned for violent offenses from 44.8 percent in

Table 9.2

Percent of Juvenile and Adult Offenders in Texas by
Selected Demographic Characteristics, 1990 and 2000

Characteristic	1990	2000
Panel A: Juvenile Offenders		
Age at Commitment to Texas Youth Commission Facilities		
<12	2.0	1.2
13	5.8	4.8
14	15.8	13.6
15	32.2	25.9
16	37.9	39.7
17	6.3	14.4
18+	0.0	0.4
Total Number	2,171	2,558
Persons Admitted to Texas Youth Commission Facilities by Race/Ethnicity [a]		
Anglo	21.8	25.2
Black	40.2	33.6
Hispanic	37.3	40.2
Other	0.7	1.0
Total Number	2,171	2,558
Panel B: Adult Offenders		
Age of Inmates On-Hand [b]		
<25	23.4	16.8
25–29	23.9	16.8
30–34	21.7	16.9
35–39	14.2	17.7
40–59	15.7	30.0
60+	1.1	1.8
Total Number	49,157	146,761
Inmates On-Hand by Race/Ethnicity [b]		
Anglo	30.8	30.7
Black	47.2	43.8
Hispanic	21.6	25.1
Other	0.4	0.4
Total Number	49,157	146,761

Sources: Texas Department of Criminal Justice 1991 and 2001; Texas Youth Commission 1990, 2002b, and 2002c.

[a]Data do not include recommitments, revocation, or reclassifications. Data do include VCP (violator of CINS probation) admissions.

[b]On-hand counts are one-day counts as of August 31 for all years.

1990 to 49 percent in 2000. The percentage imprisoned for property crimes decreased by 10.6 percent, the proportion imprisoned for drug-related offenses increased by 1.2 percent, and the proportion in the other and unclassified offense category increased by 5.2 percent.

Table 9.3

Percent of Inmates On-Hand in Adult Correctional
Facilities in Texas by Offense Category, 1990 and 2000

Offense	1990	2000
Violent		
Homicide	11.9	10.4
Kidnapping	0.9	0.8
Sexual Assault	9.9	11.2
Robbery	17.6	16.8
Assault	4.5	9.8
Total	44.8	49.0
Property		
Arson	0.5	0.5
Burglary	20.2	14.5
Larceny	4.7	2.7
Stolen Vehicle	3.4	1.6
Forgery	2.2	1.3
Fraud	0.5	0.4
Total	31.5	20.9
Drugs		
Total	18.7	19.9
Other and Unclassified Offenses		
Sex Offense	1.7	2.5
Escape	0.4	0.5
Weapons	0.5	1.2
Traffic/DWI	1.2	4.4
Public Order Crime	0.4	0.6
All Other	0.0	0.4
Unknown	0.8	0.5
Total	5.0	10.2
Total Number of Inmates	49,157	133,680

Sources: Texas Department of Criminal Justice 1991 and 2001.

Note: All counts are for August 31.

The state's juvenile and adult corrections systems have shown a rapid increase in the number of persons within them. Although some changes in the characteristics of these populations are evident, it is the large increases in the number of persons in the systems that are the most notable among recent changes.

PROJECTIONS OF THE YOUTH FACILITY AND ADULT PRISON POPULATIONS

Projections of the future populations in the Texas Youth Commission (TYC) and Texas State Prison systems were completed using rates of involvement for youth and rates of incarceration for adults, derived from the number of persons in each of the systems at a given time. The projections shown for TYC populations are of all persons involved in both residential and other types of programs. To project the number of youth in TYC programs, age-, sex-, and race/ethnicity-specific rates were developed based on year-end (August 31) populations in TYC facilities (Texas Youth Commission 2002a). Because of substantial year-to-year fluctuations, average values for the three years of 1999, 2000, and 2001 were used and divided by 2000 population values.

The projections for adults include only the number of Texas residents incarcerated in state prison facilities and do not include persons on parole, those in nonstate prisons, or other persons involved in other parts of the criminal justice system. Adult state prison incarceration rates were developed using 2000 data obtained from the Texas Department of Criminal Justice (2002) on the number and characteristics of on-hand prisoners in 2000. These values were divided by the appropriate 2000 population values to create age-, sex-, and race/ethnicity-specific incarceration rates and then applied to population projections categorized by age, sex, and race/ethnicity to obtain projections of the future number of prisoners in the Texas State Prison system. In sum, we project the number of persons who would be incarcerated, assuming that the 2000 rates of incarceration by age, sex, and race/ethnicity prevail during the projection period.

After projecting the number of persons involved in each of the two correctional systems, we next examined the cost implications of the projected changes in the number of participants. The projected costs for maintaining youths in TYC programs and prisoners in the Texas State Prison system were derived using 2000 per-youth and per-prisoner costs and assuming that these will remain constant over the projection period. All projections shown are in 2000 dollars. Costs associated with capital construction and other nonmaintenance costs were not projected. Adult prison costs were obtained from the Criminal Justice Policy Council (2001), which is mandated to estimate such costs. The costs were estimated as $40.65 per day or $14,837.25 per year in 2000. Youth costs were compiled from data obtained from the Criminal Justice Policy Council. Because our projections of TYC populations are of all those involved in TYC programs, whether in residential or other programs, we used an aggregated value of per-participant costs for projecting total TYC costs, computing an overall per-participant cost from cost estimates for different programs and the distribution of TYC youth in different types of programs in 2000. Using this sum entails the assumption that the relative mix of youths involved in the TYC programs by type of program will remain the same across the projection period. For 2000, these costs were estimated at $30,442.49 per youth per year.

As with other projections presented here, these should be seen as simply exemplary and not as substitutes for the more detailed and refined projections completed by the Texas Department of Criminal Justice, the Texas Youth Commission, or the Texas Criminal Justice Policy Council. The projections from these agencies are preferable for short-term planning purposes. Due to space limitations only projections for the 1.0 scenario are provided.

PROJECTIONS OF THE NUMBER OF PERSONS IN TYC FACILITIES

As shown in Table 9.4 (Panel A), the number of youths in TYC programs is projected to increase from 8,603 in 2000 to 17,118 in 2040. This value represents an increase from 2000 to 2040 of 99 percent. The projected rate of growth is smaller than that for the total population, reflecting the slowing growth of the juvenile age group in the population.

The data in Panel B of Table 9.4 show rapid growth in the number of Hispanics and those from the Other racial/ethnic group, the number of Anglos declines 14.6 percent, and Blacks

Table 9.4

Texas Youth Commission (TYC) Population in Texas, Percent Change in
Population, Percent of Population by Race/Ethnicity, and Net Change
in Population Using the Population Projection That Assumes 1990–2000
Rates of Net Migration (1.0 Scenario), 2000–40

Year/Period	Anglo	Black	Hispanic	Other	Total
Panel A: TYC Population					
2000	1,978	2,925	3,358	342	8,603
2010	1,969	3,554	4,582	529	10,634
2030	1,814	3,532	8,220	958	14,524
2040	1,689	3,557	10,592	1,280	17,118
Panel B: Percent Change in Projected TYC Population					
2000–10	-0.5	21.5	36.5	54.7	23.6
2010–20	-4.7	-5.8	28.1	38.0	11.2
2030–40	-6.9	0.7	28.9	33.6	17.9
2000–40	-14.6	21.6	215.4	274.3	99.0
Panel C: Percent of TYC Population by Race/Ethnicity					
2000	23.0	34.0	39.0	4.0	100.0
2010	18.5	33.4	43.1	5.0	100.0
2030	12.5	24.3	56.6	6.6	100.0
2040	9.9	20.8	61.8	7.5	100.0

**Panel D: Number and Percent of Net Change in
TYC Population, 2000–40**

	Number	Percent
Anglo	-289	-3.4
Black	632	7.4
Hispanic	7,234	85.0
Other	938	11.0
Total	8,515	100.0

Sources: Derived by the authors from Texas Population Estimates and Projections
Program 2001; Texas Youth Commission 2002a.

show a 21.6 percent increase. The number of Hispanics
increases by 215.4 percent, while the number of persons from
the Other racial/ethnic group increases by 274.3 percent. As a
result of such differentials, the proportion of Anglos declines
from 23 percent in 2000 to 9.9 percent in 2040, the percentage
of Blacks declines from 34 percent in 2000 to 20.8 percent in
2040; the percentage of Hispanics increases from 39 percent in
2000 to 61.8 percent; and the number of persons from the
Other racial/ethnic group increases from 4 percent in 2000 to
7.5 percent by 2040 (see Panel C). Hispanics would account for
85 percent of the net increase of 8,515 youth expected from

2000 to 2040, persons from the Other racial/ethnic group would account for 11 percent of the increase, and Blacks would account for 7.4 percent of the increase, while the number of Anglos in TYC programs would decline by 3.4 percent (see Panel D).

Overall, projections of the number of persons in TYC programs imply levels of growth slower than the projected population growth in the state and an increasing concentration of non-Anglo youth. Although growth is projected to be slower than that in the population, the results suggest that by 2040 the Texas Youth Commission may need a capacity capable of handling 99 percent more youth than were served in 2000.

PROJECTIONS OF PRISON POPULATIONS

Table 9.5 presents projections of the adult prison population. These data suggest that, under the 1.0 scenario, the number of persons incarcerated in state prisons could increase substantially if 2000 rates of incarceration continue for the next forty years. From the 151,868 prisoners in 2000, the number of persons incarcerated is projected to increase to 340,723 in 2040, an increase of 124.4 percent. This rate is less than the overall rate of projected population growth of 142.6 percent under the 1.0 scenario.

As is evident from the data in Panel B of Table 9.5, prisons will continue to show an increase in their non-Anglo populations. The number of Blacks would increase by 62.2 percent, the number of Hispanics by 386.5 percent, the number of persons from the Other racial/ethnic group by 339.7 percent, and the number of Anglos would decline by 4.5 percent.

As a result of such patterns, the percentage of the prison population composed of Anglos would decline from 30.9 percent in 2000 to 13.1 percent in 2040, while the percentage of Blacks would decline from 43.5 percent in 2000 to 31.5 percent by 2040; the percentage of Hispanics would increase from 25.2 percent in 2000 to 54.6 percent; and the percentage of persons from the Other racial/ethnic group would increase

Table 9.5

Prison Population in Texas, Percent Change in Prison Population,
Percent of Population by Race/Ethnicity, and Net Change in Population
Using the Population Projection That Assumes 1990–2000 Rates of Net
Migration (1.0 Scenario), 2000–40

Year/Period	Anglo	Black	Hispanic	Other	Total
Panel A: Texas Prison Population					
2000	46,910	66,124	38,235	599	151,868
2010	46,887	79,059	62,782	899	189,627
2030	45,915	101,105	135,186	1,931	284,137
2040	44,785	107,286	186,018	2,634	340,723
Panel B: Percent Change in Projected Texas Prison Population					
2000–10	0.0	19.6	64.2	50.1	24.9
2010–20	-1.0	16.2	51.6	48.9	23.8
2030–40	-2.5	6.1	37.6	36.4	19.9
2000–40	-4.5	62.2	386.5	339.7	124.4
Panel C: Percent of Texas Prison Population by Race/Ethnicity					
2000	30.9	43.5	25.2	0.4	100.0
2010	24.7	41.7	33.1	0.5	100.0
2030	16.1	35.6	47.6	0.7	100.0
2040	13.1	31.5	54.6	0.8	100.0

**Panel D: Number and Percent of Net Change
in Prison Population, 2000–40**

	Number	Percent
Anglo	-2,125	-1.2
Black	41,162	21.8
Hispanic	147,783	78.3
Other	2,035	1.1
Total	188,855	100.0

Sources: Derived by the authors from Texas Population Estimates and Projections
Program 2001; Texas Department of Criminal Justice 2002.

from 0.4 percent in 2000 to 0.8 percent by 2040 (see Panel C).
All of the net increase in the number of prisoners expected to
occur from 2000 to 2040 would be accounted for by non-
Anglos (the percentage of the net change due to Anglos is -1.2
percent), with Blacks accounting for approximately 21.8
percent, Hispanics 78.3 percent, and persons from the Other
racial/ethnic group 1.1 percent (see Panel D). With nearly 87
percent of the prisoners projected to be members of non-Anglo
groups in 2040, and all of the net increase from 2000 to 2040
projected to be due to non-Anglo populations, it is evident that
non-Anglo population growth will have an extensive impact on
the growth of the prison population if 2000 incarceration rates

continue to characterize the incarceration levels of these populations.

IMPLICATIONS FOR STATE
COSTS FOR CORRECTIONS

Table 9.6 shows the projected increase in expenditures for TYC operational costs and for the costs of maintaining the number of adult prisoners projected to be in Texas prisons in the coming years. Because the costs are based on per capita costs and are estimated by multiplying these costs by the projections of the number of persons receiving TYC services and persons incarcerated in prisons, the costs shown increase as a function of population growth in the youth and adult systems.

The absolute increase in costs will be extensive regardless of the population projection scenario. Costs for TYC services would increase from roughly $262 million in 2000 to nearly $510 million under the 1.0 scenario in 2040, while prison costs would increase from $2.25 billion in 2000 to $5.06 billion. Such costs would represent substantial additions to state appropriations for both TYC programs and for the Texas State

Table 9.6

Expenditures (in 2000 Dollars) for Texas Youth Commission Services and Adult Prison Costs in Texas by Race/Ethnicity in 2000 and Projections to 2040 Using the Population Projection That Assumes 1990–2000 Rates of Net Migration (1.0 Scenario)

Year	Anglo	Black	Hispanic	Other	Total
	Panel A: Texas Youth Commission Costs				
2000	$ 64,579,789	$ 89,384,766	$ 98,385,874	$ 9,546,352	$ 261,896,781
2010	63,110,285	108,091,093	134,806,801	15,364,766	321,372,945
2030	58,492,330	107,865,326	241,681,085	27,479,919	435,518,660
2040	54,285,651	107,989,959	310,559,385	36,945,479	509,780,474
	Panel B: Adult Prison Costs				
2000	$ 696,015,398	$ 981,098,319	$ 567,302,254	$ 8,887,513	$ 2,253,303,484
2010	695,674,141	1,173,018,148	931,512,230	13,338,688	2,813,543,207
2030	681,252,334	1,500,120,161	2,005,788,479	28,650,730	4,215,811,704
2040	664,486,241	1,591,829,204	2,759,995,571	39,081,317	5,055,392,333

Sources: Derived by the authors from Texas Population Estimates and Projections Program 2001; Texas Youth Commission 2002a; Texas Department of Criminal Justice 2002; Criminal Justice Policy Council 2001.

Prison System. The projections shown here suggest that Texas is likely to need to maintain a continuing and increasing investment in criminal justice services in the coming decades.

SUMMARY

In this chapter the implications of projected population change for criminal justice services in Texas have been examined for both the number of youth likely to be served through TYC programs and the number of adults in future Texas State Prison populations. The results suggest that:

1. Both youth and adult criminal justice services provided by the state have grown considerably in recent decades. From 1979 to 1999, the number of persons involved in youth correctional programs in Texas increased by 155.1 percent compared to a nationwide increase of 51.5 percent. Similarly, the adult prison population increased from 28,543 inmates in 1980 to 146,761 at the end of 2000. The increase in Texas' adult prisoner population was 414.2 percent from 1980 to 2000, exceeding the national growth rate of 310.6 percent.

2. When the projected patterns for youth services are examined under the 1.0 scenario, the data suggest that the growth in the number of youths in such programs will be less than the total population growth, reflecting the slower growth of the juvenile segment of the correctional population. Nevertheless, the number of youths in such programs is projected to increase from 8,603 in 2000 to 17,118. This represents an increase of 99 percent in TYC programs compared to a projected total population change of 142.6 percent. The number of Anglos in the TYC system would decrease by 14.6 percent and the number of Blacks would increase by 21.6 percent under the 1.0 scenario. The number of Hispanics, on the other hand, would increase by 215.4 percent and the number of persons from the Other racial/ethnic group by 274.3 percent. As a result of such growth differentials, the proportion of Anglos among TYC clientele is projected to

decline by 2040 to 9.9 percent, and Hispanics would account for 85 percent of the total net increase in persons added to TYC programs from 2000 to 2040.

3. The number of adult prisoners is projected to increase less rapidly than the population under the 1.0 scenario: from 151,868 in 2000 to 340,723, an increase of 124.4 percent, compared to a projected population increase of 142.6 percent. The number of Anglo inmates will decline by 4.5 percent, while the proportion of Anglos falls from 30.9 percent in 2000 to 13.1 percent by 2040. Although the projected number of Blacks is expected to increase by 62.2 percent, their proportion of the prison population will decline from 43.5 percent in 2000 to 31.5 percent in 2040. The number of Hispanics is likely to increase by 386.5 percent from 2000 to 2040, rising from 25.2 percent of all prisoners in 2000 to 54.6 percent of all prisoners by 2040. Persons from the Other racial/ethnic group will increase by 339.7 percent, growing to 0.8 percent of all prisoners by 2040. Hispanics would account for 78.3 percent of the total net change of 188,855 in the number of prisoners from 2000 to 2040.

4. Costs for TYC services would increase from nearly $262 million in 2000 to $510 million by 2040, and costs for prisons would increase from $2.25 billion in 2000 to $5.06 billion in 2040.

The growth in criminal justice programs and the costs associated with them are likely to continue to be extensive in the coming years. The aging of the population will result in slower growth in such programs than in the population, but increases in these programs are nevertheless extensive. Unless change occurs in the rates of incarceration in state prisons and of youth involvement in TYC programs, these programs will provide substantial challenges to the state.

CHAPTER 10

Summary, Implications, and Assessment of Alternative Futures

In this work we have provided an overview of the changes projected to occur in Texas' population in the coming years and of the implications of such changes for a number of public services and private-sector dimensions. Alternative projections of Texas' future population were examined as they are projected to impact the number of households and the characteristics of householders including the income, poverty, and tax revenues generated by households. Effects related to the private sector were analyzed, including effects on consumer spending, on assets and the net worth of households, and on the health care and housing industries. The effects on the number and characteristics of persons in the labor force, including the education levels, occupational skills, and salary and wages of those employed, as well as the implications for the number and percentage of unemployed persons and the demand for specific workforce training programs, were examined. The implications of population change for key service areas were also described. The effects on public elementary and secondary education and higher education, including the levels of financial need and need unmet by the household resources of students in public community colleges and universities, were discussed. The impacts on human services programs—including TANF, Food Stamps, and Medicaid—were described, as were the total and state costs associated with each. The potential effects on the number and characteristics of prison inmates and Texas Youth

Commission participants and the costs associated with such populations were also described.

For every topic, the effects of a set of projections that use population-based rates computed from data from the 2000 Census and from agency data for 2000 and which assume that these rates remain constant across the projection period, are examined. In addition, some chapters employ alternative simulations to examine the implications of alternative rates of resource acquisition or service usage. Given the range of outcomes provided by both the use of alternative population projection scenarios and alternative acquisition or use rates, a range of alternative futures was examined. An attempt was also made to ensure that the reader is aware of both the uncertainty of projections and a range of potential futures related to the material covered.

Demographic change is only one of many factors likely to affect the services and characteristics described in this volume. Economic, political, social, and other factors will impact these services and dimensions and may have as large, or even larger, effects on their scope and characteristics. The analysis provided here is not exhaustive but rather an attempt to trace the effects of changes in the size and characteristics of the population and related socioeconomic characteristics on selected aspects of Texas.

The analysis is also limited by the fact that the projections presented, like all population projections, are subject to error; by the fact that the current relationships between demographic factors and other service and socioeconomic characteristics may change in ways not anticipated; by the fact that the data used in the analysis were limited in many ways; and by the fact that only a limited set of dimensions affecting the future could be examined due to space, time, and other considerations. Despite these limitations, the analysis has revealed several key issues that may warrant the attention of private and public sector decision makers.

In this chapter we describe some of the overall implications of the trends identified in this volume. Given the summaries provided at the end of previous chapters, we will not repeat that information here. The intent of this final chapter is threefold. First, we describe the overarching population trends examined in the analysis. Second, we explicate the implications of several general alternative futures for the numerous services and other factors discussed in this work. We examine a common set of alternative projections for all topical areas and then present an education alternative in which we examine some of the benefits and cost implications related to different levels of educational attainment. Finally, we discuss some of the issues suggested by the analysis that may be of interest to public- and private-sector decision makers.

MAJOR POPULATION AND SOCIOECONOMIC TRENDS IMPACTING TEXAS

As noted in Chapter 2, Texas' population has increased rapidly, with its rate of growth exceeding the national growth rate in every decade since it became a state. It has also diversified rapidly, such that its Anglo population was only 53 percent of the total population in 2000 and Texas was not only the second largest state in the nation but also had the third largest Anglo population, second largest Black and Hispanic populations, and fourth largest population in the Other racial/ethnic group. Its population has aged such that its median age, although younger than that of the nation, has increased in each of the last two decades. Its households, like those in the nation, tend to show the fastest rates of growth in nonfamily and single-parent categories. The analyses presented in this volume project a continuation of such patterns and, in general, the pervasiveness of these patterns suggests that although their magnitude may not be exactly as projected, the direction of change is quite likely to occur as indicated and have clear implications for the services and characteristics examined herein.

All of the services and other factors examined in this volume are affected by the state's rate of population growth, and growth is likely to continue to characterize statewide patterns of population change. Because of a high rate of natural increase, Texas' population is projected to grow by more than 4.7 million persons (22.6 percent) in the next forty years even in the absence of migration (the 0.0 migration scenario). This increase of nearly 1.2 million people per decade is greater than the growth that occurred in forty-five of the fifty states in the 1990s. More likely are rates of growth of between 67.9 and 142.6 percent, resulting in an addition of between 14.2 and 29.7 million new residents. Although there is substantial variation in the absolute level of growth projected, growth is projected under all scenarios. Population growth thus is likely to have a continuing influence on the public and private sectors in Texas.

Similarly, the diversification of Texas' population is likely to continue. Between 1990 and 2000, the Anglo population increased by only 7.6 percent while all non-Anglo populations increased by rates that were at least three times that rate. About 80 percent of the state's net population growth was non-Anglo, more than 60 percent of the births in the state in the past few years have been non-Anglo, and of the total population less than eighteen years of age in Texas in 2000, 57 percent was non-Anglo. Although the total level of Anglo population growth may vary from that projected, Texas' population will be less than 50 percent non-Anglo in the next few years and is quite likely to have a Hispanic majority by the end of the projection period.

The aging of the population is largely a function of the baby-boom generation and, since this generation is fully in place, there is little doubt that the general aging of the population will occur. By 2040, between 16 and 20 percent of Texans (compared to less than 10 percent in 2000) will be sixty-five years of age or older and the median age of Texans is likely to be nearly forty.

Although household patterns are more subject to the reversal of historic trends than the other population dimensions noted here, the growth and diversification of households has continued for several decades, only slightly slowed by the population's aging. The growth in the number of households has been greater than that in the population in three of the past four decades, and projected patterns suggest that the number of households will increase faster than the population in the future. The 1990s witnessed a further decline in the percentage of married-couple households and showed substantial growth in nonfamily households. Therefore, the diversification of households appears to be continuing.

Overall, then, the major demographic trends driving the changes noted in this volume seem quite likely to continue. Although the magnitude of such changes cannot be errorlessly predicted, the direction of these trends suggest that the effects of a growing, diversifying, and aging population, and of a growing and diversifying base of households, will likely impact Texas in the coming decades. The demographic trends identified as critical to understanding Texas' population changes are overarching trends that are almost certain to affect, at least in some degree, the state's future.

The effects of these demographic factors are evident in the data for the service areas and other dimensions described in this volume. The effects of rapid population growth are evident throughout. The labor force; public elementary, secondary, and higher education enrollment; participation in TANF, Food Stamps, and Medicaid; and aggregate income, families in poverty, consumer expenditures, and state taxes all increase by at least 75 percent under the 1.0 scenario. Population growth will lead to growth in service demand and to increases (although not necessarily per household or per capita increases) in total resources in the coming years.

A comparison of the rates of growth in services to the 142.6 percent population growth rate and the 162.1 percent growth in households from 2000 to 2040 under the 1.0 scenario (see Figures 10.1–10.3) also shows the effects of the aging and diversification of the population. The slower growth in the labor force, in school enrollments at all levels, and in TYC and prison populations compared to population change show the effects of the aging of the population. Similarly, the fact that increases in the percentage of persons with diseases/disorders and disabilities, as well as the growth in households and housing expenditures, are more rapid than the population increases reflects the aging of the population because the incidences of diseases/disorders, disabilities, and home ownership increase with age. The growth in the use of most of the specialized labor force and educational programs and the increase in the number of persons in poverty and the number of TANF, Food Stamp, and Medicaid participants show the effects of higher growth rates in the faster growing non-Anglo populations. The slower-than-household rates of growth in

Figure 10.1

Percent Change in Selected Factors Compared to
Percent Change in Population, 2000 to 2040*

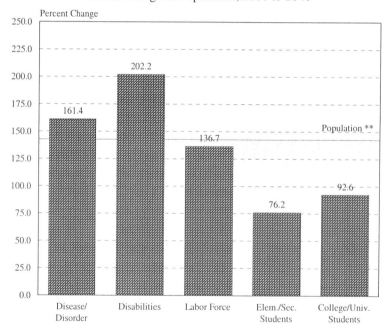

* Projections are shown for the 1.0 scenario
** Shaded background indicates population change (142.6%)

Figure 10.2

Percent Change in Selected Factors Compared to
Percent Change in Population, 2000 to 2040*

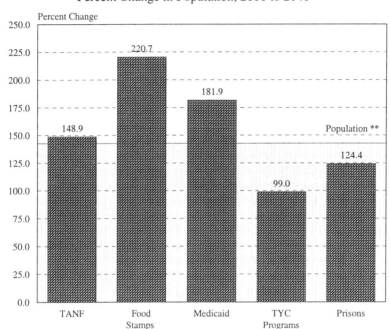

* Projections are shown for the 1.0 scenario
** Shaded background indicates population change (142.6%)

income, consumer expenditures, net worth, and tax revenues
also show the effects of the rapid growth of non-Anglo
populations, which have more limited socioeconomic
resources.

In sum, then, the effects of major population changes are
evident in the growth in the demand for services and on the
socioeconomic resources of populations. Demographic factors
will play a major role in Texas' future under existing conditions
and relationships between population characteristics and
socioeconomic resources.

THE EFFECTS OF ALTERNATIVE FUTURES
The effects noted above depend not only on demographic
change but also on the relationships between demographic and

Figure 10.3

Percent Change in Socioeconomic Resources Compared
to Percent Change in Households, 2000 to 2040*

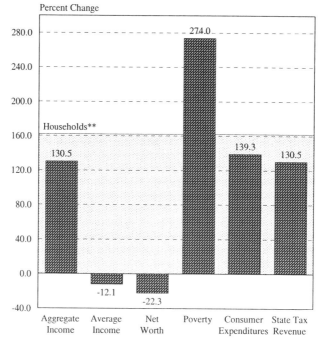

* Projections are shown for the 1.0 scenario
** Shaded background indicates household change (162.1%)

service usage and socioeconomic factors. If these relationships change, so may the implications of future demographic change. In this section we examine the implications of several alternative futures. We do not change the projected demographic patterns in any of these alternative futures, only the socioeconomic differences and service use patterns that exist between key demographic groups. Specifically, we examine the effects of changing key differentials between racial/ethnic groups. We present two sets of alternative futures, one of which examines the effects of simply altering the differences between Anglos and Blacks and between Anglos and Hispanics, and one in which we trace the effects of recent educational change on socioeconomic and service factors.

CHANGING THE DIFFERENTIALS BETWEEN ANGLOS, BLACKS, AND HISPANICS

An examination of the racial/ethnic differences noted in this work indicates that the major socioeconomic differences are between Anglos (and sometimes persons from the Other racial/ethnic group) and Blacks and Hispanics. That is, Anglos tend to have higher levels of education that translate into higher incomes (and lower levels of poverty). Moreover, with increased incomes come such factors as increased consumer expenditures, higher rates of home ownership, reduced levels of incarceration, and lower rates of use of human services and workforce training programs. The lower levels of education and income historically exhibited by Blacks and Hispanics lead to opposite patterns of service usage.

As a result, one way to examine the implications of changing the socioeconomic differences among racial/ethnic groups is to examine the effects of changing the differentials between Anglos, Blacks, and Hispanics. In this section we examine the implications of reducing differentials in Anglo and Black and Anglo and Hispanic rates of occurrence by half by 2020 and, alternatively, to completely eliminating the differentials between Anglo and Black and Anglo and Hispanic groups (that is, Blacks and Hispanics come to have Anglo rates) by 2020. Rates for the Other population were not altered from those for the base projections. Under both of these scenarios, rates remain at 2020 levels for the remainder of the projection period (through 2040). The closure to one-half is admittedly an arbitrary choice, as is the selection of the year 2020 as the date by which closure will occur. There is no clear indication of how extensive and when such closure might occur, and the period and the extent of closure is intended only to provide some acknowledgment of the fact that closure in such differentials will not be immediate. At the same time, by providing closure halfway through the projection period, we allow time to see the effects of such changes during the remainder of it.

The data in Table 10.1 show that the effects of partial and full closure are extensive under the 1.0 population projection scenario (values for the 0.5 scenario show similar proportional patterns). For example, under the 1.0 scenario, enrollment rates in workforce training programs would either decline or grow relatively slowly. Enrollment would decline from 2000 to 2040 by more than 64 percent in the WIA Youth program under full closure with Anglo rates and by 17 percent in welfare-related programs, and only in the WIA Other and WIA Dislocated Worker programs (which have relatively high enrollment rates among Anglos) would the growth rates from 2000 to 2040 still exceed 50 percent (see Panel A).

Elementary and secondary school enrollment would change relatively little because of the mandatory enrollment required at this level. However, the specialized elementary and secondary school programs show substantial patterns of change. Bilingual/ESL, Economically Disadvantaged, Immigrant, and Limited English Proficiency programs show net declines in the number of participants under full closure with Anglo rates; career and technology and special education show virtually no change; but the gifted and talented program, which is projected to increase by 48.5 percent from 2000 to 2040 under the baseline scenario, would increase by more than 129 percent under the complete-closure scenario (see Panel B).

Total public community college and university enrollment would increase from 92.6 percent from 2000 to 2040 under the baseline to 172.2 percent under the 1.0 scenario and complete-closure scenario. Public university enrollment, which has relatively large Anglo-Black and Anglo-Hispanic enrollment rate differentials, would show a percentage increase from 2000 to 2040 that is more than double that in the baseline scenario, showing an 82.5 percent growth rate between 2000 and 2040 under the baseline and 1.0 scenario compared to 195.2 percent under the complete closure (and 1.0) scenario. The number of students under the baseline rates for all public colleges and universities is 1.5 million in 2040, but under the full-closure scenario it is nearly 2.2 million. For public universities, the

Table 10.1

Comparison of Projected Changes in Service, Health, and Financial Characteristics in Texas under Baseline (2000) Rates of Occurrence by Race/Ethnicity, under an Assumption That Differences between Anglo-Black and Anglo-Hispanic Rates Close to One-Half of 2000 Levels by 2020, and under an Assumption That Black and Hispanic Rates Become Equal to Anglo Rates by 2020 and Using the Population Projection That Assumes 1990–2000 Rates of Net Migration (1.0 Scenario), 2000–40

Assumption	Number				Percent Change 2000–40
	2000	2010	2020	2040	
Panel A: Workforce Training Programs					
Title III and Title IV					
Base Projection	4,341	6,654	9,731	19,565	350.7
Partial Closure by 2020	4,341	5,629	6,456	12,366	184.9
Full Closure by 2020	4,341	4,609	3,188	5,162	18.9
WIA Adult					
Base Projection	31,239	41,911	54,143	88,234	182.4
Partial Closure by 2020	31,239	35,920	38,018	60,761	94.5
Full Closure by 2020	31,239	29,944	21,892	33,316	6.7
WIA Dislocated Worker					
Base Projection	44,148	59,464	78,306	133,604	202.6
Partial Closure by 2020	44,148	55,209	65,748	109,177	147.3
Full Closure by 2020	44,148	50,971	53,192	84,752	92.0
WIA Youth					
Base Projection	35,541	45,554	54,068	83,242	134.2
Partial Closure by 2020	35,541	36,125	31,513	47,923	34.8
Full Closure by 2020	35,541	26,702	8,950	12,599	-64.6
WIA Other					
Base Projection	1,665	2,225	2,850	4,609	176.8
Partial Closure by 2020	1,665	1,969	2,195	3,568	114.3
Full Closure by 2020	1,665	1,713	1,541	2,534	52.2
Programs Resulting from Welfare Reform					
Base Projection	156,477	206,943	261,230	410,704	162.5
Partial Closure by 2020	156,477	173,527	174,469	269,982	72.5
Full Closure by 2020	156,477	140,120	87,714	129,262	-17.4
Panel B: Educational Enrollment					
Total Public Elementary, Secondary, and Higher Education					
Base Projection	4,794,275	5,355,217	6,282,832	8,579,600	79.0
Partial Closure by 2020	4,794,275	5,418,152	6,447,588	8,890,906	85.5
Full Closure by 2020	4,794,275	5,480,717	6,611,943	9,201,802	91.9
Total Public Colleges and Universities					
Base Projection	792,048	955,529	1,083,965	1,525,809	92.6
Partial Closure by 2020	792,048	1,026,822	1,263,596	1,840,771	132.4
Full Closure by 2020	792,048	1,098,132	1,443,233	2,155,726	172.2
Public Community Colleges					
Base Projection	421,078	510,319	589,181	848,867	101.6
Partial Closure by 2020	421,078	535,329	650,454	954,767	126.7
Full Closure by 2020	421,078	560,352	711,725	1,060,660	151.9
Public Universities					
Base Projection	370,970	445,210	494,784	676,942	82.5
Partial Closure by 2020	370,970	491,493	613,142	886,004	138.8
Full Closure by 2020	370,970	537,780	731,508	1,095,066	195.2

212 The New Texas Challenge

Table 10.1, Panel B continued

Assumption	Number				Percent Change 2000–40
	2000	2010	2020	2040	
Public Elementary and Secondary Schools					
Base Projection	4,002,227	4,399,688	5,198,867	7,053,791	76.3
Partial Closure by 2020	4,002,227	4,391,330	5,183,992	7,050,135	76.2
Full Closure by 2020	4,002,227	4,382,585	5,168,710	7,046,076	76.1
Specialized Elementary and Secondary School Programs					
Bilingual/ESL					
Base Projection	498,275	628,154	861,737	1,429,125	186.8
Partial Closure by 2020	498,275	483,895	463,245	768,593	54.3
Full Closure by 2020	498,275	339,625	64,744	108,055	-78.3
Economically Disadvantaged					
Base Projection	1,956,000	2,283,807	2,879,203	4,301,098	119.9
Partial Closure by 2020	1,956,000	1,963,520	2,038,835	2,971,926	51.9
Full Closure by 2020	1,956,000	1,643,222	1,198,468	1,642,753	-16.0
Gifted and Talented					
Base Projection	336,562	346,362	395,244	499,689	48.5
Partial Closure by 2020	336,562	379,481	481,014	635,267	88.8
Full Closure by 2020	336,562	412,595	566,775	770,855	129.0
Immigrant					
Base Projection	73,804	93,667	126,300	208,854	183.0
Partial Closure by 2020	73,804	74,853	74,688	122,597	66.1
Full Closure by 2020	73,804	56,039	23,068	36,342	-50.8
Limited English Proficiency (LEP)					
Base Projection	555,470	702,915	963,568	1,600,330	188.1
Partial Closure by 2020	555,470	541,918	519,148	862,399	55.3
Full Closure by 2020	555,470	380,918	74,732	124,462	-77.6
Special Education					
Base Projection	490,220	526,604	610,813	807,324	64.7
Partial Closure by 2020	490,220	534,895	635,141	850,481	73.5
Full Closure by 2020	490,220	543,172	659,463	893,643	82.3
Title I					
Base Projection	2,012,700	2,218,796	2,774,260	4,063,972	101.9
Partial Closure by 2020	2,012,700	1,981,447	2,143,166	3,053,616	51.7
Full Closure by 2020	2,012,700	1,744,083	1,512,056	2,043,257	1.5
Career and Technology					
Base Projection	741,949	809,773	924,074	1,260,803	69.9
Partial Closure by 2020	741,949	811,864	930,341	1,273,211	71.6
Full Closure by 2020	741,949	813,944	936,605	1,285,616	73.3
Panel C: Human and Criminal Justice Services					
TANF					
Base Projection	405,287	518,244	657,457	1,008,932	148.9
Partial Closure by 2020	405,287	432,493	433,502	652,455	61.0
Full Closure by 2020	405,287	346,744	209,531	295,957	-27.0
Food Stamps					
Base Projection	1,007,067	1,383,170	1,856,883	3,229,632	220.7
Partial Closure by 2020	1,007,067	1,157,088	1,230,327	2,106,178	109.1
Full Closure by 2020	1,007,067	930,990	603,791	982,726	-2.4
Medicaid					
Base Projection	1,886,937	2,399,071	3,116,485	5,319,029	181.9
Partial Closure by 2020	1,886,937	2,092,951	2,294,481	3,872,478	105.2
Full Closure by 2020	1,886,937	1,786,829	1,472,475	2,425,909	28.6

Table 10.1, Panel C continued

Assumption	Number				Percent Change 2000–40
	2000	2010	2020	2040	
Texas Youth Commission					
Base Projection	8,603	10,634	11,821	17,118	99.0
Partial Closure by 2020	8,603	9,370	9,069	13,147	52.8
Full Closure by 2020	8,603	8,100	6,314	9,182	6.7
Prisons					
Base Projection	151,868	189,627	234,764	340,723	124.4
Partial Closure by 2020	151,868	169,509	185,292	273,378	80.0
Full Closure by 2020	151,868	149,393	135,815	206,033	35.7
Panel D: Incidences of Diseases/Disorders					
Base Projection	49,545,168	62,480,914	79,680,429	129,495,255	161.4
Partial Closure by 2020	49,545,168	63,669,222	82,951,811	135,206,702	172.9
Full Closure by 2020	49,545,168	64,857,554	86,223,160	140,918,160	184.4
Panel E: Income, Expenditures, and Tax Revenues					
Aggregate Household Income (in Billions of 2000 Dollars)					
Base Projection	$ 402.5	$ 494.3	$ 613.2	$ 927.8	130.50
Partial Closure by 2020	402.5	518.5	685.7	1,072.7	166.50
Full Closure by 2020	402.5	542.8	758.2	1,217.6	202.50
Average Household Income					
Base Projection	$ 54,441	$ 52,639	$ 50,903	$ 47,883	-12.1
Partial Closure by 2020	54,441	55,225	56,920	55,361	1.7
Full Closure by 2020	54,441	57,811	62,937	62,839	15.4
Poverty - Family Households					
Base Projection	598,325	861,246	1,212,931	2,237,880	274.0
Partial Closure by 2020	598,325	753,298	887,115	1,583,468	164.7
Full Closure by 2020	598,325	645,349	561,301	929,053	55.3
Consumer Expenditures (in Billions of 2000 Dollars)					
Base Projection	$ 274.3	$ 342.4	$ 428.2	$ 656.3	139.30
Partial Closure by 2020	274.3	349.9	450.2	699.8	155.10
Full Closure by 2020	274.3	357.3	472.2	743.2	171.00
Net Worth (in Billions of 2000 Dollars)					
Base Projection	$ 709.9	$ 845.2	$ 1,015.4	$ 1,444.2	103.40
Partial Closure by 2020	709.9	931.1	1,270.4	1,948.8	174.50
Full Closure by 2020	709.9	1,017.0	1,525.3	2,453.4	245.60
Housing Expenditures (in Billions of 2000 Dollars)					
Base Projection	$ 48.9	$ 61.1	$ 76.9	$ 120.0	145.60
Partial Closure by 2020	48.9	62.0	79.5	125.1	156.00
Full Closure by 2020	48.9	62.9	82.1	130.2	166.40
Total State Taxes (in Billions of 2000 Dollars)					
Base Projection	$ 29.5	$ 36.2	$ 45.0	$ 68.0	130.50
Partial Closure by 2020	29.5	38.0	50.3	78.7	166.50
Full Closure by 2020	29.5	39.8	55.6	89.3	202.50

comparable values are roughly 677,000 and 1.1 million. Substantial but smaller changes are evident for community colleges.

Under the same 1.0 scenario, the number of TANF and Food Stamp recipients declines and the increase in Medicaid

enrollment under the complete-closure scenario is less than
one-sixth of that under the baseline scenario. Similarly, the
TYC enrollment increase under the full closure (and 1.0)
scenario is only 6.7 percent from 2000 to 2040 compared to 99
percent under the baseline scenario, and prison enrollment
increases by about 36 percent under full closure but by more
than 124 percent from 2000 to 2040 under the baseline
projection (see Panel C).

On the other hand, aggregate household income increases
by 202.5 percent from 2000 to 2040 under the 1.0 and full-
closure scenario compared to 130.5 percent under the baseline
scenario, and average household income increases by 15.4
percent from 2000 to 2040 under the full-closure scenario
rather than decreasing by 12.1 percent under the baseline
scenario. Family poverty continues to increase under the
complete-closure scenario but by approximately one-fifth of the
amount of increase under the baseline scenario. Consumer
expenditures increase by more than 30 percent more under the
complete-closure than under the baseline scenario and housing
expenditures by about 20 percent more (see Panel E).

Finally under the 1.0 scenario, state tax revenues that are
projected to increase by nearly 131 percent from 2000 to 2040
under baseline rates would increase by more than 202 percent
under complete closure and would be more than $21 billion
more per year than under the baseline scenario.

In sum, the data for these two scenarios show that change in
differentials among racial/ethnic groups could substantially
alter the effects of population change on Texas. In particular,
closure between Anglo, Black, and Hispanics groups could
substantially increase those effects generally perceived as
positive (such as increased income) and reduce the negative
effects (such as increases in human services and prison
populations).

AN EDUCATION ALTERNATIVE

As noted in Chapter 7, one of the reasons for the emphasis
placed on education is that it is so closely tied to

socioeconomic success. The average income for a household in which the householder is a high school graduate in the United States in 2000 was $45,368, but the average income for a householder who is a college graduate was $84,029 (see Figure 7.1). Higher levels of education are clearly related to socioeconomic success. Such success, in turn, tends to be associated with lower levels of public service usage particularly for those services that are usually required by persons or households that have a lack of socioeconomic resources. What effect would increasing educational attainment levels have on Texas?

In this final set of alternatives we examine the implications of changing rates of educational attainment on selected service and socioeconomic factors. Educational attainment rates by race/ethnicity were computed for the population twenty-five years of age or older from the 2000 Census (see Table 10.2). Given these data, three alternative scenarios of attainment were developed (see Table 10.3) with the results applied to the population twenty-five years of age or older in the alternative population projection scenarios used throughout the volume. Under one of the alternative projections, 2000 rates of attainment by race/ethnicity were assumed to prevail throughout the projection period—that is, the Anglo, Black, Hispanic, and Other populations' 2000 attainment rates were assumed to continue unchanged from 2000 through 2040. The second alternative assumed that 1990–2000 percentage changes in the number of persons within each educational attainment category within each race/ethnicity group continued for each decade from 2000 to 2040. The values so computed were controlled to the total projected population twenty-five years of age or older. These projected values and the percentage of persons twenty-five years of age or older projected to be at each educational level within each race/ethnicity group are shown for the years 2010 and 2040 in Table 10.2. The third scenario assumes that the projected Anglo proportions by attainment level as projected and shown in Table 10.2 apply to the Black and Hispanic groups (for example, Anglo rates in 2010 apply to

Table 10.2

Number and Percent of Persons 25 Years of Age or Older in Texas by Level of Educational Attainment
and Race/Ethnicity in 2000 and Projections to 2040 Using the Population Projection That Assumes
1990–2000 Rates of Net Migration (1.0 Scenario)

Educational Attainment Level	Anglo		Black		Hispanic		Other		Total	
	Number	%	Number	%	Number	%	Number	%	Number	%
2000										
Less than High School	957,552	12.7	332,414	24.0	1,726,690	50.7	90,520	21.0	3,107,176	24.3
High School	1,939,975	25.7	412,996	29.9	747,931	22.0	68,920	16.1	3,169,822	24.9
Some College and Associate	2,384,508	31.6	423,000	30.6	624,105	18.4	88,641	20.6	3,520,254	27.5
Bachelor and Above	2,268,766	30.0	214,275	15.5	303,894	8.9	181,993	42.3	2,968,928	23.3
Total	7,550,801	100.0	1,382,685	100.0	3,402,620	100.0	430,074	100.0	12,766,180	100.0
2010										
Less than High School	690,545	8.4	282,710	16.4	2,613,077	46.0	154,488	19.3	3,740,820	22.8
High School	1,945,279	23.8	521,330	30.1	1,322,457	23.2	109,615	13.7	3,898,681	23.8
Some College and Associate	2,705,479	33.0	594,677	34.4	1,133,743	20.0	144,747	18.1	4,578,646	27.9
Bachelor and Above	2,850,493	34.8	330,146	19.1	614,837	10.8	391,781	48.9	4,187,257	25.5
Total	8,191,796	100.0	1,728,863	100.0	5,684,114	100.0	800,631	100.0	16,405,404	100.0
2040										
Less than High School	202,278	2.2	120,392	4.3	6,276,216	32.1	471,407	13.4	7,070,293	20.1
High School	1,531,809	16.6	725,908	25.6	5,066,097	25.8	270,705	7.6	7,594,519	21.6
Some College and Associate	3,086,352	33.4	1,143,860	40.5	4,709,964	24.1	386,876	11.0	9,327,052	26.5
Bachelor and Above	4,415,464	47.8	835,946	29.6	3,528,622	18.0	2,399,148	68.0	11,179,180	31.8
Total	9,235,903	100.0	2,826,106	100.0	19,580,899	100.0	3,528,136	100.0	35,171,044	100.0

these groups in 2010, Anglo rates in 2020 apply to these groups in 2020, and so forth). Rates for the Other group remained as projected. Due to space limitations values are shown only for the 1.0 scenario.

Given the projections of persons twenty-five years of age or older by level of educational attainment, we projected total income, consumer expenditures, prison populations and costs, and human services participants and costs under the alternative population projection scenarios using data (averaged from the 1999–2001 Current Population Survey) on income and consumer expenditures by level of educational attainment and 2000 data (from the agency sources noted in the chapters above) on human services and prison populations by educational attainment level. Income, consumer expenditures, incarceration, and human services usage rates by race/ethnicity and educational attainment level for persons twenty-five years of age or older were computed for 2000 and applied to the three scenarios of educational attainment for the population twenty-five years of age or older. All projections are for the population twenty-five years of age or older so they are not directly comparable to data presented elsewhere in this volume. The restriction to the population twenty-five years of age or older is necessary because census data on educational attainment are limited to members of that age group. Because of this restriction, the data can only be used comparatively to indicate the effects of increased educational attainment.

The data in Table 10.3 suggest that increasing educational attainment would lead to substantial change in key socioeconomic and service factors. These data show that maintaining the educational progression of the 1990s under the 1.0 scenario would result in a population twenty-five years of age or older in 2040 that would generate $143 billion more income than under 2000 attainment levels and that completely closing the educational attainment gap would result in more than $317 billion more in annual income than under the 2000 alternative scenario.

The second part of Table 10.3 shows the effects of alternative levels of educational attainment on consumer expenditures. Increased education at the levels of the 1990–2000 period would increase consumer expenditures by more than $100 billion per year in 2040 under the 1.0 scenario compared to those under the 2000 attainment level and by nearly $224 billion per year under the scenario that assumes Anglo rates. Increased educational attainment would clearly impact the state's private sector.

Increased educational attainment would not only increase the income and expenditures of Texas residents, it would reduce state costs in several key areas. Under the 1.0 scenario, prison populations are reduced by nearly one-third under the 1990–2000 trends in attainment scenario and to less than one-half the baseline levels under the scenario that provides Anglo levels of educational attainment for all persons twenty-five years of age or older. Similar patterns are found in terms of the number of participants in the TANF, Food Stamp, and Medicaid programs. Costs are reduced accordingly. Under the 1.0 population projection scenario and the attainment scenario that assumes that Texas increases its rates of educational

Table 10.3

Projected Aggregate Income, Consumer Expenditures, and Prison and
Human Services Populations and Costs for the Population 25+ Years of
Age in Texas under Alternative Assumptions of Educational Attainment
Using the Population Projection That Assumes 1990–2000 Rates of
Net Migration (1.0 Scenario), 2000 and 2040

Economic or Service Factor	2000 Attainment Differentials	1990–2000 Trends in Differentials	Anglo Trends in Differentials Apply to all Groups
Aggregate Income			
2000	$ 251,003,110,398	$ 251,003,110,398	$ 251,003,110,398
2040	621,420,399,115	764,801,856,645	938,439,061,623
Consumer Expenditures			
2000	$ 210,437,031,544	$ 210,437,031,544	$ 210,437,031,544
2040	528,409,337,699	629,290,664,927	751,866,155,896
Prison			
Populations			
2000	126,515	126,515	126,515
2040	341,068	227,969	134,539
Costs			
2000	$ 1,877,134,686	$ 1,877,134,686	$ 1,877,134,686
2040	5,060,511,184	3,382,433,047	1,996,188,779
Human Services			
TANF			
Participants			
2000	122,772	122,772	122,772
2040	469,976	356,127	179,697
Costs			
2000	$ 90,344,231	$ 90,344,231	$ 90,344,231
2040	345,841,238	262,063,175	132,233,633
Food Stamps			
Participants			
2000	323,194	323,194	323,194
2040	1,256,109	959,744	481,898
Costs			
2000	$ 51,245,641	$ 51,245,641	$ 51,245,641
2040	199,168,643	152,177,008	76,409,746
Medicaid			
Participants			
2000	397,959	397,959	397,959
2040	1,353,742	950,713	485,228
Costs			
2000	$ 999,143,721	$ 999,143,721	$ 999,143,721
2040	3,398,799,426	2,386,926,609	1,218,247,382

attainment at the level of the 1990–2000 trends throughout the
projection period, state costs would be reduced from the levels

under the 2000 attainment scenario by approximately $1.7 billion for prisons, $84 million for TANF, $47 million for Food Stamps, $1 billion for Medicaid, for a total of nearly $2.8 billion per year. Under the 1.0 population scenario and assuming Anglo attainment levels for Anglo, Black, and Hispanic groups, the savings from the 2000 attainment scenario levels would be more than $3 billion for prisons, nearly $214 million for TANF, nearly $123 million for Food Stamps, and nearly $2.2 billion in Medicaid costs, with a total savings approaching $5.5 billion per year.

The data in this section suggest that education appears to pay not only through increased income and consumer expenditures but also through reduced public costs. Education is only one answer to changing the socioeconomic differentials among racial/ethnic groups in Texas, but the data presented here suggest that it may have substantial potential to address the challenges likely to result from the state's projected future population patterns.

IMPLICATIONS FOR THE FUTURE OF TEXAS
The alternatives examined above suggest that the state's demographic and socioeconomic characteristics will change rapidly in the coming years. Their implications may be substantial and deserve the attention of private and public sector decision makers.

Population Size and Change
For public sector decision makers, the change in the size of Texas' population will be of substantial importance. Growth likely will be extensive but not the same everywhere. Many parts of the state that have shown rapid growth will likely continue to do so, but others may show reduced growth and still others renewed growth. The projections presented here suggest that the variation in growth may be substantial but that growth is likely throughout the state, leading to the need to anticipate new infrastructure, service, and other requirements.

Careful examination of change in population characteristics is also essential. Different types of populations will have different types of needs that will require detailed analyses and preparation to ensure effective service delivery. Under a wide variety of alternative scenarios, Texas' population growth seems likely to continue to form a challenge for the public sector.

For the private sector, Texas' population growth will lead to continuing expansion in markets for nearly all types of goods and services. Market niches tied to the state's changing demographics will likely become of increasing importance. Moreover, there seems little doubt that the variation in population growth across the state will necessitate careful market analyses. What seems apparent, however, is that Texas will remain a growing market during periods in which many other states may show only marginal growth, and the state's population increase suggests substantial private-sector opportunities.

Aging of the Population

The aging of the population will have many of the same effects in Texas as in other parts of the nation, with a growing elderly population placing increased demands on health care, long-term care, and other services. At the same time, the aging process in the state is tempered by relatively rapid growth in young, largely non-Anglo populations, which means Texas is likely to remain somewhat younger than many other parts of the nation. In addition, the marked age differentials between Anglos and non-Anglos suggest that the state's elderly population will be disproportionately (to the total population) Anglo, while its younger population will be disproportionately non-Anglo.

For public sector decision makers, this aging factor suggests that increasing parts of state and local service demands and budgets will involve health, long-term care, and other needs of older populations. Under any scenario examined in this volume, the increases in the demands for, and costs of, services for the elderly are projected to be substantial. In Texas, as in nearly all other parts of the nation, the needs of the elderly are likely to place pressures on other service areas with slower-growing requirements resulting from slower growth in younger populations. For Texas, however, there is the potential for tension between age groups to be accentuated by differences in race/ethnicity. This is not to suggest that there are not common interests across racial/ethnic and age groups, but the fact that the state's older population is disproportionately Anglo and its younger population disproportionately non-Anglo raises the potential for differences in perspectives on the levels and forms of services required for the elderly and for youth to be seen in racial/ethnic terms as well. The demographic reality of age and race/ethnicity differentials may become a factor impacting the decision-making process at both the state and local levels.

For the private sector, the realities of the state's age structure suggest that Texas, like the nation as a whole, will be a growing market for health care and other services for the elderly. The fact that its age structure is marked by substantial differentials by race/ethnicity may also suggest that Texas' young and older markets will be increasingly distinct, with markets for children and young adults also becoming increasingly non-Anglo markets while markets for older persons remain more closely tied to Anglo populations. The projections presented here suggest that, over time, all age groups in Texas will become increasingly diverse but that during the interim period, private-sector marketers may find themselves challenged by the fact that they may need to develop more specialized and diverse product and service forms to adequately meet Texans' demands.

Change in Texas Households

The number of Texas households has increased rapidly and is projected to continue to grow rapidly in the future. As in other parts of the nation, Texas households have changed substantially, coming to have increasingly diverse forms and reduced proportions of traditional married-couple-with-children families. Although the state's household patterns are such that they may partially abate the effects of such changes, the overall increase and diversification of Texas households is likely to continue. Since single-parent and other nontraditional forms of households often make more extensive use of public services, patterns of household change may accentuate public sector service requirements in the coming years, and serving Texas households will increasingly require serving diverse forms of households with a diverse range of services.

At the same time, higher rates of growth among non-Anglo households in the state—particularly Hispanic households, which have larger proportions of married couples—suggest that demographics may reduce the proportion of need resulting from other household forms. The diverse patterns of growth in the state are likely to offset some of the changes resulting from overall household change.

Although Texas household forms may be less diverse than those in other parts of the nation, the growth in the number and diversity of Texas households will likely require increasing attention by public agencies to ensure that the needs of an increasing range of household types are addressed. For the private sector, projected patterns of growth in the number of households in the state suggest that Texas will remain a strong market for goods and services and may represent a stronger market for family-oriented products than that in many other parts of the nation. As with aging effects, the fact that married-couple families are more likely to be concentrated in specific racial/ethnic groups suggests additional need for specialized products that are both household-type and racially/ethnically unique. Household change will present a variety of opportunities for the state's private sector.

Racial/Ethnic Diversification

The analysis presented here shows that the diversification is the dominant demographic pattern impacting Texas. The state will become more diverse, becoming less than one-half Anglo in the next few years, and is likely to be a majority Hispanic by 2040, with only one-third to one-quarter of the population being Anglo by 2040 and between 52 and 59 percent Hispanic. Given the current socioeconomic differentials among racial/ethnic groups, this growing diversity presents a major challenge to Texas.

For the public sector, unless the socioeconomic differences among racial/ethnic groups change, the growth in non-Anglo populations will increase the demand for nearly all forms of state services and result in a relative reduction in the resources available to pay for them. The state's non-Anglo populations will increasingly become *the* Texas population. What this pattern suggests is that the state's future will be increasingly tied to its non-Anglo populations and that how non-Anglo populations grow and change will largely determine its future.

For the private sector, increasing diversity means that Texas will be a major and growing market for many forms of racially/ethnically distinct products. Texas is a major Hispanic market and will likely become increasingly so in the coming years, but it is also the state with the second largest Black population and fourth largest population of persons from the Other racial/ethnic group. Texas demographics make it a major market area for the development of increasingly diverse and culturally oriented goods and services.

The Socioeconomic Future

In this volume we have described the effects of population change on a variety of service and socioeconomic conditions in Texas. We have examined demographic effects given existing socioeconomic differentials among age, households, and particularly racial/ethnic groups. We have noted that such socioeconomic differences are a product of a wide variety of historical, discriminatory, and other factors and are related to, but not necessarily dictated by, demographic factors. Population change leads to predictable patterns of change in socioeconomic conditions to the extent that socioeconomic differences among population subgroups remain unchanged.

The baseline patterns of population change presented here suggest that, in the absence of changes in the socioeconomic resources of population groups that show reduced levels of education, reduced incomes, increased levels of poverty, and related increased rates of use of a variety of state services, demographic change in Texas is likely to produce socioeconomic change. Under these baseline conditions of population change, Texas would have a population that not only will be poorer, less well educated, and more in need of numerous forms of state services than its present population but also less able to support such services. It would have a population that is likely to be less competitive in the increasingly international labor and other markets.

At the same time, our analysis has shown that if socioeconomic differentials between demographic groups were to be reduced through increased education and other means, Texas' population growth could be a source of increased private and public sector resource growth. Coupled with such growth would be increased competitiveness and a population whose diversity may create a competitive advantage relative to that of other states in competing in international markets.

CONCLUSION

We began by noting that demography is not destiny but that it plays an important role in determining the future. In fact, in many ways, how well Texas meets the challenges of the twenty-first century may well depend on the extent to which it can alter the determinative effects of its changing population and ensure that population growth also leads to extensive and inclusive patterns of socioeconomic growth.

References

Ascher, W. 1978. *Forecasting: An Appraisal for Policy Makers and Planners*. Baltimore: Johns Hopkins University Press.

Bouvier, L. F., and D. Poston, Jr. 1993. *Thirty Million Texans?* Washington, D.C.: Center for Immigration Studies.

Brody, H. 1993. "Great Expectations: Why Predictions Go Awry." *Journal of Consumer Marketing* 10, no. 1: 23–27.

Bureau of Labor Statistics. 2002. *2000 Consumer Expenditure Survey*. Microdata release on CD-ROM (SAS data sets).

Bureau of Labor Statistics and U.S. Bureau of the Census. 2002. *Current Population Survey: Annual Demographic Survey* (March Supplement). Available at http://www. bls.census.gov/cps/ads/sdata.htm.

Cohen, J. W., S. R. Machlin, and S. H. Zuvekas. 2000. *Health Care Expenses in the United States, 1996*. MEPS Research Findings 12. AHRQ Pub. No. 01-0009. Rockville, Md.: Agency for Healthcare Research and Quality.

Criminal Justice Policy Council. 2001. *Limes to Limes: Comparing the Operational Costs of Juvenile and Adult Correctional Programs in Texas*. Prepared for the 77th Texas Legislature. Available at http://www.cjpc.state.tx.us/ reports/opercpd/CostPerDay2000.pdf.

Davern, M. E., and P. J. Fisher. 2001. "Household Net Worth and Asset Ownership: 1995." In U.S. Census Bureau. *Current Population Reports, The Survey of Income and Program Participation, Household Economic Studies.* Series P70-71. Washington, D.C.: U.S. Government Printing Office.

Kintner, H. J., T. W. Merrick, P. A. Morrison, and P. R. Voss. 1994. *Demographics: A Casebook for Business and Government.* Boulder, CO.: Westview Press.

Murdock, S. H. 1995. *An America Challenged: Population Change and the Future of the United States.* Boulder, CO.: Westview Press.

Murdock, S. H., and D. R. Ellis. 1991. *Applied Demography: An Introduction to Basic Concepts, Methods and Data.* Boulder, CO.: Westview Press.

Murdock, S. H., E. Wray, B. Pecotte, J. Jordan, D. Fannin, N. Hoque, and K. Effah. 1998. *An Analysis of First-Time Admissions to College; Junior/Community/Technical and Senior Colleges/Universities; and to Select and Other Senior Colleges/Universities in Texas Using Enrollment Data for 1995–1997.* College Station: Center for Demographic and Socioeconomic Research and Education, Department of Rural Sociology, Texas A&M University.

Murdock, S. H., N. Hoque, M. Michael, S. White, and B. Pecotte. 1997. *The Texas Challenge: Population Change and the Future of Texas.* College Station: Texas A&M University Press.

———. 1996. *Texas Challenged: The Implications of Population Change for Public Service Demand in Texas.* Austin: Texas Legislative Council.

————. 1995. *An Assessment of the Implications of Population Change for Public Service Demand and Costs in Texas.* College Station: The Center for Demographic and Socioeconomic Research and Education, Department of Rural Sociology, Texas A&M University.

Murdock, S. H., R. R. Hamm, P. R. Voss, D. Fannin, and B. Pecotte. 1991. "Evaluating Small-Area Population Projections." *Journal of the American Planning Association* 57: 432–43.

National Center for Health Statistics. 2002a. *2000 National Health Interview Survey.* Public Use Data Release. Hyattsville, Md.: U.S. Department of Health and Human Services.

————. 2002b. *National Nursing Home Survey, 1999.* Available at http://ftp.cdc.gov/pub/Health_Statistics/ NCHS/Datasets/NNHS.

————. 2001. *Health, United States, 2001: With Urban and Rural Health Chartbook.* Hyattsville, Md.: U.S. Department of Health and Human Services.

Pol, L. G. 1987. *Business Demography: A Guide and Reference for Business Planners and Marketers.* New York: Quorum Books.

Pol, L. G, and R. K. Thomas. 1992. *The Demography of Health and Health Care.* New York: Plenum.

Siegel, J. S. 2002. *Applied Demography: Applications to Business, Government, Law, and Public Policy.* San Diego: Academic Press.

Skrabanek, R. L., S. H. Murdock, and P. K. Guseman. 1985. *The Population of Texas: An Overview of Texas Population Change, 1970–1980.* Austin: Texas State Data Center.

Smith, S. K., J. Tayman, and D. A. Swanson. 2001. *State and Local Population Projections: Methodology and Analysis.* New York: Kluwer Academic Publishers.

Texas Comptroller of Public Accounts. 2002a. *2000 Annual Cash Report.* Available at http://www.window.state.tx.us/comptrol/san/fm_manuals/cr00_manual/cr2000vol1_financial.html.

———. 2002b. *1998 Annual Cash Report.* Available at http://www.window.state.tx.us/comptrol/san/fm_manuals/cr98_manual/tab0598.html.

———. 2002c. *Texas Economy: Spring 2000 Forecast.* Available at http://www.window.state.tx.us/ecodata/forecast.

———. 2001. *Tax Exemptions and Tax Incidence.* Available at http://www.window.state.tx.us/taxinfo/incidence.

———. 1998. *Disparity in Texas Higher Education: Recruitment, Admissions, Retention, and Financial Aid.* Austin: Texas Comptroller of Public Accounts.

———. 1995. *Texas Financial Update.* Austin: Texas Bond Review Board.

Texas Department of Criminal Justice. 2002. "On-hand Population: Demographic data for adult prisoners confined on June 30: 1980–2001" (machine-readable data files), Texas Department of Criminal Justice, Huntsville.

———. 2001. *Statistical Report: Fiscal Year 2000.* Huntsville: Texas Department of Criminal Justice.

———. 1991. *Statistical Report: Fiscal Year 1990.* Huntsville: Texas Department of Criminal Justice.

———. 1981. *Statistical Report: Fiscal Year 1980.* Huntsville: Texas Department of Criminal Justice.

Texas Department of Health. 2002. "Health Professions Resource Center." Available at http://www.tdh.state.tx.us/dpa/coverpg.htm.

Texas Department of Human Services. 2001. *Expanded TDHS Annual Report Data: Fiscal Years 1995–1999.* Austin: Program Budget and Statistics, Client Self Support, Texas Department of Human Services.

———. 1999–2001a. "Monthly Client Files for 1999, 2000, and 2001" (machine-readable data files), Texas Department of Human Services, Austin.

———. 1999–2001b. "Monthly Medical Eligibility Files for 1999, 2000, and 2001," (machine-readable data files), Texas Department of Human Services, Austin.

———. 2000. *Expanded TDHS Annual Report Data—2000.* Austin: Program Budget and Statistics, Client Self Support, Texas Department of Human Services.

Texas Education Agency. 2002a. "Academic Excellence Indicator System, 2000–01 AEIS Reports." Available at http://www.tea.state.tx.us/perfreport/aeis/2001/index.html.

———. 2002b. *Pocket Edition: Texas Public School Statistics.* Available at http://www.tea.state.tx.us/perfreport/pocked.

———. 2001. "Demographic data for public school students for 1980–2000" (machine-readable data files), Texas Education Agency, Austin.

Texas Health and Human Services Commission. 2002. "Nursing Facility Program, 1999: Rate Analysis for Long-Term Care Services." Available at http://www.hhsc.state.tx.us/medicaid/programs/rad/NF/SummaryCRData.html.

Texas Higher Education Coordinating Board. 2002a. "Financial Assistance by Income Group, Fiscal Year 2001" (machine-readable data files), Texas Higher Education Coordinating Board, Austin.

————. 2002b."Financial Aid Data Base Program File, Fiscal Year 2001" (machine-readable data files), Texas Higher Education Coordinating Board, Austin.

————. 2002c. *Statistical Report 2000.* Available at http://www.thecb.state.tx.us/DataAndStatistics/.

————. 2002d. *2000–2001 College Student Budgets.* Available at http://www.thecb.state.tx.us/reports/pdf/0111.pdf.

————. 2001a. "Demographic Data for Public Community College and University Students for 1980–2000" (machine-readable data files), Texas Higher Education Coordinating Board, Austin.

————. 2001b. "Enrollment of Texas Residents in Texas Public Community Colleges and Universities, School Years 1999–2000, 2000–2001" (machine-readable data files), Texas Higher Education Coordinating Board, Austin.

————. 2001c. *Closing the Gaps: The Texas Higher Education Plan.* Available at http://www.thecb.state.tx.us/AdvisoryCommittees/HEP/HEplanFinal.pdf.

————. 1990. *Statistical Report 1990.* Austin: Texas Higher Education Coordinating Board.

Texas Legislative Budget Board. 2001. "Summary of Legislative Budget Estimates." Available at http://www.lbb.state.tx.us/LBE/2002-2003/Art07_0101.pdf.

Texas Population Estimates and Projections Program. 2001. *Projections of the Population of Texas and Counties in Texas by Age, Sex, and Race/Ethnicity for 2000–2040.* College Station: Texas State Data Center.

Texas Workforce Commission. 2002a. "Labor Force Training Program Participants: 1999, 2000, and 2001" (machine-readable data files), Texas Workforce Commission, Austin.

———. 2002b. "Welfare-to-Work Status Report as Required by Rider 40." Available at http://www.twc.state.tx.us/welref/rider40.pdf.

———. 2001a. *Workforce Investment Act: Program Year 2000 Annual Report: An Investment in Texas' Economy.* Austin: Texas Workforce Commission.

———. 2001b. Texas Workforce Commission letter, 09-01, available at http://www.twc.state.tx.us/boards/wdletters/letters/09-01.pdf.

Texas Youth Commission. 2002a. "On-Hand Populations: 1995–2001" (machine-readable data files), Texas Youth Commission, Austin.

———. 2002b. *Youth Commitment Profile: Fiscal Year 2000.* Available at http://www.tyc.state.tx.us/research/profile.html.

———. 2002c. *Youth Commitment Profile: Fiscal Year 1995.* Available at http://www.tyc.state.tx.us/archive/Research/profile1.html.

————. 1990. *Annual Evaluation Report: Fiscal Year 1990.* Austin: Texas Youth Commission, Department of Research and Planning.

U.S. Census Bureau. 2002a. "Census 2000 Summary File 3" (machine-readable data files), U.S. Census Bureau, Washington, D.C.

————. 2002b. *Consolidated Federal Funds Report, 1995–2000.* Available at http://harvester.census.gov/ cffr/index.html.

————. 2001a. "Census 2000 Redistricting Data (Public Law 94-171)" (machine-readable data files), U.S. Census Bureau, Washington, D.C.

————. 2001b. "Census 2000 Summary File 1" (machine-readable data files), U.S. Census Bureau, Washington, D.C.

————. 2001c. "Census 2000 Summary File 2" (machine-readable data files), U.S. Census Bureau, Washington, D.C.

————. 2000. *County Population Estimates and Demographic Components of Population Change: Annual Time Series, July 1, 1990, to July 1, 1999 (CO-99-8).* Washington, D.C.: U.S. Census Bureau.

————. 1991a. "Census of Population and Housing, 1990: Summary Tape File 1" (machine-readable data files), U.S. Census Bureau, Washington, D.C.

————. 1991b. "Census of Population and Housing, 1990: Summary Tape File 2" (machine-readable data files), U.S. Census Bureau, Washington, D.C.

————. 1991c. "Census of Population and Housing, 1990: Summary Tape File 3" (machine-readable data files), U.S. Census Bureau, Washington, D.C.

————. 1983. "Census of Population and Housing, 1980: Summary Tape File 3" (machine-readable data files), U.S. Census Bureau, Washington, D.C.

————. 1982. "Census of Population and Housing, 1980: Summary Tape File 2" (machine-readable data files), U.S. Census Bureau, Washington, D.C.

U.S. Department of Agriculture. 2002. "Food Stamp Program Participation and Costs." Available at http://www.fns.usda.gov/pd/fssummar.htm.

U.S. Department of Education, Office of Post Secondary Education. 2000. "The EFC Formula, 2000–2001," Available at http://www.fafsa.com/fm/2000-01_FM.pdf.

U.S. Department of Health and Human Services. 2002a. "United States: AFDC/TANF State-by-State Welfare Caseloads Since 1963." Available at http://www.acf.dhhs.gov/news/stats/caseload.htm.

————. 2002b. "Federal Matching Percentages." Available at http://aspe.hhs.gov/health/fmap.htm.

————. 2001. "Fourth Quarter ACF-196 Report, Fiscal Year 2000." Available at http://www.acf.hhs.gov/programs/ofs/data/q400/q4fy00.xls.

————. 2000a. *HCFA-2082 Report, 1999–2000.* Washington, D.C.: U.S. Department of Health and Human Services.

————. 2000b. *1999 HCFA Statistics.* Washington, D.C.: U.S. Department of Health and Human Services.

————. 2000c. *State Health Workforce Profiles: Texas.* Health Resources and Services Administration. Washington, D.C.: U.S. Government Printing Office.

U.S. Department of Justice, Bureau of Justice Statistics. 2002. "Key Facts at a Glance: Correctional Populations: 1980–2001." Available at http://www.ojp.usdoj.gov/bjs/glance/tables/corr2tab.htm.

U.S. Department of Justice. 2001a. *Census of Juveniles in Residential Placement Databook: 1999*. Washington, D.C.: Office of Juvenile Justice and Delinquency Prevention.

————. 2001b. *Prisoners in 2000*. Washington. D.C.: Bureau of Justice Statistics.

————. 1994. *Prisoners in 1993*. Washington, D.C.: Bureau of Justice Statistics.

————. 1992a. *Prisons and Prisoners in the United States.* Washington, D.C.: Bureau of Justice Statistics.

————. 1992b. *National Juvenile Custody Trends: 1979–89.* Washington, D.C.: Office of Juvenile Justice and Delinquency Prevention.

————. 1989. *Children in Custody: 1975–1985.* Washington, D.C.: Bureau of Justice Statistics.

————. 1988. *Historical Statistics on Prisoners in State and Federal Institutions, Year-end, 1925–86.* Washington, D.C.: Bureau of Justice Statistics.

Index